THE SIMPLE ACT OF PLANTING A TREE

The best time to plant a tree
was twenty years ago.
The second best time is now.

ANONYMOUS

THE
SIMPLE ACT
OF
PLANTING
A TREE

*A Citizen Forester's Guide
to Healing Your Neighborhood,
Your City, and Your World*

TREEPEOPLE

with
ANDY AND KATIE LIPKIS

Jeremy P. Tarcher, Inc.
Los Angeles

This book is dedicated to

Citizen Foresters everywhere.

May we reforest the earth!

Library of Congress Cataloging-in-Publication Data

Lipkis, Andy.
    The simple act of planting a tree :
a Citizen Forester's guide to
healing your neighborhood, your
city, and your world / TreePeople
with Andy and Katie Lipkis.
        p. cm.
    Includes bibliographical references.
    ISBN 0-87477-602-3 (paper) : $12.95
    1. Tree planting—Citizen participa-
tion. 2. Urban forestry—Citizen
participation. 3. Trees, Care of—
Citizen participation. 4. Trees
in cities. I. Lipkis, Katie.
II. TreePeople (Firm) III. Title.
SB436.L56 1990   90-11133
635.9'77'091732—dc20   CIP

Jeremy P. Tarcher, Inc.
5858 Wilshire Boulevard, Suite 200
Los Angeles, CA 90036

First Edition

Design: Deborah Daly, Daly Design
Editor: Nicky Leach
Production Editor: Paul Murphy

Zones indicated beneath tree drawings
throughout the book refer to map on
page 176.

The service mark *TreePeople* is registered
and protected under California and federal
laws, and the term *Citizen Forester* is pro-
prietary to TreePeople.

Back cover photo by Carl Studna.
Other photographs by David Bohrer,
Jon Earl, Bruce Flint, Cathryn Berger
Kaye, Jerold Kress, Andy Lipkis, Katie
Lipkis, George Ollen, Jeff Share, and
Ben Swets. Drawings on pages 44, 133,
135, 136, 137, 144, 148, 149, 157, and
158 are by Mark Beall. Cartoon on
page 115 is reprinted with permission of
Richard Wallmeyer, Wallmeyer Car-
toons, *Press-Telegram*, copyright 1984.
Captioned drawings of trees are by
Anne Spaulding. Charts on pages 34
and 56, photos on pages 167 and 172,
and drawings on pages 54 and 55 are re-
printed from *A Planter's Guide to the
Urban Forest* with permission from Fern
Tiger and Associates, copyright 1983.
Chart on page 16 is reprinted with permission of Jeremy Rifkin. Photograph
and article "Andy vs. the Bureaucratic
Deadwood" on page 40 are courtesy of
the *Los Angeles Times*, April 23, 1973.

Manufactured on recycled paper in the
United States of America.

Contents

Acknowledgments

This book is the product of four years of Citizen Forester Trainings held at the TreePeople headquarters in Los Angeles. Heartfelt thanks to every graduate of the training for they are the real authors of the work. Many people's energy has gone—knowingly or unknowingly—into creating this book, including Fred Anderson, Mark Beall, Caryn Diamond Bosson, Jon Earl, Jeri Eckhart, Katherine Gould-Martin, Mary Greenstein, Teri Hannigan, Margaret Pott Hartwell, Scott Hayman, Alex Pancheco, Phil Porush, Ellie Rosenthal, Murray Rosenthal, Rick Ryan, Walter Teller, Joseph Turner, Lorna Weinheimer, and David Winkelman. Thanks also to TreePeople's former, current, and future staff, board of directors, volunteers, and members, and countless others who have become so much a part of the fabric of TreePeople that there is no separation.

Thanks to Cor Trowbridge who almost lost her mind deciding what was technically correct for inclusion in Chapters 6 and 7, and to those urban-tree experts who guided her, including Alden Kelley, Phil Barker, Richard Harris, Clyde Hunt, Gary Moll, Paul Rogers, Rowan Rowntree, and Bob Skiera.

We extend our gratitude to California ReLeaf, the American Forestry Association's Global ReLeaf campaign, and a handful of imaginative urban foresters for feeding the roots, embracing the work, and holding the vision, and to Jeremy Tarcher, whose personal commitment to the empowerment of individuals made the publication of this book possible in an indecently short period of time.

To those who suffered while we wrote—parents, friends, staff, and Phoebe Lipkis—we ask your forgiveness. Yes, Phoebe, the book is now done.

Our congratulations to the dynamic Deborah Daly of Daly Design for a stupendous-looking book, and to Tarcher staff, including Robert Welsch, Daniel Malvin, Karen Kallis, and Paul Murphy, for patience and persistence.

The following deserve special mention as it is their financial support that has fed the development of TreePeople's Citizen Forester Training:

    The McKesson Foundation
    The men and women of McDonnell Douglas—West
    The Laird Norton Foundation

Foreword

In the battle to save the planet, tree planters are on the front lines. The act of planting trees, as thoroughly detailed in this book, has broad societal effects that go far beyond forest boundaries and city limits. Against the backdrop of the many developments contributing to the environmental degradation of the planet—shrinking forest cover, cropland degradation, growing population, accumulation of greenhouse gases, and a thinning stratospheric ozone layer—no single action can turn the tide. Yet, planting trees and nurturing them to maturity is one thing an individual can do to put society on the track to a sustainable future.

The advantages for the local community or city are readily apparent. Tree-lined streets are inviting and aesthetic, and urban forests provide a local getaway for city dwellers who routinely spend their weekends in search of wooded seclusion. These obvious benefits only hint at the broader implications. Livable cities can be energy efficient, enticing people to live closer to their jobs and to stay in the area during their leisure time rather than trying to escape at every opportunity. The trees that beautify also moderate city temperatures, reducing energy consumption for air conditioning and making summer heat less oppressive.

Tree planting also fosters community spirit and pride, bringing people together for a meaningful purpose that can build the bridges and promote the understanding that brings the neighborhood together. The initial efforts of the tree planters compound themselves as others find in the trees a deeper appreciation of the community as well as natural beauty. It is the beginning of the formation of new values that is the foundation for city-wide transformation. The newly organized group can further push for bike paths, improvements in public transportation, and changes to make the area less congested, less polluted, and more livable.

Global deforestation is proceeding at an appalling rate, estimated at 150 square miles daily. Besides leading to the extinction of thousands of plant and animal species each year, deforestation contributes to greenhouse warming. Trees that are growing remove the primary heat-trapping gas, carbon dioxide, from the atmosphere, using it to produce wood in their growth. Cutting down trees begins the process of releasing carbon back into the atmosphere. If the area is not reforested, there is a net buildup in carbon dioxide. Worldwide deforestation currently accounts for roughly one-fourth of the carbon dioxide released into the atmosphere.

Although deforestation is primarily a problem in the tropics, industrial countries are still the primary source of carbon dioxide, due to the use of fossil fuels and greenhouse gases such as chlorofluorocarbons and nitrous oxide. With a business-as-usual scenario, the buildup of these gases in the atmosphere is projected to cause a rise in global temperatures of five degrees Fahrenheit by late in the next century. Such a change would cause a major disruption of natural ecosystems and agriculture and result in the flooding of coastal areas. Reversing the deforestation of the earth can slow global warming as trees take carbon dioxide out of the atmosphere, thus serving as a sink for excess carbon dioxide.

Trees affect regional climates because of their part in the hydrological cycle. In one study, researchers found that three-quarters of the rain that fell in a forested region of the Amazon Basin was returned to the atmosphere through evaporation and transpiration from the trees, with only one-quarter of the rainfall leaving the site as runoff into the streams to return to the ocean. The moisture recycled into the atmosphere replenishes clouds, moving the precipitation further inland. On deforested land, the ratio of evaporation-transpiration to runoff is roughly reversed, with three-quarters of the rainfall leaving the land. In vast areas of the interior of Africa, shrinking tree cover has seemingly weakened this link in the hydrological cycle, resulting in reduced rainfall and more frequent drought.

The increase in runoff from deforested slopes is a disaster for communities downstream. Without the trees to slow runoff, the rain carries away topsoil and can cause flooding. In India, the frequency of severe, crop-damaging floods has more than doubled since 1960. In the Philippines, extensive logging for tropical hardwoods has resulted in flooded agricultural land as well as irrigation reservoirs nearly filled in with the soil that eroded from once-forested land.

In many countries today, winning the battle against envi-

Heritage Live Oak
(*Quercus virginiana*)
zones 7–10

ronmental degradation and economic decline depends on planting trees and planning families. Unfortunately, although much of the Third World has recognized the need for reforestation, successful efforts to reverse the loss of forests are rare indeed. South Korea, which has reforested its once-denuded hills and mountain sides, planting an area of fast-growing pines roughly two-thirds its area in rice, is the only developing country to reverse its deforestation. Among the industrialized nations, Australia has announced a major tree-planting program for the decade to restore two-thirds of the tree cover lost since European settlement, around 1 billion trees, and the United States has vaguely defined plans to plant 10 billion trees—a laudable goal if achieved.

Every tree planted is another step forward in the battle to save the planet, not only because of its environmental contributions, but because individual actions help to build the political momentum needed to push governments to take broader action. TreePeople is a pioneer in this area. Started in 1973 by a fifteen-year-old boy with a love of planting trees, its initiative has grown and grown, to the point where Los Angeles is adopting its plan to forest the entire city.

In this book, *The Simple Act of Planting a Tree*, TreePeople shares with us years of practical experience in planting trees in urban settings. From it, we can learn not only how to plant trees and nurture them until they mature, but how to bring nature into the urban environment, how to rebuild a sense of community, and how to make a difference in a world in need of change. This book is about changing the way we view our environment and the world.

Lester R. Brown
Worldwatch Institute

Preface

Several years ago, before the current progress on nuclear disarmament, we took a break from work to examine our situation and recommit ourselves to serving humanity in the best possible way. We explored what that meant and realized that people who are happy and healthy, who are in touch with their own true power and ability to contribute, whose lives produce satisfaction, are people unlikely to make war. To us, a world at peace is a thriving world where people live in a healthy environment with food to eat and the freedom of choice and expression. In pursuing what we, as two individuals, could do to bring this about, the most powerful option was also the most practical: to keep doing what we do and to share it with others.

The publicity surrounding TreePeople often is focused on our so-called heroic work. Although the personal attention is flattering, it misses the point. This work is wonderful and miraculous, but it is available to everyone. It might be novel to allow ourselves to be hailed as environmental, tree-planting saviors, but this work is profoundly local and personal, and everyone who embarks on this journey is a hero—or none of us are.

Our work feeds us. Planting and caring for trees, taking on challenges bigger than ourselves, building bridges of cooperation, solving problems creatively, seeing communities grow and strengthen, watching people come into their power, having a purpose, and knowing that we have made a difference in the lives of others produces a satisfaction so deep and fulfilling we feel like millionaires. In a sense, we are. Instead of dollars earned, millions of trees are planted and nurtured, lives are touched, and kids are turned on to caring.

We have the chance, quite simply, to be the first to live in final accord with our Spaceship Earth—and hence in final harmony with each other. The Ancient Greeks, the Renaissance communities, the founders of America, the Victorians enjoyed no such challenge as this. What a time to be alive!

NORMAN MYERS

This is the true joy in life: the being used for a purpose recognized by yourself as a mighty one; the being thoroughly worn out before you are thrown on the scrap heap; the being a force of nature, instead of a feverish selfish clod of ailments and grievances, complaining thatthe world will not devote itself to making you happy. I am of the opinion that my life belongs to the whole community, and as long as I live it, it is my privilege to do whatever I can. I rejoice in life for its own sake. Life is no brief candle to me; it is a sort of bright torch which I have got hold of for a moment and I want to make it burn as brightly as possible before handing it on to future generations.

GEORGE BERNARD SHAW

I (Andy) started the work of TreePeople when I was fifteen years old. Although the vehicle was trees, my motivation was not a love of trees and the environment, but the search for a life of meaning in a world that appeared self-serving. In high school, I was starting to feel my power while the world was broadcasting the message that I couldn't really do anything or affect anything. It was frustrating and painful.

In the midst of this, I learned that the forest where I spent my summers was being killed by the drifting smog from Los Angeles. I spent three weeks with two dozen summer camp peers working like crazy to repair a piece of the dying forest by planting smog-tolerant trees. Instead of sitting around figuring out what to do for entertainment, we swung picks at rock-hard ground and shoveled cow manure. When it was done, we watched birds, squirrels, grass, flowers, and trees return to what had been a dead parking lot. Caring friendships developed while we were having what amounted to one of the highest times of our lives, and the experience filled me with ideas for repairing what I saw as an environmentally and socially-damaged world.

What followed was three years of repeatedly starting and failing before my project began to take shape. I had a lot of barriers to confront. I couldn't find role models; in fact it was quite the opposite. People who cared about the environment were portrayed on television as weird outcasts, and people who expressed concern over an issue were do-gooders. I didn't want to look like a freak. Although I was drawn to the work, I resisted it. If it worked, would I get stuck doing this for life?

I (Katie) was definitely not a do-gooder. In fact, I was a pretty average, sort of ignorant person who rode a motorcycle and jumped out of airplanes.

When I met Andy, I'd never even planted a tree. I'd had a lot of fun working my way up the advertising ladder, grabbing a Clio award on the way, and had reached the rung called "Is that all there is?" I was a yuppie before the yuppies. With everything in front of me, life started to crumble. The trappings of corporate power had me trapped. How could I survive without a huge salary? What could I do to earn money? Copywriting was so easy!

Ironically, I also felt powerless. With so much on earth to be done, my nine-to-five seemed like just marking time. I was happiest volunteering, giving something back, using my powers of persuasion for things that could make the world a better place and relieve the suffering of others.

I began to understand the difference between what society defines as power and success and what power and success truly are, as demonstrated by individuals who feel and see and touch the positive changes they're making in the world. I wanted to find a way to share and nurture the blossoming of real power in others. In a moment of rare objectivity, while standing in my air-conditioned office next to my *ficus* that I didn't even know was a *ficus*, I was able to say, "When you've given this up, and the money starts looking attractive, remember this instant; the money's not worth it!"

A conference came to Melbourne, Australia, where I was living, and one of the speakers was a young man whose dream was to see a million trees planted in Los Angeles. "What do you do?" he asked. "I write," I replied. "Boy, oh boy, could TreePeople use a writer!" he exclaimed. We were married and are living happily ever after.

Introduction:
What's So Simple?

What a strange notion, that an act supposedly so simple, holding the key to solving many of the problems that plague the inhabitants of the earth the world over, should take so much prep time and so many pages of this book. If the answer is trees, what's holding us back? Let's just get up out of our armchairs and *go do it*! Right?

Not so fast. Many transformational acts are simple. Few are easy. So it is with establishing trees, growing forests, creating canopies—whatever we wish to call this simple act of planting. Doing it right will take you on a journey during which you'll discover not only which trees you like but also which neighbors you can count on, which bureaucrats you can call by their first names, what it takes to get a tree into the ground, and what it takes to keep it alive. Getting pregnant is pretty simple. It's more difficult to go through labor and birth. But the hardest part is raising the children, giving them just enough of what they need and not smothering them. So it is with trees in cities. It's easier to dream than to plant and harder still to maintain.

Planting a tree is *a nice thing to do*. It helps maintain the status quo. However, it can also be a powerful act of defiance, embodying the leverage that galvanizes people to take action. It separates gesture and sentiment from true commitment. It gently but ruthlessly extracts commitment from the gesture. Trees demand care—our continued involvement, interest, and nurturing. Without it, they die. Planting has the ability to transform our own behavior and that of our culture.

Tree planting takes the simple act of an individual and elevates it, revealing the truth about where true power rests in the world. The result of a single person's planting can be monumental, and when individual acts are added up, the result is powerful evidence of what one can do for the world. For some reason, this

> No town can fail of beauty, though its walks were gutters and its houses hovels, if venerable trees make magnificent colonnades along its streets.
> HENRY WARD BEECHER

work causes people to move beyond political, philosophical, cultural, racial, and economic differences to cooperate together. The colossal amount of energy that's generated in that coming together can be used to accomplish extraordinary feats.

As such, it is the perfect drive mechanism, the first step in the healing of our nation and environment. When we plant and care for trees, alone or together, we begin to build an internal place of peace, beauty, safety, joy, simplicity, caring, and satisfaction. The results encourage us to take on larger challenges. After a while, we discover that we've established a richer inner and outer world for ourselves, our families, our neighborhoods, our cities, and our world.

This book will draw an analogy between trees and people, partly because trees have personalities just as people do, and partly because the magic we will explore is created only out of the synergy between trees and people.

Working with living things—people as well as trees—takes patience and persistence. It's not neat and tidy. Part of the challenge in putting together this book was to pinpoint those ideas and facts we felt would be helpful while guarding against the *cookie-cutter* approach. There's no such thing as a typical American city when it comes to street-tree planting. In Los Angeles, we have it pretty tough at the time of this printing with laws mandating such local customs as the use of root barriers, which aim to help prevent broken sidewalks, and the pounding in of steel poles instead of wooden stakes as an extra measure against vandalism. But other cities have their own special requirements, such as Atlanta, where Trees Atlanta must plant enormous trees as a guard against vandalism and must do it at 2 A.M. to comply with rules that require the entire street to be blocked off for such a performance. Have you ever tried to keep people enthusiastic at 2 A.M.?

The Simple Act of Planting a Tree is strangely not a book about planting trees, although we hope it will inspire you to put a few in the ground and rear them well. If five years from now you've changed the face of your city by planting and establishing a green canopy, our purpose will have been served beyond our dreams. If you've transformed your backyard into a forest, we'll be delighted. However, if you've not planted one tree but, excited by the concepts and ideas expressed here, you've started a neighborhood watch, a citizen advocacy group, a babysitting co-op, or even if you've volunteered at your kids' school library, we've still done what we set out to do. This book is about community—establishing it, tapping into it, and using it to nurture responsibility for our global environment.

TAKING BACK OUR POWER

The Emerald Isle?

In 1984, Jan Alexander, an Australian woman returning to her adopted home of Ireland, passed through Los Angeles taking TreePeople literature as a souvenir.

That winter, Ireland suffered its worst winter storms in forty years. Many trees were destroyed, and many that survived were cut down as the meaning of the word *liability* hit landowners. Jan wrote the *Irish Times* demanding more respect for the hardwoods of Ireland and announced her intention to begin replanting them. Crann is the Gaelic word for tree and the name of the organization she started in 1986. Crann has trained twenty young people in forestry, started a nursery to supply trees to projects throughout Ireland, launched its first urban initiative with the planting of 10,000 trees in Dublin, produced literature and a video, and is finalizing plans for the planting of 50,000 oak trees in a rural county south of Dublin.

In recognition of her role in generating interest in tree planting, the Irish Government appointed Jan Alexander to the State Forestry Board in 1989.

Most people are *on* the world, not in it—have no conscious sympathy or relationship to anything about them—undiffused, separate, and rigidly alone like marbles of polished stone, touching but separate.

JOHN MUIR

As your perspective changes, or as you implement your first project, you'll wonder how the bulk of the human population can know so little about the natural environment and, specifically, about the plant kingdom—our more ancient cohabitants of this planet. With plants and trees being so critical to our survival, how is it that we don't see them? How can urban dwellers walk past street trees that are being strangled by tree ties and not want to cut them with a pair of clippers, or at least report them? How can we overlook the bad maintenance practices that destroy the urban forest canopy, and with it part of our children's inheritance, without making tree care a priority in our local government?

We are right in the middle of a beautiful ecosystem and we don't even see it.

We cannot separate ourselves from the environment; it is actually as much a part of us as we are of it. The air we breathe, the water we drink, the food we eat, all become a part of us. As we pollute the earth, we damage ourselves, our own bodies. It's increasingly difficult for us to pretend that environmentally caused illnesses such as skin and other cancers, auto-immune-system disorders, and lung disease have nothing to do with the way we've been treating ourselves and the extensions of our bodies—the environment.

The words *community* and *commons* are from the same root. Traditionally, the commons in England were used to graze cows —common land, respected and maintained by all for the good of all. What happened to our concept of common spaces? They are all around us still—the streets, parks, air, beaches, ocean, rivers, streams, and forests—but for some reason we don't feel personally responsible for them.

Much of what happened was the result of our moving out of villages and into cities. No longer did everyone know everyone else's business. Every now and then, a person could actually get away with a transgression and not be found out. Cities granted anonymity. And, in a strange way, with anonymity comes powerlessness.

Under the notion that they could do a better job than all of us, we gave up many of our responsibilities to governments and institutions. In doing so, we also gave up much of our power. *They* handled things just fine for a while. *They* had the responsibility for fetching the water, food, and energy, and getting rid of the waste. *They* were also taking care of the common resources of land, water, air, and trees. We figured we weren't supposed to stay involved, because *they* knew more about it than we did. It is convenient to not have to be responsible for everything, but it's not so pleasant to lose individual power.

The larger cities became, the less in touch we were, the more damage we unwittingly created, and the less it seemed to matter whether we were decent citizens or not. The prevailing feeling was "If I don't do it, somebody else will," and no corresponding negative feedback to this attitude developed. Inevitably, we lost the ability to discern the difference we made. We assumed we had no control over our environment and, therefore, no role to play in either preserving or enhancing it. Many of the problems now facing our inner cities—problems in the face of which *they* are the powerless ones—stem from having given up our individual responsibility for ourselves and our surroundings. Gang wars. Drug abuse. Teen suicide. The school dropout rate. Graffiti. Urban youth is shouting out: I want to matter!

These days, most who live in large cities have inherited its problems: pollution, bad planning, too much concrete, and not enough community life. This sense of a bad inheritance exacerbates an already depressing situation, adding to our conviction that there's nothing we can do to change it.

This book is here to help you put together two pieces of a horribly complex puzzle. On the one hand, we present an environment that's crying out for our attention, love, and nurturing, and is hurting from our neglect. On the other, we see a society in breakdown over a lack of positive outlets for its energy, its members suffering from a perceived lack of personal power. Society is saying "Help!" The planet is starting to fray around the edges. It's time for us to get involved.

Environmental damage is now being equated with a basic threat to personal health and human survival. However, protecting the environment used to be regarded as an altruistic act —the work of the do-gooders. We submit that doing good is not just about our own survival on the planet; it actually feels pretty good too.

This book is peppered with stories about people who only really found themselves when they got out and started working in the community. Brilliant leaders who had never stood before an audience of more than two. Mothers who've linked with other mothers, kids with cops, environmentalists with four-wheel-drive clubbers. The synergy of people cooperating with one another can form the magic that produces miracles. When those people are neighbors, the magic is only beginning. From tree planting and care to sharing fruit and rich compost and having monthly cookouts and block-club activities, as we begin to recycle our

I am only one, but still I am one. I cannot do everything, but still I can do something; and because I cannot do everything, I will not refuse to do the something that I can do.
EDWARD EVERETT HALE

Volunteers in 1984 protecting the roots of nursery-surplus fruit trees distributed by TreePeople to deserving families.

The way to live our vision on a daily basis is to understand that right now is the only time we have.

JOHN HANLEY

energy instead of being drained by strenuous work, we're revitalized. Instead of feeling alienated, we create family. Instead of feeling helpless, we find power. Instead of wondering why we're alive, we have purpose.

But where to start? What are we allowed to do? Don't you need a college degree to be able to do serious urban tree planting? What about money, permission, resources, contacts, supplies, a network? Where are they? How do we find them? These are the questions this book will answer.

You'll understand how to start this work right from where you sit. You'll read about successes and failures and how the challenges are met. You'll learn what happens when we reconnect with nature and our own power. You'll see how when we recycle our energy, we can link up natural cycles that have been broken. You'll discover how this work, simple as it is, is a basis—practically a prerequisite—for mobilizing our society to take on the larger environmental challenges that face us.

This book is both a sit-down-and-read-it book *and* a champing-at-the-bit book. It's not just for pragmatists but also for those who use new appliances without reading the instructions. Most of the book can be taken in by the fireplace in an evening or two and may see you getting impatient to pick up a shovel, or at least the phone. The workbooks are best attacked with pencil in hand and creative juices flowing—whether that be during your coffee

A Man with a Mission

Dr. Alfred Swanson, a noted international speaker on hand surgery, has addressed audiences in fifty countries over the last thirty years, and the environmental degradation he witnessed around the world started getting to him. He began slipping environmental slides into his presentations and demanding five minutes on the subject with every audience. In 1985, he formed the International Tree Corps- then realized his personal planting project should begin with his Western Michigan neighborhood. In 1989, he gave each of 10,000 lucky local fifth graders an eight- to twelve-foot maple or sycamore sapling to take home and plant. In 1990, he added first graders to the program with each receiving a one-foot-tall Colorado Blue Spruce. He plans to reforest the first and fifth grades through the year 2000. "If 20 percent of the population starts planting trees, we've reached a critical mass," says Dr. Swanson, who received a letter from one of last year's fifth graders vowing to send him photographic updates every year for the next ten years.

break, in the supermarket line, around a community conference table, on the bus, or in the middle of a phone call.

Flip back and forth. Participate as you go along. This book is not just a nice idea, but a practical guide to get you out into your community, talking to your neighbors, introducing yourself to your trees or to their absence, and doing something about planting and taking responsibility for what's there.

In putting the pieces together, we have attempted to follow a logical chronology, which is not, however, the only way that planting and care projects develop. In fact, once you start on this course, you'll find yourself guided better by problems than by logic; you'll proceed based on which problems arise first to be solved. Since you likely are a person open to alternatives, you may find an alternative way to read this book, other than from beginning to end. Where it seems helpful, we refer you to another chapter or section of the book where a particular thought or situation is explored in more detail. Chop and change at will. This process after all is organic.

Community tree planting and care is a nonpartisan, nonreligious open door through which anyone can step. What may start out as a fun way to spend a few weekends, or a way to get to know your neighbors, can become a powerful tool for one's personal growth. The combination of learning and playing with hard work, tough challenges, and the creation of something real and positive in the physical world can be enough to change peoples' lives.

Your urban forest—whatever its condition—needs you. Even with the best government-managed urban-forestry program imaginable, there's still a role for you as an advocate. When the going gets tough and nobody is listening to you, however, you'll feel some doubt about this role. But check back with the trees because it is they, after all, that are your inspiration.

Happy reading. But don't get too comfortable in that armchair. There's a whole lot of planting to do!

1

The Urban Forest Possible

*W*hat is a forest? A forest is made up of trees, of course, but it's also the plants—including fungi and microflora such as lichen—that grow under and around the trees. It's the birds and animals; the bugs and microorganisms; the air; the streams, rivers, and lakes; the rain, fog, and snow; the soil, the rocks, the mountains, and the minerals. It is the products of the forest: the fresh air, clean water, protected soil, recreation, fish, game, edible seeds and nuts, and of course fiber, both timber and pulp.

The forest creates less tangible products as well, which are rarely valued and hard to quantify. These include wilderness and wildness, solitude, emotional and physical restoration, beauty, nature, and a reconnection with one's spirit and spirituality as well as one's sense of adventure.

A WALK IN THE WOODS

It's right before dawn. You slip out of bed, pull on your sweats, and go for a walk through the forest. The birds get up just before you to herald the sunrise. It's hard to see them, but they're everywhere in the lacy and varied canopy overhead. The cacophony of sound is bracing. The air too is crisp, fresh, and clear. You take a deep sniff. Is that wet pine leaves or eucalyptus? There's a rustle in the tree above. A squirrel leaps three feet, clutching an acorn in its teeth. How peaceful and calm it is here! You feel nurtured and relaxed, yet delightfully exhilarated. What a way to start the day! There's a new smell—of bacon frying and coffee brewing. It's feeding time for the dominant animal species of this, the urban forest.

WHAT IS THE URBAN FOREST?

Many agencies have spent years trying to define it. Most differ somewhat in their opinions, but they generally agree on what constitutes an urban forest: trees and vegetation in and around a town or city environment.

In the city, the only part of the forest managed by public agencies is that which grows on public land such as streets, highways, parks, and public buildings. But like the natural forest, the urban forest is actually an entire ecosystem. All areas—private homes, condos, apartments, roof gardens, commercial and retail property (including their parking lots and landscaped areas), flood-control channels, hillsides, utility rights of way, abandoned rail lines and the edges of active lines, airports, and spandrels (the no-man's-land open spaces covered by trees, weeds, or trash)—are parts of the urban forest. It is a whole system. If a disease infects the trees on your street, it will likely spread to the vegetation around your home, and vice versa. You can't effectively help the urban forest without dealing with the whole, including factors outside your city and somewhat outside your control. If your water is imported, weather patterns hundreds of miles away

I never saw a disconcerted tree. They grip the ground as though they liked it, and though fast rooted, they travel about as we do. They go wandering forth in all directions with every wind, going and coming like ourselves, traveling with us around the sun two million miles a day.

JOHN MUIR

Elm Action

When Dutch Elm Disease hit Minneapolis, Don Willeke, lawyer and cofounder of the Twin Cities Tree Trust, mobilized a massive citizen lobby that resulted in a state matching fund of $60 million to help cities organize a war against the disease. Most other stricken cities lost nearly all their trees, but by acting quickly, the people of Minneapolis slowed the spread of the disease and saved nearly half of their old elms. They have also planted nearly 1 million large trees in the past fifteen years to ensure a dense urban-forest canopy. According to Don, the key was to involve politicians: "People underestimate their power to move government to action. They think as long as they're doing tree work, they don't need to get their hands dirty with politics." During the effort, citizens visited their representatives to plead for the trees. Now 100,000 mature elms lining the streets of Minneapolis stand as testimony that their strategy worked.

might have an impact on you. Likewise, laws and public policies legislated thousands of miles away can affect your forest.

An urban forest would function like a rural forest if it weren't for the rather inconvenient (for the trees) existence of the city and its human activity. Because the natural cycles that guarantee its functioning have been broken, the urban forest needs us to survive. For example, new trees are always being planted in natural forests through the process of natural seeding. There is a mix of ages of trees. When older trees die, the maturing younger ones are right there to fill in. Since concrete and the lack of a natural ecosystem prevent trees from reseeding themselves in most parts of the urban forest, it becomes our job to *constantly* plant new trees. We must interplant along our streets and in our parks to guarantee that there's a generation ready to succeed our old beauties. It's the same story with nutrients, water, and pest control; we must provide that which does not occur naturally in cities.

Take a Peek

Perhaps the best way to view your urban forest is to look at it from above. If you're afraid of taking off or landing, checking out your forest is a great airplane activity for those tense sixty seconds! For a longer, more studied view, find the tallest building in town, a good hillside, or a detailed aerial photo. Notice the elements that we label *city*: the buildings, streets, parking lots, cars, and freeways. Now look at the forest instead of the city. The trees are probably obvious, but what about the meadows and clearings? Lawns, gardens, parks, parkways, golf courses, and cemeteries play a major role in the city forest, along with the wildlife, birds, bugs, and bees.

Now that you've mentally checked it out, what have you found? Was your city carved out of the forest, or was the forest planted into your city? If you don't have much of a forest at all, then your role is clear. You need to help create it wisely and establish it firmly. If your city or community is blessed with heavy forest cover, your job is just as magical, only different. How old are the trees? How well have they been maintained? Is there an inventory on them? What's the replacement plan? What's the ratio of trees lost to trees planted each year? (The national average is four trees lost for every tree planted.) Trees grow old and die. Disaster strikes communities who've become complacent about tree cover and have dropped planting from their list of priorities. Can a tiny sapling adequately replace a 100-year-old elm? Foresight will keep your community shaded in the manner to which it has become accustomed.

Who is taking care of your forest? Who's the guardian of the whole ecosystem? Who's monitoring what's happening? Who's reporting what to whom, and when? Where do government agencies, landscape professionals, and gardeners go for reliable information on what to do? How and where do lay people plug themselves in? Are there gaps between that which the agencies are able to manage well and that which is clearly the jurisdiction of private individuals? If you've never really seen the forest from this perspective before, you've probably not clearly been able to see your stewardship role.

THE URBAN FOREST POSSIBLE

Already the forests in our cities contribute a lot to our lives, physically, aesthetically, emotionally, and spiritually. Everybody has a tree story in their past. If we now contribute a little extra energy to them, they'll give us even more.

Trees shade and cool our streets and buildings, creating beautiful green towers to soften the harsh urban environment. A big tree can provide a day's oxygen for up to four people. Trees contribute to a community's sense of place. They increase property value. They provide fruit. They give us beautiful shapes, flowers, fall colors, and scents, and they provide homes for birds (who sweeten the air with their voices), butterflies, squirrels, and other wildlife. Their flowers are a food source for bees, and their branches hold many a tree house. In colder climates, trees can help insulate homes from cold winds as well. Trees catch rainfall, slow storm runoff, and prevent soil erosion. (See Chapter 2 for a complete list of the benefits of trees.)

Not so obvious are the emotional and healing benefits to people. A study at a hospital in Pennsylvania revealed that surgical patients whose rooms had a view of trees and greenery took fewer painkillers and recovered quicker than those whose windows faced a brick wall. Is there any doubt that an abundance of trees in the city makes it a saner place and keeps its residents a little more balanced?

HOW TREES COOL OUR CITIES AND OUR PLANET

The entire urban forest canopy plays a leading role in cooling our cities and keeping our energy costs down by breaking up *heat islands*, thereby lowering peak summer temperatures by five to

Trees Release Me

Trees can't be used as the scapegoat for unrepentant polluters. For instance, although many studies have shown trees to be valuable as sinks for trace contaminants—trees lining freeways are especially valuable in absorbing lead and exhaust fumes—we need to consider what happens to the leaves after they've taken up particulate matter from the air. If leaves are removed and burnt, the contaminants end up back in the atmosphere. If they're buried in landfills, the pollutants may leach into soil or ground water. If the leaves are used for mulch or compost (in the case of evergreens, leaves stay on the tree but are cleaned by rainfall), the soil eventually gets the pollutants back again. What's more, some trees cannot withstand air pollution and will die or suffer chronic stress. The message? Give trees a break. Don't ask them to clean a mess that was avoidable in the first place.

Mental Tarzan

As you begin to know trees by name, you'll almost unconsciously start labeling them as you walk or drive through the city. Your attention will be drawn to them rather than to the urban hardscape. Ultimately, you may find yourself mentally swinging from tree to tree like Tarzan in the urban jungle.

nine degrees. A heat island, primarily an urban phenomenon, is an area of exposed, heat-absorbing surfaces, such as tarmac and concrete, that without tree cover absorb the sun's energy and radiate it back as tremendous heat. They can be found all over the city—in our parking lots, streets, and buildings.

According to research conducted since 1988 at Lawrence Berkeley Laboratory (LBL), proper planting and shading of these urban surfaces can achieve an energy saving of up to 50 percent of the electricity used for summer air conditioning. Used in this way, an urban tree becomes an effective machine for combating global warming and cutting utility costs. Hashem Akbari and Arthur Rosenfeld, researchers at LBL, report that one urban tree does the job of between ten and fifteen rural forest trees in keeping greenhouse gases from the air.

Just as global warming and the hole in the ozone layer are linked, so too are trees in their ability to combat these environmental ills. The shade produced by trees on city streets and campuses can help shield us from harmful ultraviolet rays, which are more prevalent without the protective ozone layer.

Exploiter vs. Exploited

"You're from Los Angeles, huh? (Sympathetic sigh.) Oh, they really need you down there. You know, our son went down there; he built three shopping centers, and we were ready to go down and see the job he'd done. Suddenly we had a call from him saying he was coming back to Spokane; said there were no trees down there and too much traffic and congestion and people and buildings and . . . well, the trouble is, you lose hope in a city like that. It doesn't seem like anyone can affect anything at all. . . . Now he's building houses in Spokane."

POP ECO-PSYCHOLOGY: COMPLETING THE BROKEN CYCLES

Imagine the earth is a ball you're holding in the palm of your hand. Look at its precious resources: clean air, clean water, energy, abundant food, animal life. Notice that all the elements on the earth seem to coexist in a state of balance. This rule applies not just to the whole but to its parts. The forest ecosystem in its natural state is a perfect example of nature in balance.

This *state of balance* is actually a dynamic set of processes that make up cycles. In natural ecosystems, everything—energy, information, nutrients, water—flows in a cycle.

Let's follow an energy cycle. Plants grow using energy from the sun, carbon dioxide from the air, and nutrients from the soil. During photosynthesis, plants transform the sun's energy into biomass: leaves, stems, and wood. Anything that falls to the ground, be it leaves, broken branches, or the plant or tree itself when its life is through, decomposes and returns the energy to the soil, making it available for the growth of other plants. One simple and complete cycle.

The cycle expands to include the animal kingdom, which consumes the food the earth produces. Animals—humans included—are a part of the bigger cycle. We eat plants, convert and use some of the plant energy, and then, through elimination or death, pass the remainder of that energy back to the earth to be used as fertilizer for the growth of more plants. Another complete cycle.

If a cycle is broken, the energy is diffused. For instance, during a forest fire, heat, carbon dioxide, and smoke are produced as waste products. That waste, or diffusion, is what scientists define as pollution.

For millions of years, humans were able to live on the earth as a part of natural cycles and systems. Whatever damage or disruptions people caused could be handled by nature. As technology advanced, people learned how to manipulate the environment and to disrupt cycles permanently.

Instead of recycling the energy we use back into nature, we break the cycle and think we can throw away that energy. Our waste becomes pollution: sewage fouling rivers, lakes, and oceans; litter making our common land look like a trash can; and garbage filling our canyons and

turning them into ever-increasing and harder-to-reach landfills. The level of pollution—poison—has risen to the point where it is affecting our health and killing off forests and animals.

Human energy has more than just a physical presence. We also express and recycle our energy in the form of love, service, art, dance, prayer, and so on. Likewise, wasted human energy is represented by more than just physical pollution. We feel boredom, frustration, anger, alienation, depression, and pain. Until recently, our physical pollution has been out of sight and therefore out of mind—flushed or buried from view. On the nonphysical plane, ridding ourselves of our deep boredom, anger, or pain has required sophisticated distractions, such as harmless spectator sports or, more drastically, gang activity and drug abuse. No wonder we're an addicted society!

Our role in the breaking of cycles began when technological advances made it possible for humans to manipulate the environment. It gained new proportions when we moved beyond villages into large cities, where a degree of anonymity could be translated into not being accountable and *not counting*. Aside from breaking the energy cycle on a massive scale, urban dwellers broke the negative feedback loops. As long as we could put our waste somewhere else, we didn't have to face the damage it was causing and so didn't change our behavior.

Now that we see a crisis before us, both environmentally and socially, we have a chance to get back in touch with our personal power and responsibility to change our ways. Imagine what can happen when that human energy is focused! The answer doesn't lie *out there*. There will never be enough money to hire teams to clean up the planet for us, any more than there will be enough money to rid us of the scourge of drugs. The answer lies in mobilizing every single one of us to heal—not as a punishment, but as a powerful gift to ourselves. Tending our own mess, like tending our own trees, is a continuing discipline. As with most messes, once we get involved in cleaning up, we can appreciate the need for prevention.

Humans are the only creatures capable of comprehending and relinking the earth's cycles. From an ecological perspective, we do have a role to play above enjoying ourselves, consuming the earth's resources, and destroying its life-support systems. Consequently, the three Rs many of us remember from childhood have become the four Rs for the nineties: reduce, reuse, recycle, and replant.

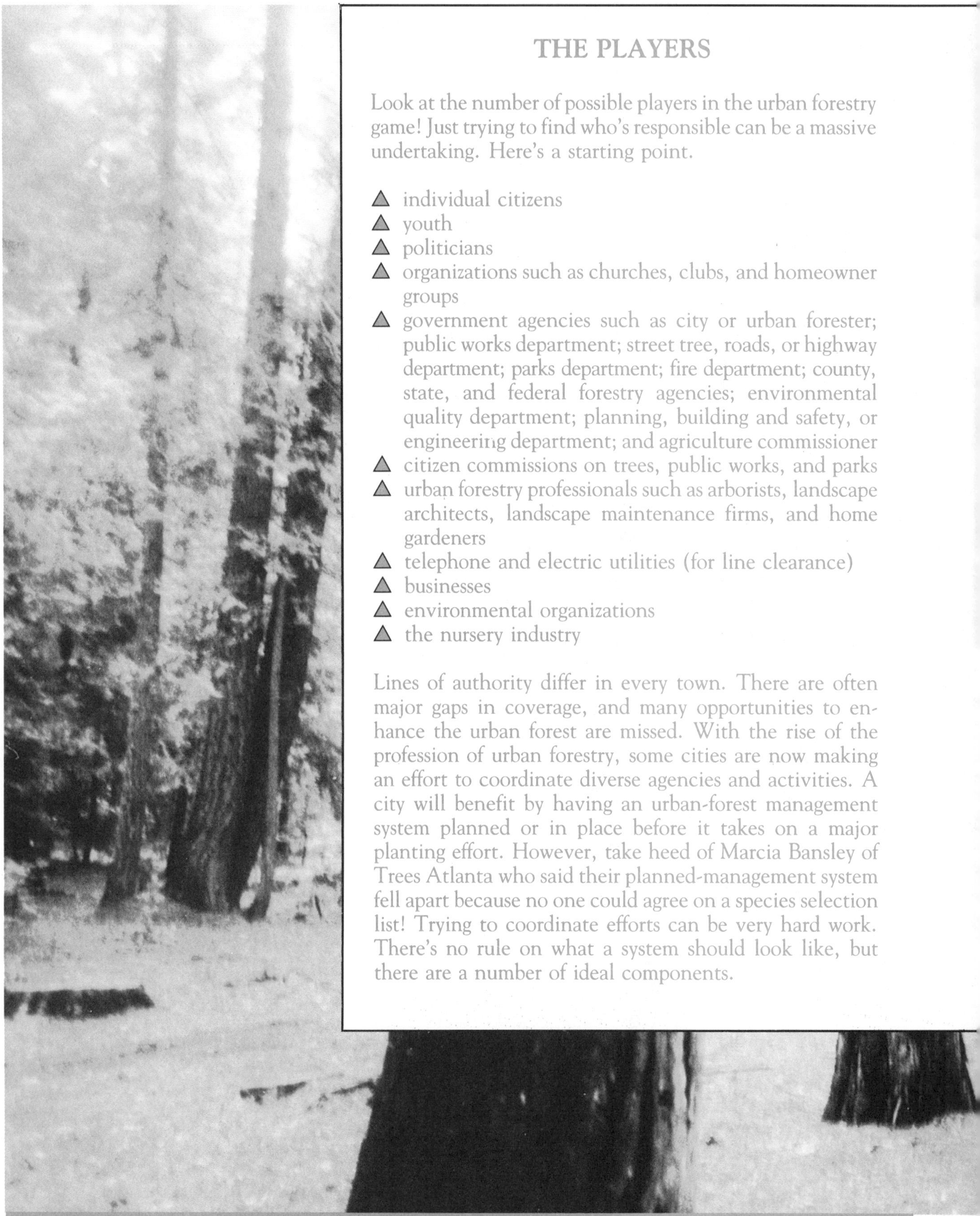

THE PLAYERS

Look at the number of possible players in the urban forestry game! Just trying to find who's responsible can be a massive undertaking. Here's a starting point.

- △ individual citizens
- △ youth
- △ politicians
- △ organizations such as churches, clubs, and homeowner groups
- △ government agencies such as city or urban forester; public works department; street tree, roads, or highway department; parks department; fire department; county, state, and federal forestry agencies; environmental quality department; planning, building and safety, or engineering department; and agriculture commissioner
- △ citizen commissions on trees, public works, and parks
- △ urban forestry professionals such as arborists, landscape architects, landscape maintenance firms, and home gardeners
- △ telephone and electric utilities (for line clearance)
- △ businesses
- △ environmental organizations
- △ the nursery industry

Lines of authority differ in every town. There are often major gaps in coverage, and many opportunities to enhance the urban forest are missed. With the rise of the profession of urban forestry, some cities are now making an effort to coordinate diverse agencies and activities. A city will benefit by having an urban-forest management system planned or in place before it takes on a major planting effort. However, take heed of Marcia Bansley of Trees Atlanta who said their planned-management system fell apart because no one could agree on a species selection list! Trying to coordinate efforts can be very hard work. There's no rule on what a system should look like, but there are a number of ideal components.

City forester: Overall program manager whose role is to integrate the work of public agencies and the private sector.

City or government agency: Has planting, management, and maintenance responsibility and funding to do it.

Ordinances: Some ordinances protect trees or prescribe minimum legal tree cover in, for instance, commercial parking lots. Others may mandate certain densities of plantings with development projects or percentage of sun required on city streets. Some city ordinances even mandate tree-pruning standards and require certification of tree-care professionals. (Contact the American Forestry Association, TreeNet, or the International Society of Arboriculture for information. See Resources.)

Citizen tree commission: Holds the vision of a city forest, provides community input, and contributes to the planning and management process. Can be set up in a policy-making or advisory capacity.

Citizen action component: Includes youth involvement in planning, planting, light pruning, and care; advocacy; and the contributions of citizens through environmental or community-service private nonprofit groups.

Public education: Handled by public or private sector.

Neighborhood-level outreach, organizing, training, and action: Best handled by a private organization.

Tree inventory: Organized list of all trees on public lands. Should include maintenance history and prescribed policy and schedule for maintenance and replacement.

Tree or forest master plan: A planning document that guides selection of species, planting styles, sizes, and formats. Could include special neighborhood identities. The creation of this document can be a profound process for building community involvement and commitment.

Just how these components come together can be tailored to the needs, resources, size, and spirit of a given community. Depending on the players, much can be the responsibility of local government or a local nonprofit.

Current Emission of CO2 by Source

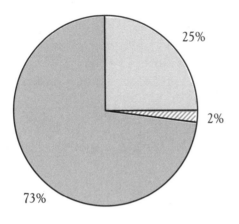

25%

2%

73%

☐ Fossil fuel combustion

☐ Deforestation

▨ Cement production

Top Three Sources

Fossil fuel combustion

1. United States
2. USSR
3. China

Deforestation

1. Brazil
2. Indonesia
3. Colombia

Cement production

1. China
2. USSR
3. Japan

THE GREENHOUSE EFFECT AND GLOBAL WARMING

Carbon dioxide (CO_2) and other gases form a natural shield in the earth's atmosphere and behave in a similar way to the glass in a greenhouse. The sun's rays penetrate the shield, hit the earth, and are reflected as longer-wave heat. The shield then traps some of the reflected heat that would otherwise radiate into space.

This process is a natural phenomenon. Without this *greenhouse effect*, global temperatures would be sixty degrees (Fahrenheit) cooler—unlivable for us. However, with the overabundance of greenhouse gases, which include water vapor, methane, and nitrous oxide, as well as carbon dioxide, the natural blanket surrounding the earth is thickening and, as a consequence, global temperatures are rising slowly but dangerously.

We are losing tropical rain forests—the lungs of the earth that along with other plants absorb carbon dioxide and release oxygen—at an alarming rate. An area roughly the size of a football field is cut down and burned every second; an area the size of a city block is cut down every minute. We're not only losing the forests' ability to absorb and store carbon but are also releasing more carbon dioxide into the atmosphere during the slash-and-burn process.

World energy use is the main contributor to increased atmospheric CO_2. Conservative estimates say that each year we burn enough fuel to release nearly six billion tons of carbon dioxide into the air. The United States, with only one-twentieth of the world's population, produces nearly one-quarter of the annual global CO_2 from burning fossil fuels.

The 1980s have witnessed the four hottest years this century, with 1988 being the warmest year on record. Present global temperatures are the highest since mankind has been keeping records. The rate of global warming in the past two decades is higher than at any earlier recorded time. Moreover, in addition to destroying the ozone layer, which protects the earth from the sun's ultraviolet rays, chlorofluorocarbons (CFCs)—widely used in aerosols, refrigerators, air conditioners, and foam packaging—are responsible for 15 to 20 percent of the global warming phenomenon.

PICTURE THIS

Thousands line a major boulevard in teams of four to ten people, removing concrete from neatly trimmed, square holes cut in the sidewalk. They dig, measure, determine the sun's direction to enable them to orient the tree's limbs, and mix soil amendments and nutrients into the native dirt.

When the preparation is done, they assemble around a waiting tree. They move it toward a hole, and while some support its branches, others quickly and gently remove the pot from the tree's rootball. All help lower the tree into its new home, steadying it while the hole is filled. The soil is packed in, and stakes are pounded into position on either side. The people use special rubber ties to secure the tree between the stakes—loose enough to allow the tree to sway in the wind and build its own trunk strength, but tight enough to provide protection from a host of urban stresses it will encounter in its first, most vulnerable years.

Then the final touches. While some sweep and clean up the surrounding area, others fashion a basin around the tree's base using surplus soil from the hole. The team gathers to inspect the work for quality. They take turns pouring buckets of water into the basin. To complete their work, they dedicate the tree by giving it a name, which they write on a small strip of bumper-sticker material. They sign their names to another sticker, then affix both stickers to the stakes. Before moving on to the next tree, they commit to plans for watching over and caring for this one. Stepping back, one can see the boulevard in the midst of a profound transformation. As teams complete their planting, they polish the job by collecting and recycling litter, and sweeping the sidewalks. Tomorrow they'll be back to paint out the graffiti.

Down the road at the shoe warehouse, on company time before the lunch break, employees are pruning and weeding the trees they planted eighteen months before around their parking lot. Some of the faster-growing species they selected are already beginning to shade the building and reduce air-conditioning needs and every day the *early birds* get the pick of the cool, shaded parking spaces. The employees then sit down to enjoy lunch in the scented herb-and-fern-garden picnic area they created just off the parking lot.

Street Trees Bear Fruit

It's not common, but in Coral Gables, Florida, the avocados that line some streets are tended by civic and church groups who glean and distribute the fruit to the needy. The trees are well mulched to prevent the avocados from splattering if they fall. From 1980 to 1985, Massachusetts had a state-mandated fruition program that also relied on gleaning groups to keep the trees clean. However, a city in California just removed its fruit-bearing street trees because citizens (adjacent owners) weren't harvesting or cleaning up the fruit that had dropped and become a hazard. If you can provide solutions to the problems your city might face, this fruity idea bears thinking about!

The bell rings. It's the end of another school day. Students flow out of the classroom doors. While most leave, a couple go to the bicycle compound. Mounted on specially engineered forest-care bikes, they ride to the boulevards and business districts in their assigned territory. One student checks with a local shopkeeper before hooking up a hose and filling the fifty-gallon tank on his bike. He adds some nutrient concentrate and pedals up the sidewalk to feed and water the trees. Another loosens tree ties that are beginning to strangle their charges and prunes suckers that have sprouted. She then rides to the neighborhood compost station to deposit the prunings before riding home.

On another day, students are making preparations for future forests that will shelter their schools and surrounding communities. Working with neighbors and local businesspeople, they survey streets, parking lots, and open spaces to determine the number and species of trees required to form a green canopy. They receive guidance from city foresters and planners and will ultimately gather the whole community to shape their collective dreams into action plans.

They plan to collect funds, materials, and supplies to plant seeds, transplant seedlings and then raise thousands of trees in nurseries built in school yards. Students will spend a portion of every day working in the nursery and caring for the larger trees they've planted around their campuses and communities.

On Sunday after the service, several families gather to harvest peaches, plums, and apricots from the trees they planted in the community orchard at their church. They each take their share, then deliver the remainder to a local food bank for distribution to clients. Just a month before, this part of town held its annual Jacaranda Festival to celebrate the brilliant display of the purple-flowered theme tree planted by residents along the length of the streets in a square-mile block. The festival attracts tourists from around the country, drawn to the town not only by the beautiful floral display but also by the general aesthetic quality and high standard of care of its well-planted streets.

This is not Ecotopia nor even a futuristic community-living complex in Scandinavia. It's what is possible in cities throughout the United States and the world as citizens take back their power and begin to take responsibility for the urban environment.

The sky's the limit in this urban forest. The number of trees lining highways and freeways, in parks, parking lots, streets, school yards, and private homes can be increased dramatically.

CITY HARVESTS

Trees For Life

Balbir Mathur says he is simply an observer of miracles. Since 1983, his organization, Trees For Life, has planted more than one and a half million trees in India. "Trees For Life is not really about planting trees but about regenerating the spirit of people," he says. Trees For Life was the result of a childhood promise Mathur made to the generous lemon tree in his backyard: to plant thousands more like it so that others could enjoy its fruit. Although its focus is India, Trees For Life is based in Wichita, Kansas, where its Grow-A-Tree kit provides school children with fruit-tree seeds and the instructions to plant and care for them.

We know urban trees grow old and eventually die, just like rural-forest trees. But why do they end up in our landfills, or simply sold as firewood, instead of being used to provide the more typical forest products we know? There are inspiring examples in Northeastern cities where tree trimmings are recycled as mulch. And now with the advent of portable, mini sawmills, urban trees can be turned into usable wood and lumber. A mill can be pulled with a pickup truck right to the site of a cut or fallen tree, or can be used in a municipal equipment yard where trunks and debris are hauled. Lumber from these mills, some of which are almost fully automated, can be used for furniture, crafts, toys, and small construction projects.

The lumber from a city-owned mill could be made available to inner-city high-school and junior-college wood shops and carpentry-training programs. In Los Angeles city schools, students must pay for the wood they use for projects in shop classes. One inner-city wood-shop teacher at Jordan High School, upon receiving an award for his outstanding work with students, commented that if he could only be given enough wood for student projects, he could keep them all out of gangs and off the streets! This wood could help develop carpentry and job skills, as well as supporting cottage industries for small crafts.

Recycling urban wood is not just an opportunistic idea. Can you imagine growing trees on abandoned urban land parcels with the specific intent of selectively harvesting the wood and replanting the crop? Think of the places, such as along highways and freeways, where trees could be doing double duty!

In Oslo, Norway, some of the parks are also well-managed, lumber-producing forests. People play and ski in them, but the city foresters also harvest mature trees and sell them for lumber. The true value of this program lies not with the wood harvested but the example of sustainable forestry that's set and the reminder to urban dwellers that we should be able to protect far off, unseen tropical hardwoods.

HOLDING THE RAIN

As our cities continue to sprawl, the increase in paved areas causes enormous runoff, erosion, and storm-water problems. Instead of rainwater being caught and slowed by trees and shrubs and slowly percolating into the ground, rainwater hits asphalt, concrete, or bare, compacted ground with full impact and rushes off wherever gravity takes it.

Most cities have developed complex and expensive flood-control systems to carry away the resulting runoff. Once done effectively, continued urbanization now threatens to outstrip the ability of the flood-control system to handle the runoff. In Los Angeles, the Army Corps of Engineers is in the midst of planning an emergency project to raise by ten feet the walls of the Los Angeles River and the bridges that cross it. The Corps has determined that, because of increased paving and construction, major portions of the city will be threatened during a one-hundred-year flood (or greater), because the Los Angeles River at its current capacity could surely overflow its banks.

What's more, the runoff from urban areas carries with it toxic substances, such as oil from the streets, which go on to pollute our waterways and lakes and the bays and oceans into which they feed.

The polluting of our water in this way is as tragic as the loss of the urban watershed to development. In areas like Los Angeles, where water must be imported, it's folly to send valuable rainwater to the ocean when it could be captured and used where it falls, channeled into tanks or swales (minidams) for irrigating the local urban forest. Forestry is also known as watershed management. It therefore follows that urban forestry can be used as urban watershed management, saving on importation of water and protecting waterways downstream. Proper planting and design of parking lots and sidewalks, along with the installation of devices to trap and store rainwater, can help solve the problem.

Man alone of all the creatures of earth can change his own pattern. Man alone is the architect of his own destiny.

WILLIAM JAMES

River Birch
(*Betula nigra*)
zones 4–9

THE MAN WHO PLANTED HOPE AND GREW HAPPINESS

Jean Giono writes of a humble shepherd named Elzeard Bouffier who lived alone in a deserted and barren region of the southern French Alps in the early part of this century. It was his opinion that the land was dying for want of trees. Confessing to no pressing business of his own, he had resolved to remedy this state of affairs. Every day, while tending his sheep, he planted acorns. When the author met him, he was growing beech trees in a nursery near his cottage and was considering birches for the valleys. Ten years later, the oaks and birches had formed a young forest. Formerly dry streams now ran with water. The wind scattered seeds and, with the water, willows, rushes, meadows, gardens, and flowers reappeared. The transformation took place so gradually it caused no astonishment other than the delight of discovery by the local administration of what appeared to be a *natural* forest. Thirty years later, the earlier barren landscape was unrecognizable. Along with the forest and water came a changed climate, a healthy agriculture, and a new, energetic population. One unlearned peasant, armed with a greatness of spirit and the tenacity of benevolence, had completed a work worthy of God.

Australia suffers the effects of drought regularly on a countrywide basis. Not coincidentally, it's also badly devoid of tree cover. Coastal and inland areas have been largely deforested to make pastureland for the wool and cattle industries. Water is a precious commodity. In most semirural areas, *mains* water is way too expensive for anything but drinking. In extreme circumstances it has to be trucked in. Many households—even in the suburbs—collect rainwater for their own use. Australians are conscious of the value of water and use a variety of simple rooftop collection systems to supply themselves with drinking and bathing water, as well as water for animals and irrigation.

THE CITIZEN FORESTER POSSIBLE

Whether you put a ficus in a pot in your living room or launch a grass-roots action group in your city, your energy, inspiration, love, creativity, time, talent, resources, and your concern for this

Trainers Ellie Rosenthal (top left) and Mary Greenstein (top right) with graduates.

earth are crucial right now. The need is clear. The way forward is simple but certainly not easy.

In Los Angeles, a Citizen Forester is a person who has taken very specific TreePeople training. Citizen Forester is a term trademarked by TreePeople. It is used to represent an individual citizen who is *volunteering* to serve the community. The term is specific and is in no way meant to imply possession of professional forestry skills or license to practice professional forestry. TreePeople expects its graduates to join in the task of fostering environmental stewardship in the community, and the organization is committed to that task. Reading this book is a different matter. We don't have your name and address, and no one is there to cajole you to pick up a shovel. In this book the term *citizen forester* is used in a broader sense. Here are a few examples, from the simplest to the most gung-ho, of what might happen to you as a result of reading this book.

The Backyard Forester

People in glass houses shouldn't throw stones. And people in any sort of house with land around it should start their planting right outside their door. It's the simplest way to start. It will involve you in the wonderful discovery of your favorite trees, and you won't have to deal with permits, volunteers, fund raising, publicity, or any of the other things that can sometimes stump even the most fervent planter. But you *will* learn what it takes both to plant and care for trees.

Your own home, or a nearby vacant lot, can provide you with tons of opportunity to create a highly diversified and intensive urban-forest microenvironment. You can turn your yard into a wildlife or bird refuge—the National Wildlife Federation has a special program to encourage exactly that—or create an orchard that produces a surplus to share with food banks.

Don't discount this idea if you're a renter. Not all landlords will pay for your garden improvements, but many will welcome your work. They may ultimately benefit, but you're the first beneficiary, and approaching life with a giving spirit invariably sets you up to receive at least as much as you give.

The Multiunit Forester

Whether it's patios, common areas, window boxes, terraces, rooftops, outside the parking garages, or around the building itself, there are plenty of areas with landscape potential around apartments and condominiums. With the permission of the owners, it's possible to cut concrete to make room for planting. Obviously a little less satisfying, but also less threatening, is to use containers, such as pots, boxes, and large planters.

The Neighborhood Forester

Once you've done the work for yourself and your family, think about moving beyond your own property to take on the role of creating community around tree planting. Having learned the basics, you can help get your neighbors started in planning, planting, or in taking extra care of the trees around their homes.

It will depend on the layout of your properties, but you might want to coordinate the planting of a particular species right inside the property line, all the way along the street. Whether you aim to line your street with trees, or populate your neighborhood with a tree species that will attract specific birds, there are many opportunities for action.

The Scout

At some point, it's a good idea to inventory the needs and resources that exist in your area. Look out for vacant lots, parking

CITIZEN FORESTERS

TREEPEOPLE

lots, graffiti-covered walls, traffic islands—neighborhood eyesores. City hall likely has no clue about the specific blights or needs of your community.

The Citizen Pruner

In New York, Citizen Pruners are trained by the Street Tree Consortium and certified by the city to carry an ID card that authorizes them to prune trees whenever and wherever needed and to liberate trees girdled by tight support wires.

Perhaps you can create something similar. Bone up on pruning techniques (see Chapter 7 and Resources or sit in on a nursery demonstration or community-college class) and begin with your trees and with your neighbors' trees—with permission, of course, or on request. Carry with you wire cutters and pruning shears. Where you can't assist a needy tree, or if you don't feel your work would be appreciated, carry a notepad so that you can mail in problem reports to the proper authority. We don't encourage vigilante action. However, if your local agency is overburdened, it may welcome responsible maintenance action on the part of trained citizens. What's more, all agencies appreciate hearing about disease and pest problems so they can head off a potentially deadly infestation before it takes hold.

The Citizen Activist

Get involved in local politics. Sit on a tree board, work with your city to create or enhance a professional urban-forestry management program, be a guardian of your forest by watching out for inappropriate tree removal or bad pruning techniques. Help organize a way to protect them. One long-time TreePeople volunteer digs in the city's capital-improvement plans, discovers where street widening (and tree removal) is proposed, and notifies neighbors so that they can respond accordingly. He also pays close attention to notices of public hearings, spreads the word about them, and attends to speak on behalf of the trees. He is one man operating alone. In Seattle, one woman has formed an organization called Plant Amnesty "to end the senseless torture and mutilation of trees and shrubs that many people incorrectly refer to as pruning." With a sense of humor but a serious mission, Plant Amnesty delights in telling bad horticultural jokes and tales of hope and horror. Remember, angels can fly because they take themselves lightly!

Scouts Honor

Scouts love merit badges. It's only logical that when a scout learns the terms and principles of urban forestry and carries out a tree-planting-and-care project, he or she should be honored with a badge. In the early 1980s TreePeople worked with the Angelus Girl Scout Council to develop Urban Forestry Merit Badges. Hundreds of girls participated in an educational program with TreePeople, then went on to work with the Los Angeles County Forester and Fire Warden to plant a special grove in an inner-city regional park. Completion of both phases of the program earned each scout a special urban-forestry badge. Senior scouts, too, commonly take on special projects with TreePeople to earn their final title of Eagle Scout.

The ReLeaf Coordinator

Once you've been doing this for a while, you may be ready for the big league. New groups are popping up all the time, responding to their founders' inner calls and to the growing need for citizen involvement in urban environmental healing. The American Forestry Association is running a campaign called Global ReLeaf and provides guidelines for new local groups. There's a lot of support out there. There are also many other people with great ideas.

Sooner or later you'll bump into someone in your city who's in the same situation or, maybe even better, has already got something together on a bigger scale. Perhaps your city already has a tree-planting organization, or an urban forester. (If so, put this book down *now* and go work with them!) Try not to act too much like the newly converted around the old salts. Your role may be as facilitator or problem solver. Perhaps you'll be a leader or simply a planter. Maybe the most important thing you can do will be to put forth your ideas and get out of the way. Look to nature for guidance. There's room for a wide variety of ideas. They don't have to compete. Diversity is the strength of the forest. Cooperation is the key. Have fun!

Tree Huggers

When commercial loggers began large-scale felling of trees near Reni in northern India, their chainsaws were slicing through the very roots of local society and threatening the livelihoods of local communities. In an astonishing display of courage and determination, the women of Reni wrapped their arms around the trees to protect them from felling, sparking off the Chipko Andolan movement (the "movement to hug"). Eventually, following an inquiry, the government declared 12,000 square kilometers of the sensitive watershed region of the Alakananda basin off-limits to loggers. Today, the Chipko movement runs reforestation programs in other villages where livelihoods are threatened.

GLOBAL RELEAF

In the summer of 1988 the American Forestry Association and TreePeople sat around a conference table in Washington, D.C., to discuss how the American people could be moved to take a stand against the growing gloom of global warming. The result of that meeting (and an inordinate amount of research, coordination, and fund raising on the part of Neil Sampson and Gary Moll) was the launch of Global ReLeaf, a national campaign to encourage the planting of 100 million trees in U.S. cities by 1992. Recognizing the essential role of community groups in the realization of the goal, AFA has built a network of local and regional organizations under the ReLeaf banner, providing fledgling groups with information on how to get started and acting as a clearinghouse to link individuals with their nearest organization. (See Resources.)

2

Whenever Two or More Are Gathered: Organizing Your Community

Never doubt that a small group of concerned people can change the world. Indeed, it's the only thing that ever has.
MARGARET MEAD

*B*y now you may have started thinking there's real potential for improvement in your neighborhood. The question is, what are you going to do to make it happen? More important, what do you do first? It may seem obvious, but before you do anything, research your neighborhood.

HOLD ON A MINUTE!

For all you know, someone may already be planting or planning to plant. You may not know because existing efforts are often underpublicized. Nonetheless, time and energy have been expended and lessons may already have been learned. As we alluded to at the end of the last chapter, community efforts require, above all else, cooperation, trust, and goodwill, so it's most important to avoid unintentional offense by announcing a project that apparently ignores an existing one.

Can you play a role in the existing effort? Does it match your goals? If not, are the principals willing or able to adapt their project to include your ideas and goals, or you theirs? There is neither time nor money for competition in this arena. If it is truly not possible to work with an existing effort, be sure to make your own project distinct and complementary rather than competitive.

If you're on your own out there and want to start something more than you can handle with just a couple of neighbors, seek out organizations such as chambers of commerce, homeowners associations, and citizen-planning commissions, who may have a strong interest in taking part in projects that support their missions. Other organizations like garden clubs, scout troops, religious groups, local schools and PTAs, service clubs, corporate-

How's Your Community Doing?

American Forests Magazine tells us that a community can divide the average life span of its trees into the total tree count (including vacant planting locations) to come up with the approximate number of trees that should be planted annually to replace those being lost. New York City, for example, has 700,000 trees or tree spaces in its inventory. Dividing thirty-two (the life span of an average urban tree) into that number yields 21,875 trees that New York should be planting each year. As a whole, the U.S. isn't doing too well. In our cities on average, we are planting one tree for every four lost.

volunteer programs, and neighborhood-watch groups might want to use a street-tree planting to further benefit the community.

It's likely that groups such as these will be able to tap many of the resources needed for tree projects, like volunteers and fund-raising capability, not to mention friends in high places. To help you find out what organizations exist in your community, refer to *The Encyclopedia of Associations* published by Gale Research.

As we've said earlier, when you make the commitment to working and getting along with others to create a tree project, you're already having a positive effect on the lives of others. Once you know how to inspire and unite people toward a common goal—in this case to *green* your community—you'll rapidly find there are many issues about which you and your neighbors feel strongly. A single individual facing city hall has come to symbolize the impossible fight. But an organized group is more visible with the potential to directly influence city decisions. A group dedicated to planting trees in the neighborhood will get a reputation as a group dedicated to public service. Tree projects can be just the beginning. Don't worry about what an organization should look like or be. Just take it a step at a time and look for ways to accept others into the fold.

What's It Worth?

Dr. Rowan Rowntree with the U.S. Forest Service estimates that our current urban forest may already be saving this country $4 billion in energy costs. But what about the smaller scale? Another study shows that property value can increase as much as 20 percent with the addition of trees.

The Council of Tree and Landscape Appraisers uses the concept of replacement value to put numbers on individual tree values. Their formula starts with an assigned *basic value* for a tree's shade production and other functions, based on the diameter of the trunk. By that standard, the 1988 value of a ten-inch-diameter tree, for example, was $1,729. The tree's health, location, and species are factored into the final figure.

In 1985, the American Forestry Association did a rough estimate of the annual values that an average fifty-year-old urban tree would supply: air conditioning, $73; soil erosion and stormwater control, $75; wildlife shelter, $75; and air pollution control, $50. Total value in 1985 dollars: $273. Total value, compounded at 5 percent for fifty years: $57,151!

MORE THAN YOUR OWN BACKYARD

Some distinct advantages encourage broadening your tree project into a community activity—even if that means taking on one another's yards. A large-scale tree project will have a greater impact on the look of your neighborhood and provide substantial benefits for the environment as a whole.

WHAT DO TREES REALLY DO FOR US?

1. Provide oxygen.
2. Clean the air by absorbing odors and pollution.
3. Conserve energy by shading and cooling homes and buildings and breaking up urban heat islands, thereby reducing the need for air-conditioning.
4. Reduce water consumption and increase atmospheric moisture.
5. Prevent water runoff and soil erosion by breaking rainfall and holding soil.
6. Produce food and mulch.
7. Provide a canopy and habitat for wildlife.
8. Transform barren areas and provide buffers from harsh urban landscapes.
9. Increase property values and improve business traffic.
10. Add unity, identity, landmarks, and pride to communities working together.
11. Absorb noise, dust, and heat.
12. Reduce glare.
13. Provide visual barriers and fire and wind breaks.
14. Provide fuel and craft wood.
15. Serve as a vehicle for personal and community activism.
16. Provide employment.
17. Turn vacant lots into parks and playgrounds.
18. Provide protection against the increase in cancer-causing ultraviolet rays due to the depletion of the ozone layer.
19. Serve as friends, companions, playmates, and teachers.
20. Provide spiritual and creative inspiration.
21. Dramatically accentuate seasons in the city.
22. Act as symbols of life, peace, hope for the future, and life-style change.
23. Produce a sense of rootedness, connectedness, and community.

If you decide to plant trees on public property, remember that consolidation means you can reduce paperwork. Most cities require tree permits but will sometimes issue a blanket permit for a group of trees. It is best if you can purchase bulk supplies, because the cost per tree decreases every time you add one to your project. If you need to hire a contractor to cut cement sidewalks, you'll save money if the work is performed under one contract at one time, even if your sites are spread around the neighborhood a little. Cutting tree wells at different times will certainly add to the cost.

How do you interest your neighbors in a tree project when, with our busy lives, just getting together for dinner can be a challenge? In this chapter, you'll read concrete suggestions for capturing local interest and support, which will be the first of many changes in your neighborhood.

GOAL SETTING

Before you let your neighbors in on your ideas, set your own goals. Tree projects take many forms. You may want to simply fill in the gaps in your already-planted street, or perhaps plant the next generation if your street trees are mature. Or you may feel like tackling a large-scale planting along the whole street, either on private property or on city-regulated sidewalks. Perhaps you have trees in dire need of maintenance. Though this is usually the responsibility of the city, it's often neglected due to lack of resources. Are there parking lots nearby that ought to be shaded? Are there businesses that would like trees on the sidewalk in front of their buildings? Decide what you think will best benefit your

Restoring the Earth

The practice of environmental restoration —putting back what was originally there— is becoming recognized as an important facet of environmental activism. Restoration can be as simple as a group of neighbors replanting a decimated hillside with native-tree species, or one family's reclamation of their own backyard with the grasses and plants that grew there before suburbia took over. On a larger scale, restoration projects have brought back tracts of forest and prairie; saved members of endangered species; and purified dirty rivers and waterways, replanted their banks with original vegetation, and restocked them with fish. Laws require corporations and developers to reverse some of the environmental damage they create, and sophisticated technology can make enormous undertakings possible. However, not all damage can be fixed, and complex ecosystems are not easily replaced. Critics warn against restoration being held out as a cureall. A recommended book, *Restoring the Earth* by John J. Berger, recounts inspiring restoration success stories. See Resources for details.

THE VISION PROCESS

I do it best while listening to classical music, walking, hiking, or bike riding with something to occupy the linear part of my brain.

I put on rock music and lie down and roll myself from side to side like I'm in a trance. That's when the good stuff comes to me.

I have to keep my eyes closed so that reality doesn't block the creative flow of my imagination.

It doesn't matter how you do it, but creating your vision can be the most powerful part of your entire project, and it deserves a lot of respect. If you've never taken anything past the good-idea stage, try this.

Think about the project and envision it as complete. Examine all the elements as they would be if the project were finished. Spend some time savoring those images. Now work backwards. Build a bridge back to the present. From the point of completion back, at every phase, see if you can see who is doing what and what resources or tools are being used. Without limiting yourself by wondering how you can afford it, list the kinds of people and resources you envision you'll need. As the vision unfolds, ask yourself, "How might we do that?" Limiting thoughts will come up, but don't let them stand in the way of this process.

neighborhood and see if others agree. Don't work on details now—the next chapter covers step-by-step planning—but get an idea of what you want to accomplish.

Who do you want to involve? Are the residences on your street largely privately owned? Are there apartment dwellers who would welcome involvement in a communal project? Consider the role you want to play in the project. Project leader, planting supervisor, or mere visionary? If you're not clear early on, it might be difficult to get others interested.

Think carefully about your commitment to follow through. Planting and caring for trees is a powerful way to make a difference in a community, but your enthusiasm will face obstacles along the way, and you need to be prepared. Keep in mind that the greater the obstacles, the more rewarding the end result!

Simply ask the question and let your imagination create answers. Notice the information you're getting. Some of it may seem easy to accomplish and some may seem crazy or preposterous. That's perfect. If it helps, make notes.

Now return to the conscious world and begin to build the bridge, in concept form, from the present reality to the envisioned completed project. Visit the site and try linking your vision with what's currently there.

Next comes the difficult, exciting part. Begin to talk with people close to you. The more you have to put your idea into words, the clearer and sharper it will become. People may challenge you or criticize or laugh at your plan. That's okay. Take the feedback, hold the comments at arm's length, and evaluate whether or not they give additional perspective or information that will ultimately help you.

Do you need to alter your plan or your communication of it so that people better understand it? Is it something that's still not solid enough for others to see? That's also fine. Remember that others—even family—can be threatened by a burst of inspiration and expression that may have them reevaluating their lives. A first response can be defensive or even offensive. Don't lose heart. Others have their own processes to go through too.

Another valuable part of sharing your idea is that often your friends and family have resources, suggestions, or energy to add. When others start holding the vision, the goal becomes much more real.

CANVASING THE NEIGHBORHOOD

Plan on putting together a core group of committed individuals early on. Discuss your ideas with people you know. Garner their support before you bring in others you don't know. Talk to your neighbors. Give them an idea of what you'd like to accomplish. Go door to door. Introduce yourself and chat about your ideas. The goal is to get people thinking about the potential and dreaming of what the neighborhood could be. You may want to start by writing a letter to everyone on your street, making copies, and hand delivering them. The more personal the contact with people, the greater the response will be. You can put letters in mailboxes, but that's just one more piece of mail to sift through or to toss. If you hand deliver, your neighbors can attach a face to the project.

If you are not used to communicating in this way with strangers, selling your idea to them may seem daunting. If you're going door

Breaking New Ground

The Canadian city of Toronto has decided to reduce its carbon emissions 20 percent by the year 2005—as called for at a landmark global warming conference held in the city in 1988. The Toronto Special Advisory Committee on the Environment has called for the following: increased parking fees, enforced vehicle-emissions standards, more bike lanes, expanded carpool programs, and refitting city buildings with energy-efficient fluorescent bulbs. The exact carbon-reducing potential isn't known, but the plan will offset at least 20 percent of the city's carbon dioxide emissions because of a massive tree-planting program. By planting 495,000 acres of red pine in Ontario over the next ten years, Toronto will trap an average of 500,000 tons of carbon in each of the next forty years. Within the city limits, Toronto plans to make a net addition of 1,500 trees per year. Public support grew out of an awareness among residents that steps to save the global atmosphere would also improve the air they breathe. It's the ambition of the plan, along with its successful marriage of local and global environmental concerns, that distinguishes it as a shining example of how to formulate global-warming policy.

World Watch Magazine
MAY-JUNE 1990

NEIGHBORS UNITED ASSOCIATION

Tree Planting Petition

Members of our community have expressed interest in ways to maintain and/or increase property values and beautify our neighborhood, as well as control noise and pollution.

In an effort to address these issues, Neighbors United Association has chosen to plant trees along Guthrie and Sawyer as its' "1989 Beautification Project". We feel this action will enhance our neighborhood and create a more pleasant environment in which to live.

****

By signing this petition, I agree to have trees planted along Guthrie Avenue from Crescent Heights through Point View Street, and the 5900 block of Sawyer.

I understand and authorize the following:

1) I have reviewed and agree to the proposed plans for the planting of tree(s) on my adjacent property.

2) The type of trees approved by the City of Los Angeles is a Jacaranda on Guthrie, and a **Bradford Pear** on Sawyer.

3) The pruning of the trees will be done by the City of Los Angeles as needed.

4) I will be responsible for watering and routine care of the tree(s) on my adjacent property.

5) The cost of the tree planting will be paid by a "Neighborss United" fund raiser and volunteer efforts.

Your support in our "1989 Beautification Project" is appreci

Neighbors United
119 PO Box 35103
Los Angeles, Ca. 90035

Would you be interested in the BEAUTIFICATION of our community?

Would you be interested in reducing:

  a) Noise Level?

  b) Exhaust fumes?

  c) Glare?

  d) Dust emission?

HOW can we do all of this TOGETHER?

L E T S   P L A N T   T R E E S

WHERE: On Sawyer, between Fairfax & Point View

B E N E F I T S

1. Less Pollution

2. More oxygen as trees breathe

3. Summer cooling

4. Much much more but MOST OF ALL

5. Neighborhood BEAUTIFICATION & P R I D E

Contact: Dolores I've got a plan

120

The Organizing Process

Create your vision.

↓

Talk to friends and neighbors.

Develop a group; identify and set goals· for a project. ← Hold meeting about trees.

↓

→ Create a structure (schedule meetings, assign work).

↓

Notify officials of your idea and ask for assistance.

↓

Establish good working relationships with: property owners; city, county, or company officials; and tree experts.

↓

Define the project: choose a practical site, develop a timeline for the project, get necessary permissions, select species, consider maintenance needs, define what's needed to get the job done.

↓

Raise the necessary resources.

↓

Organize and accomplish the planting.

↓

Plan for and follow through with maintenance.

↓

Pull in help if you get stuck.

to door in your neighborhood, you're doing it in the best way possible—but that doesn't mean it's a pushover. Some people are very wary about opening the door to anyone they're not expecting. If they appear irritated, cautious, or downright rude, don't take it as a personal affront. You may have inadvertently taken them away from an activity that needed their concentration. Apologize, ask if you can continue or whether you should call back at another time, and move on—either with the purpose of your visit or to the next house! It's hard but necessary for you to protect yourself from being hurt by rejection. Talk to yourself under your breath on the way to the front door, shield yourself with an imaginary veil, go in pairs, meet before or after for coffee with the committee so you can blab about how it all went—whatever works. But do it. (For further information, see page 77.)

Spend time getting to know more about your neighborhood and the people who live there. Think of the places where people gather: a cafe, the laundromat, a local bank, a school, the post office, the day-care center, the park, or even a driveway down the street. Who hangs out there and who knows all the gossip? The goal is to find those people who have a hand in everything and to share your idea with them. They'll often know who to talk to and will probably help spread the word.

LET US BEGIN

Now bring together as many people as possible! Invite them over for coffee, tea, or dessert some evening, or perhaps on a Sunday afternoon.

This initial gathering can be very informal. You might consider making a map of the neighborhood so that on arrival everyone can mark down their particular residence. You can then make copies and distribute the maps. Since you've called the meeting, it's up to you to be prepared with some material, ideas, or information. If you think your project will be on public land, make a quick call to the responsible agency for an idea on how long the permit process will take. (See Chapter 3.) It will help you set a timeline if your meeting goes that route. Have a clear idea of what you'd like to see happen but stay open to suggestions. Don't have your idea so developed that no one can contribute to the creative process. Ask people to share their ideas and dreams for the neighborhood. Support them in making the project their own because, believe it or not, their support is vital to your success. If it's all your idea, then it's all your project!

Planning the Meeting

Have an agenda for your initial meeting. You may not plan to lead the whole project, but you're the one who's taken the initiative. Here's a suggested outline for a preliminary meeting.

1. When people arrive, give out name tags. It helps break down barriers.

2. Start the meeting by introducing yourself and thanking the people for coming. (Acknowledging that you need their support is a key element in helping them feel part of the project.) Let them know your purpose. Tell them when the meeting will be over and don't keep anyone longer than an hour and a half. Post your agenda on a large piece of paper or hand it out. Have everyone introduce themselves to the group. Which house is theirs? What ideas or dreams do they have for greening the neighborhood? Discourage a gripe session.

3. Acknowledge that this time, for convenience, you'll facilitate the meeting. Ultimately, you can have other people host and lead meetings, but don't push it until others show their interest, ability, or energy.

4. Begin your agenda, which might look something like the agenda at left.

5. For the What's-Possible section, it would be good to have a reference book with pictures of different tree species or a sketch of your street that highlights possible planting spots. Others can then add their ideas. If you've really done your homework, you might have some slides of your favorite trees in the neighborhood.

6. During the discussion-brainstorm, record the ideas on a posted piece of paper. Brainstorms should only focus on the positive to encourage people to feel comfortable enough to share ideas. Don't comment. Don't commit sabotage. The purpose is to emerge with possibilities and to encourage others to contribute. Brainstorming generates ideas; it does not evaluate what is realistic. Encourage people to be outrageous and to dream, as opposed to commenting on the ideas of others. What may look outrageous in this setting might be a fresh new practical solution when you come to implementation. Once ideas are recorded, go back and discuss them. Highlighting strengths helps others feel appreciated and involved. All it takes is a little insensitivity now to lose someone for the rest of the program.

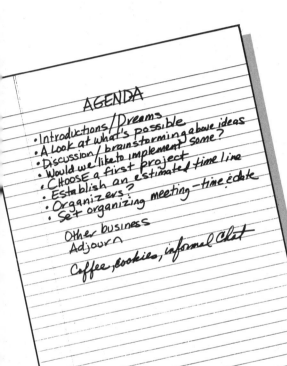

AGENDA
• Introductions/Dreams
• A Look at what's possible
• Discussion/brainstorming above ideas
• Would we like to implement some?
• CHoose a first project
• Establish an estimated time line
• Organizers?
• Set organizing meeting — time & date

Other business
Adjourn

Coffee, cookies, informal Chat

TreePeople invites you to your General Volunteer Meeting Wednesday June 6, 1990

Join the staff and volunteers for this month's special volunteer meeting, a fluid evening on why watering trees is investing in L.A.'s future. You will be entertained by a revealing slide show highlighting events of the last two months. This is the season that's saturated with opportunites to stay cool with TreePeople -- all of our volunteer programs have events planned for the upcoming months!

TreePeople's meeting place is Coldwater Canyon Park, at the intersection of Mulholland Drive and Coldwater Canyon Avenue, 1.5 miles south of Ventura Boulevard in Studio City.

NEW VOLUNTEER ORIENTATION 7:00 PM
EVERYONE ELSE 7:30 IN THE COMMUNITY ROOM
818-753-4600 FOR MORE DETAILS
12601 MULHOLLAND DR, BEVERLY HILLS, CA 90210

Local Tree Planting Meeting

March 10, 1990

Dear Neighbor:

My roomate and I live off Bronson Street near Sunset and are very interested in planting more trees in the neighborhood. We feel that it would add beauty and noise protection as well as help to clean the air.

I have contacted a group called Tree People and am training on the best way to organize a successful planting including: community support, city permits, tree types, and care of new trees. With your help we will be able to plant dozens of trees on a weekend before the end of April (Earth Day)!

Whether you live or work in the neighborhood, I would really like to hear from you. Your advice, volunteer time, or contribution will make all the difference!

Please join us for a short meeting,

Thursday March 15, 1990 7:00 PM
Denny's Restaurant (back room)
5751 Sunset Blvd. (@101)

Call me with your questions and ideas.

Chris Paine

7. Make it clear that, while everyone will be needed for the project, a few will have to help organize. Don't try to do it all yourself. You'll probably burn out and be discouraged forever from planting! Try recruiting one or two people to work with you on the following tasks:

△ contacting the local government agency for regulations and beginning the process of getting a permit, including a list of approved trees for your street, if necessary, assuming your work will be on land that requires government approval

△ contacting the neighbors who haven't yet been reached

△ collecting information on trees, prices, nurseries, and other supplies

△ locating tools

△ fundraising

△ planning, producing, and running additional meetings

△ coordinating the planting day, the block party, and the barbecue

△ organizing other volunteers, resources, and publicity

8. This group may express reservations about getting involved before they know how much time or money they'll have to devote to the project. Perhaps you'll have some sample costs to share. But even if you don't, try to steer people away from getting stuck by worrying where money, energy, or time will come from. Be prepared for their concerns by reading Chapter 3 before the meeting.

9. Establish an estimated timeline for planting.

10. Set a date and time to meet with the organizing group. If it doesn't feel like an undue amount of pressure, try creating a list of action items to accomplish by, or report on, at the next meeting.

11. Wrap up the formal part of the meeting. Create a roster of names, phone numbers, and addresses.

12. Let everyone know that you, or one of the new organizers, will be back in touch for another meeting on types of trees and so forth, unless decision making has been delegated to the organizing committee.

13. Adjourn the meeting. Be prepared to chat and munch for a while afterward, as important informal discussion is likely to take place.

Books Are Made From Trees, Right?

In April 1986, an arsonist set fire to the Los Angeles Central Library. Once the flames were out, a rescue operation was mounted, using TreePeople's skills to co-ordinate the hundreds of volunteers who wanted to save the remaining books from irreversible water damage. The operation set a record for library evacuation. ARCO—headquartered opposite the library—provided a bank of phones and offices to house the telephone operators coordinating the rescue. A small bank twenty miles away happened to have a phone number one digit short of the rescue hotline. An irate bank manager called ARCO and asked for Andy Lipkis. "You'd better send someone down here right now to handle this mess! We're getting calls from people who want to volunteer at the library and it's interfering with our work!" Andy explained that the library fire was interfering with TreePeople's work too—and ARCO's and most of all the library's. He suggested the bank become a part of the rescue team and assign a staffer to give phone instructions. There was an almost audible shift in the manager's attitude. He got the point and began to give, instead of complain.

The process doesn't have to be this organized, but it helps when you are hosting a lot of interested people. An additional step would be to ask someone from a local tree group, or your city's urban forester, to speak to your gathering.

After the Meeting

After your first meeting, move quickly to obtain results. Collect information vital to the project or establish contacts in city agencies. The faster you move, the better. People need to see progress. On your roster, make a note of those who expressed interest in the project, those who offered to plant, and those who are part of the organizing committee. Stay in touch!

Resources

Be aware of the vast resources at your fingertips. Your neighbors are a primary resource. By offering them a chance to put their skills to work, you let them know how valuable they are to the effort. Neighborhood groups you're not working with directly may nevertheless be helpful when it comes to specific tasks.

If you followed our advice, you checked out what community organizations already exist in your neighborhood. Don't overlook your city-council representative or county supervisor. It's their job to facilitate community activity. Call their offices. Not only can they help you contact existing organizations but they can often facilitate your work with government agencies and the consequent red tape! If you don't know who your elected officials are, your local public library will probably carry a Public Officials Roster with this information. Newspapers and flyers may also provide leads. Don't forget to ask your friends and neighbors for suggestions.

Getting Formal

We suggest you call the offices of your state attorney general for further information on incorporating as a nonprofit if that's what you think you'll eventually want to do. States will vary in their requirements, but most have literature to help you establish yourself. The Internal Revenue Service is another good source of information on the laws, policies, and standards regarding fundraising.

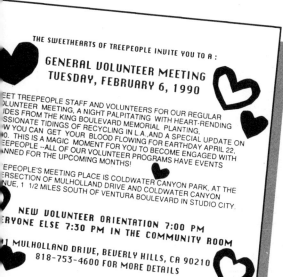

THE SWEETHEARTS OF TREEPEOPLE INVITE YOU TO A:

GENERAL VOLUNTEER MEETING
TUESDAY, FEBRUARY 6, 1990

EET TREEPEOPLE STAFF AND VOLUNTEERS FOR OUR REGULAR
OLUNTEER MEETING, A NIGHT PALPITATING WITH HEART-RENDING
IDES FROM THE KING BOULEVARD MEMORIAL PLANTING,
SSIONATE TIDINGS OF RECYCLING IN L.A., AND A SPECIAL UPDATE ON
W YOU CAN GET YOUR BLOOD FLOWING FOR EARTHDAY APRIL 22.
O. THIS IS A MAGIC MOMENT FOR YOU TO BECOME ENGAGED WITH
EEPEOPLE—ALL OF OUR VOLUNTEER PROGRAMS HAVE EVENTS
NNED FOR THE UPCOMING MONTHS!

EPEOPLE'S MEETING PLACE IS COLDWATER CANYON PARK, AT THE
ERSECTION OF MULHOLLAND DRIVE AND COLDWATER CANYON
NUE, 1 1/2 MILES SOUTH OF VENTURA BOULEVARD IN STUDIO CITY.

NEW VOLUNTEER ORIENTATION 7:00 PM
RYONE ELSE 7:30 PM IN THE COMMUNITY ROOM

1 MULHOLLAND DRIVE, BEVERLY HILLS, CA 90210
818-753-4600 FOR MORE DETAILS

For further support, many states also have organizations that may offer classes or provide information on establishing a non-profit, including grant writing. For example, the Foundation Center in New York has information on the types of grants available and how to seek funding—both private and public. For information, see listing in Resources.

TreeUtah

SALT LAKE CITY

P.O. Box 11506 • Zip 84147-0506

TreeProject

SACRAMENTO
Tree
FOUNDATION

·Founded·
·1982·

The Community of Trees

TREEPEOPLE

WHAT'S IN A NAME?

Each week in the world, a forest the size of London disappears. Hence was founded the organization called The Forest of London after a fortuitous visit by Andy and Katie Lipkis in 1984. Crann, an organization created to replant the hardwoods of Ireland, took its name from the Gaelic word for tree. Andy Lipkis founded the California Conservation Project in 1973 because, as a long-haired, bearded teenager, he wanted an official-sounding name, but the public insisted on calling the group "the tree people." The worldwide Men of the Trees, founded by Richard St. Barbe Baker, was the name he gave to the volunteers from a tribe of Kenyan dancing warriors he creatively enlisted in 1920 for a reforestation campaign. The title, Global ReLeaf, a project of the American Forestry Association, was derived from a poster entitled "Urban Releaf," created by Doyle, Dane, Bernbach for TreePeople's Million Tree Campaign in 1982. Whatever your project, there's a perfect name. Sit with your vision long enough, and your name will come to you!

PUBLIC SPEAKING

Later on, if you get bitten by this bug, you may be asked to make presentations to groups interested in tree planting or maintenance. Your purpose will be to provide information, direction, and in some cases to assist others in organizing their project. Improving your speaking skills will also help you more eloquently lead planting and maintenance demonstrations, recruit volunteers, and raise money.

We've all heard speakers who read their presentation in a dull, monotonous tone. The fear of speaking should be the fear of being boring! You have the basic natural skills for speaking. The trick is developing fluency. The first step is to visualize yourself speaking the way you'd like to. Believing you can do it makes a difference. Joining an organization like Toastmasters, which helps improve public speaking skills, can be helpful. Meanwhile, this section can set you on the right path.

In preparing your speech, be clear about your purpose. What would you like to come out of the talk? Know your audience's interests and the kind of support they'll require. If possible, ask the contact person in advance. If you feel comfortable, invite questions of the group before you speak, so you can address their concerns in your presentation. Write the questions or pointers on a chalkboard if one is available.

Preparation will give you confidence. Have an outline in big type or reference cards as reminders of important points. It's better to speak from your heart and talk about what you know. Don't lecture. Interact with the group. Encourage them in their strengths and work with them through their weaknesses.

Give a brief introduction before you cover your main topics, then offer a conclusion. In the introduction, give a preview of the subjects so the audience will be able to follow your thoughts. Your main topics should stem from your assessment of the group. In the conclusion, it is helpful to give a summary of what you have talked about and to include suggestions for action.

In general, assume the group knows nothing about the topics you're covering. Give explanations of terms you use, such as *greenhouse effect* or *sucker growth*. Try to relate stories or anecdotes that illustrate your experience with tree projects.

Tips

△ Dress appropriately for the group and the setting. If everyone will be in business suits, dress professionally. If people are casual, your attire can be more relaxed. When in doubt, dress up rather than down. If they can accept you at first glance, they will listen to what you say.

▲ Thank the group for inviting you and for their interest.

▲ Tell about your involvement in tree projects and experiences.

▲ Use visual aids—anything from a seedling or shovel to pictures or a brochure.

▲ Take time to collect your thoughts before you get up to speak. Review your notes, take some deep breaths, remember why you're there and what you want to accomplish.

▲ The audience is hungry for information but will not bite! Be yourself. Relax. If you're nervous, turn it around and use the

ROOTS IN ECOLOGY—Andy Lipkis with a few of the 8,000 smog-resistant trees he plans on replanting.
Times photo by Harry Chase

Andy vs. the Bureaucratic Deadwood

BY MICHAEL SEILER
Times Staff Writer

Andy Lipkis, a 19-year-old college freshman very much into ecology, had this idea a couple of years ago: The trees in the San Bernardino National Forest are dying from the smog that drifts east out of Los Angeles, so find some smog-resistant trees and replant them there.

After all, Lipkis thought, the experts say the forest in the Big Bear-Lake Arrowhead-Barton Flats area could be dead in as little as 20 years if nothing is done.

A pure case for a bit of individual initiative, right? One young man could get the ecological bandwagon rolling.

It wasn't quite that easy. There were some complications along the way. Like the bureaucracy of the California Division of Forestry.

Lipkis discovered a few months ago that the division had 20,000 smog-resistant Sierra redwoods and sugar pines, all under a year old, growing in its tree nursery up near Davis.

Andy told the forestry people his plan. They said that it was a nice idea, but rules are rules, and the division does not give its baby trees away. If they're not sold, they're plowed under.

They cost two and one-half cents per tree and Andy wanted all 20,000 trees.

Tight Student Budget

Which is more money than a kid on a tight college-student budget can handle.

He went to a few of the bigger corporations that talk a good ecology game. But Andy, an environmental studies major at Cal State Sonoma, had no luck in coming up with the $500 needed to buy the trees.

And while he was making the rounds, time was slipping away.

"They (the forest division administrators) said I had to get the money by March 16 or they'd kill the trees," Andy said.

"They were going to plow them under to replant

Please Turn to Page 7, Col. 1

energy. Just don't get nervous about being nervous. Accept it. Have fun. You can even tell people you're nervous.

△ It's okay not to know every answer. Refer people to a source such as your local tree group if you have one or other pertinent organizations, or offer to find out and then get back to them.

△ Many public speakers practice in front of a mirror to observe their body language. If you gesture too much, it may be distracting. If you don't move at all, it can be boring. Also, listening to yourself on a tape can increase your awareness of tone and rate of speaking. If you have access to a video camera, so much the better!

△ Speak to the person in the back of the room and everyone will hear you.

△ Eye contact is very important, especially in small groups. Try to speak to each individual using your eyes to make a connection. As a speaker, you'll develop your own unique speaking style. Concise and accurate information is the key to being an effective speaker regardless of your personal style.

The more comfortable you are with the facts and information you are delivering, the easier it will be for you to refine your presentation. A technique to use for subjects you are not familiar with is to learn the material from a brochure or article, even memorize it, then begin saying it your own way. The more practice you have, the more readily words will come to you.

Every presentation is a practice for the next one, so make notes to yourself. What worked? What didn't? How could you do it better? You can be your own best critic. Your speaking skills will improve quickly if you take the opportunity to evaluate yourself in a constructive way and then practice.

Citizen Foresters need to communicate to groups at various levels. Whether you are speaking to a group formally or informally, doing a demonstration, or just answering questions, people will look to you for leadership. Interaction requires listening as well as speaking. Listening is a first step to being listened to.

If you're interested in your topic, your audience probably will be too. Think of what inspires you and speak from that perspective. Speaking is sharing information, knowledge, and experience. People relate to what you're saying if you're both excited and focused.

If you lose your train of thought, pause. If you don't remember something, move on and come back to it. When people look restless, suggest a stretch break or ask a question. You are in charge of your presentation. Keep believing. Good luck!

3

Getting It Together: Planning and Funding Your Project

I have a high regard for our species, for all its newness and immaturity as a member of the biosphere. As evolutionary time is measured, we arrived here only a few moments ago and we have a lot of growing up to do. If we succeed, we could become a sort of collective mind for the Earth, the thought of the Earth. At the moment, for all our juvenility as a species, we are surely the brightest and brainiest of the Earth's working parts. I trust us to have the will to keep going, and to maintain as best we can the life of the planet.

LEWIS THOMAS

Mark Christensen and David Creigh, VIPs from the Southern California Gas Company and Hiuka America, dig in on Martin Luther King, Jr. Boulevard.

*A*re you getting eager to start remaking your neighborhood? Don't go any farther until you've read this chapter! It deals with time-consuming issues that, if heeded, will lead to a much more successful project with your long-term goals of tree survival and community enhancement standing a far greater chance of being reached. Successful tree events require careful forethought. Missing a critical step here could result in failure—no one showing up on the big day, people feeling alienated, weird press coverage—all through problems that could have been avoided. (The workbook contains checklists and room for specific notes to help you focus on *your* project. You'll have your own way of tackling the work in hand, so proceed now as suits you best.)

SITE SELECTION

If your group is interested in a neighborhood planting, you've probably brainstormed a number of possible sites at your initial meeting. Did you overlook your own yards? There's no reason why this can't be a group project, buying in bulk and *making light* of some heavy work. Remember, one of the primary purposes of this book—and of urban tree planting as far as we're concerned—is to create community, and you can do that just as easily on private property. Again, you won't have to consider rules and regulations—just sensible locations!

Possible Locations

Perhaps you want to replace manufactured fences with living, green ones or create a new neighborhood identity. Consider plant-

Energy-Efficient Landscaping

There is no quiet place in the white man's cities. No place to hear the unfurling of leaves in the spring, or the rustle of insect's wings. . . . And what is there to life if a man cannot hear the lonely cry of the whippoorwill or the argument of the frogs around the pool at night? . . . Whatever befalls the earth befalls the sons of the earth. If men spit upon the ground, they spit upon themselves. This we know—the earth does not belong to man, man belongs to the earth. Like the blood which unites one family. All things are connected. Whatever befalls the earth befalls the sons of the earth. Man did not weave the web of life; he is merely a strand in it. Whatever he does to the web, he does to himself.

CHIEF SEATTLE, 1856
UPON SURRENDERING
HIS TRIBAL LANDS

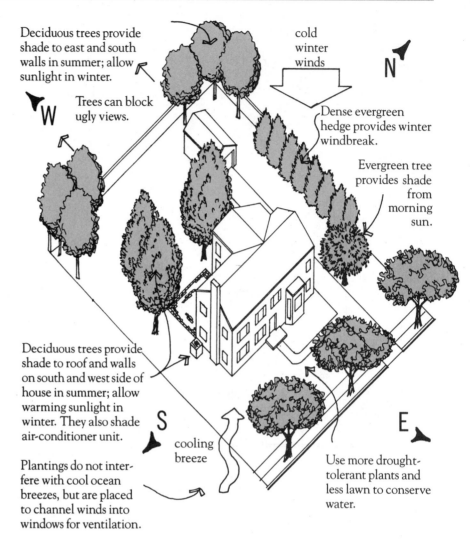

Deciduous trees provide shade to east and south walls in summer; allow sunlight in winter.

Trees can block ugly views.

cold winter winds

N

Dense evergreen hedge provides winter windbreak.

Evergreen tree provides shade from morning sun.

Deciduous trees provide shade to roof and walls on south and west side of house in summer; allow warming sunlight in winter. They also shade air-conditioner unit.

Plantings do not interfere with cool ocean breezes, but are placed to channel winds into windows for ventilation.

S

cooling breeze

E

Use more drought-tolerant plants and less lawn to conserve water.

Make sure you consider a tree's mature growth, height, and spread in relation to the amount of space you have. Keep trees three to five feet from sidewalk or paving.

ing for function as well as design. Remember, shade trees will help keep your homes cool and will transpire moisture, so look for spaces where they can block direct sun; three on the west and south sides of each house will do nicely. They'll create natural air-conditioning or cut artificial air-conditioning costs (and thereby carbon dioxide and other emissions from power plants). A species note for winter warmth: choose a dense evergreen to plant on the north side to block winter winds; choose deciduous for the south side to let in winter sunlight. If you want to intercept noise, wind, eyesores, or dust, think about planting in clusters or double rows. Always plant food-producing trees as far away as possible from streets or old refuse sites. Toxic lead does not decompose and may be drawn into the fruit. If you want to hold a slope, use closely spaced conifers.

Once your yards are green havens and your patios and rooftops are converted and shaded, move on! Street parkways (the strips of grass running between the sidewalk and the street, also known as tree lawns, nature strips, and green belts) or paved street sidewalks are usually regulated by your local government. They're a good choice but will almost certainly require permits to plant, so consider first planting in front of houses near the sidewalk. It might achieve a similar effect, and you won't need anyone's permission but the homeowners', who are likely all on your committee.

Consider also a median strip (the center of the street) or even traffic islands. These are regulated too, but they're one of

Climbing the Infrastructure Tree

"City trees need attention—not just admiration." So says the tree lady of Gainesville, Florida, who blew the whistle on her utility company, which was bypassing a local ordinance requiring replacement, inch for inch, of any trees removed because they posed a threat to its equipment. Inch for inch means replacing a mature tree with two or three smaller ones, if necessary, in an appropriate place. "Poems extol the virtues of trees, but who's out there protecting them?" she demands. Kay Hanna went from citizen activist to chair of the local tree committee, then had the whole of her committee boosted to City-Tree-Advisory-Board status, reporting directly to the city commission. The headline in the local paper read, "Lady Will Do Anything To Save Trees." You bet.

the obvious choices in shading streets. Are there any undeveloped parklands or other areas of waste ground that have little foot traffic? They're probably in a more native state and may be appropriate for planting seedlings. Hillside slopes too steep for development can be planted to help hold the soil and add greenery.

Once you start looking, you'll be surprised at the nooks and crannies that can be made better by trees. Some are conspicuous, like planting in and around the stalls of a parking lot, or in a school yard, where trees will cool the blacktop and shade the kids from those extra ultraviolet rays we're receiving through the damaged ozone layer. But don't overlook the subtle locations either, like alleys behind houses or the spaces between buildings or those no-man's-land areas known as spandrels. Consider temples, churches, or other private buildings; vacant lots; city or county parks; flood control channels to combat erosion; landfills; railroad rights-of way; graffiti-covered walls (try vines or espaliered trees); freeways to absorb fumes from traffic; industrial sites to combat pollution; or perhaps the bare strips of land beneath high-tension power lines.

What Makes a Site Practical?

As the American Forestry Association's Gary Moll says, giving trees a home means giving them space to grow both above and below the ground. First look up. Then look around. Are there overhead wires or obstructions that will limit the height or spread of the tree? Is it a place where spreading branches might get bumped by trucks or buses? Look down. Measure how much space there is for the root crown (the dimension of the trunk at ground surface). Think of the tree's root system and determine whether there's room for it to spread. Are there any underground pipes or utilities? These considerations are important. You and your neighbors won't appreciate a tree whose roots are breaking your pipes. Utility companies too are particularly concerned about tree placement. Original bad placement can lead to very bad feelings between communities and utilities who spend $800 million each

A tenacious *ficus* hangs on in an inappropriate location, pruned by every truck that wooshes by.

year in this country just maintaining and removing trees that are interfering with overhead service.

Be sure that the trees you want to plant are appropriate for your location—the right tree in the right place (see page 50).

Check out the long-term availability of the site. It should be available and intact for a significant part of the trees' lifespan. Are they likely to be cut down in their prime to make room for development, expansion, or street widening? Property owners may encourage tree plantings to improve the site's value if they intend to sell the property. The trees' future would then depend on the next owner. This possibility may lead you to consider a temporary project using container trees that could be moved to a permanent location when the current site is developed.

You must get permission—and with luck, enthusiastic cooperation—from the property owner to plant trees on the site. Unauthorized plantings are illegal—and stupid! They provide no guarantee that the trees will be allowed to grow, and a full guarantee that you or your group will get a bad name. Government agencies have a right to, and will, remove trees for which permits have not been granted. TreePeople knows of at least one painful instance where an individual paid a professional contractor to

I owe an allegiance to the planet that has made me possible, and to all the life on that planet, whether friendly or not. I also owe an allegiance to the 3½ (three and a half) billion years of life that made it possible for me to be here, and all the rest of you too. We have a responsibility to the largest population of all, the hundreds of billions of people who have not yet been born, who have a right to be, who deserve a world at least as beautiful as ours, whose genes are now in our custody and no one else's.

DAVID R. BROWER

plant seven beautiful, expensive trees—of the wrong species for that location. It was done in the spirit of helping the city, but in this case the city didn't appreciate the help.

Finally, the site should provide access for tree maintenance and periodic watering until the trees are well established and pose no unusual danger to volunteers or maintenance workers, such as a steep site that's extremely susceptible to slides.

Taking Care of What's There

If you're interested in tree care rather than planting, you probably have in mind a problem site that needs attention. In a way, it's a much more mature route to take—recognizing that we should appreciate and care for what's already there before we add to the maintenance burden of the community.

Be realistic. Leave the pruning of large old trees to professional tree trimmers. Instead, concentrate on finding sites where your group can pull weeds and water trees or remove stakes and ties that are strangling trunks. This activity will have a significant impact, and the trees will love you for it at least as much as the community will. Younger trees are usually a good bet for maintenance as they require great care during the first three years following planting. Even drought-resistant trees need consistent watering while they're sending down roots and becoming established. Pruning is also more manageable with smaller trees and can be a worthwhile project. If maintenance is a big problem in your city, find out why. What's the city's tree maintenance budget? Don't automatically point the finger at the responsible department. Perhaps they need help from citizens to advocate more training for employees or a bigger budget to hire more trimmers. Have your role be one of assistance, rather than hindrance, to a well-managed department.

Your group may be interested in looking after neglected trees on private land. Make sure you don't end up simply being a replacement for the local tree trimmers. The goal here is to improve the quality of community trees. Can or should the landowner take care of these trees? Your first step is to contact the person or firm that owns the land and explain that the trees are in need of care. This step may even involve showing a representative or the grounds keeper what's needed. Depending on the reaction, you have several options.

You may decide that you'd like to take charge of caring for the trees; perhaps the community enjoys them and would be interested in doing the work. Maybe you can help the landowner

TreePeople knew of an enterprising and concerned arborist who created a Tree-In-Trouble report slip that he would fill out and slip in the mailbox on any property where he spotted a tree that needed help. He suggested he or other professionals do the work.

develop a maintenance schedule and train the employees (or a recreation, horticulture, or garden club set up for employees) to care for the trees. Yet again, the best solution may be to refer the landowner to an arborist who can care for the trees.

However you work with landowners, approach it as a mutually beneficial partnership. Don't provoke a confrontation. Chances are, the landowner will be as interested as you in improving the appearance of a valuable property and will appreciate your concern if it's tactfully expressed.

SPECIES SELECTION

Choosing trees should be one of the most difficult yet rewarding processes of your entire project. It's vital you choose a tree that both meets your goals and can thrive within the constraints of the planting site.

Fall in Love

The fact is, this relationship is like a marriage. With luck, it will last as long—in fact longer—than most marriages. Ideally, we marry people we're in love with. Thus we need to embark upon a love affair with trees, allowing ourselves to be seduced by their magic. The really marvelous part about this relationship is that you don't need to restrict your affair to one tree! Most tree lovers have a healthy list of their favorites and, like a good marriage, they've come to love these trees because of their finer points and regardless of their drawbacks. Knowing the good and bad of your favorites means you'll be able more skillfully to match the tree with the location. You'll know not to recommend a deciduous tree to an obsessively tidy lawn fanatic, or a tree with buttressing roots for a sidewalk planting.

But there's more to it than that. Expecting any book to provide the definitive guide to the best trees is like asking a mentor for a list of the best people in the world. Fortunately, that list would be different for everyone. There's no such thing as a perfect person. We're loved for who we are, in spite of our weaknesses.

It's the same with trees. Nobody can really explain why his or her favorites are on a pedestal. They just are.

Before you fall in love with just any old oak, pine, or spruce, it's important to know a few things about yourself. What are the qualities you like in a tree? Do you want it strong and independent? Or do you want it to be more sensitive and vulnerable, dependent on you for loving care and attention?

The tree which moves some to tears of joy is in the eyes of others only a green thing which stands in the way. Some see nature as all ridicule and deformity . . . and some scarce see nature at all. But by the eyes of a man of imagination, nature is imagination itself.

WILLIAM BLAKE
IN A LETTER TO DR. TRUSLER

ONE MAN'S MEAT IS ANOTHER MAN'S POISON

It was Saturday morning. Katie was deep in the heart of the manuscript for this book when Andy burst in through the front door: "I need your help—quickly!" Her husband's face was trickling blood all over his hands. "The chorisia!" he panted.

The Floss Silk tree, *Chorisia speciosa*, is Katie's favorite. It's tall and elegant with bright green leaves and showy pink flowers in the fall. It also has a fat, spiny trunk, so it's not good around kids. In 1985, she'd planted a seedling in the garden of a rental property. A vigilant neighbor and TreePeople volunteer called six months ago to say the tree was going to be removed; the new tenants were afraid of its spiny trunk. At the Lipkis's request, the neighbor containerized the tree, and it was moved to their present house. During the move, this twelve-foot beauty flipped its trunk in Andy's face and cut his forehead. Bad tree? Silly Andy? Or the wrong person in the wrong place at the wrong time?!

The Case for Natives

If you like an independent that doesn't require much attention, look for native species that are meant to grow where you are. In fact, if you're planting in a natural area, use only natives. They are environmentally sound, provide and maintain food supplies and habitat to native birds and wildlife, and have the least impact on resources. Don't introduce exotic species in forests or undeveloped urban areas. They may grow well but could require extreme amounts of water or care that make them an inappropriate choice. They may drop leaves that inhibit the growth of other vital plants. In working to restore damaged ecosystems, native species should be given the highest priority. If natives won't suit your location, look next for trees from similar climate regions.

Cruising

There are tree-selection and planting guide books available for most areas. (See Resources.) Consulting them is a vital piece of the selection process as you'll get a good idea of what's appropriate or historic for your area. But books alone are not sufficient. Learning characteristics—even viewing illustrations and photos far superior to those provided in this book—can only give you limited experience of a tree you might be spending the rest of your life with.

The best way to select a tree is to personally meet its family before you make a commitment. Unlike choosing a mate, you have a chance to see how your intended will behave and what it will look like after one year or five, ten, twenty-five, or even fifty years. Go out looking for trees that attract you. You can cruise the streets for an idea of those that seem to do well or are accepted in your community. Go to your planting site and see what thrives around it. If you don't recognize the species, cut a sample or take a picture and ask a nursery for identification. Or go to where you'll find variety, panache, and labels—the arboretum or botanic garden. Often a college campus or regional park will have a large selection of trees. Check them out. How do they look? How do they behave? Do they drop leaves, fruit, branches? Do they have potentially damaging roots? Ask the grounds personnel what it's like working with specific trees. What about their long-term care including pruning and feeding? Do they have any personality problems?

Go to those who know. Ask your city, county, or state forester. Quiz botany or biology teachers, garden-club members, or certified arborists. If you don't get anywhere, go back to books that can help you identify the trees in your area. Books that lead you through a series of steps to determine the species are called keys. Ask an expert for one that will work locally.

If your site includes overhead wires, call your utility company. Many are now publishing excellent free booklets to help you choose trees that won't grow past thirty feet in twenty-five to forty years. If you want to plant larger trees, see if you can set them to one side or the other of the wire, and choose a narrow or conical tree.

If you're planting street trees on public property, you may have the entire selection procedure made simple for you; your city might have a master tree plan that specifies the kind of tree for each street or determines the species based on what's been planted in the past. Save yourself hours of frustration. Check first. In special situations, officials may consider a newer tree if they're convinced of its safe attributes and good chance of survival.

Basic Prep

Get to know the planting site and the qualities that will limit or guide what you ultimately select. Once you've found some trees you like, go back and recheck how they'll fit your site. If your

Most of the things worth doing in the world had been declared impossible before they were done.

LOUIS BRANDEIS

Maidenhair Tree
(*Ginkgo biloba*)
zones 4–9

LIFE IS NOTHING BUT PROBLEMS

Yes! It's true! Life is just one thing after another. When you deal in the petty, your problems are petty. When you choose to have your life's purpose be about something other than yourself, your problems tend to follow suit—they become big, beautiful, and worldly! When President Kennedy declared that Americans would be on the moon in ten years, there was no preworn path to follow. What the president created through this declaration was a mass of problems. Those problems defined the job to be done. Had he not made the commitment and created the problems, America would not have made it to the moon within the decade.

Community forestry is fraught with problems. But you'll be that much nearer to achieving your goal once you recognize that these very problems are in fact gifts—there to be confronted and solved. Problems often bring with them special energy. When solved creatively, they can move your project closer to reality than you could ever have imagined. The bigger the problem, the more energy it has to propel a committed individual toward the goal.

After three years of developing his project, Andy Lipkis was ready to go. He'd lined up hundreds of summer campers who were ready to plant 20,000 seedlings that he'd located in a state forestry nursery. But there was a hitch: he had to buy the trees, and as a student he didn't have the required money. The trees couldn't be given away, and any surplus trees were to be destroyed to clear the seed beds for the next season's crop. When Andy checked with the nursery, he discovered they'd begun plowing the trees under—killing them. It looked to Andy as if his project were washed out. Three years' effort was down the drain! After several minutes of mourning, he decided against throwing in the towel and mounted a media rescue effort that saved 8,000 of the trees. The resulting coverage attracted enough donations, equipment, and volunteers to powerfully launch the organization and complete the first year's program.

Now that your vision's out in the open, lack of funding, bureaucratic resistance, neighborhood apathy, and your own insecurity or weaknesses can all look like problems that are saying *stop!* Usually, they're just telling you what needs to be handled next.

Tree Shape

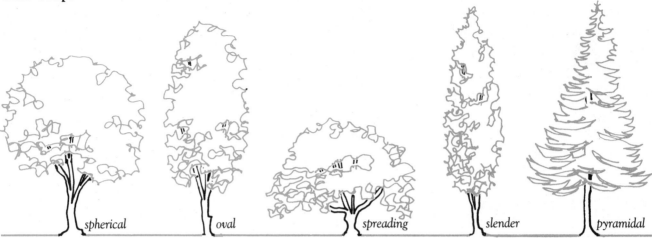

spherical   *oval*   *spreading*   *slender*   *pyramidal*

Goodies for Gophers

When Culver City acquired some wild land for a park, city-hall officials asked for TreePeople's help to build it and to involve kids so they'd have an investment in protecting it. We talked with every student at every Culver City school, and the municipal bus company brought the kids to the park for a half day of planting. The educational and logistics aspects of the program were successful, but survival proved a problem. Due to inadequate site preparation, we discovered too late that the apparently vacant hillside was actually high-density housing for hungry gophers! The city's promised irrigation system never materialized, so we spent several years hand watering the site as, cartoon-style, trees were pulled underground and devoured. Still, a number of trees, transplanted by TreePeople into wire-mesh baskets, stand as testimony to the students' accomplishment.

site's already chosen, look at it now through different eyes. What light—both natural and man-made—does it offer? Is the site in full sun or partially shaded? Is it completely shaded by a tall building? Does it receive artificial light from street lamps all night long? Is it in a spot, such as against a white wall or in a parking lot, where it would receive an extraordinary amount of reflected sunlight or heat that could scald? Is the site vulnerable to turbulent wind or constant wind from one direction? Are your trees likely to have to stand up to fog or salt?

List all the constraints, then think of the shapes and qualities you're after. For example, if you require a tree to grow in the shade of a tall building, think about seeking out a true understory forest tree—one that grows to medium height under the largest trees in a forest or rainforest.

Do you want a tall, columnar tree or one with an oval or spreading, umbrella-shaped head? Do you want it to let in winter sunlight but also provide summer shade? Do you want flowers, fruit, nuts, scent, birds, butterflies, wildlife?

This may seem arduous but it pays off. Even with twenty years of planting experience behind us, when it came time to replant the Lipkis driveway, we went through the process above. It actually took a couple of visits to our favorite trees to get to know them and their finer habits—looked at afresh as we tried fitting them to our specific site. Trees that were Andy's favorite just didn't work along the driveway. We finally settled on five species that are working wonderfully.

Tree Size

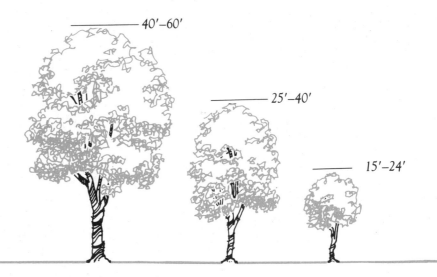

40'–60'

25'–40'

15'–24'

Specimen Selection: Choosing Your Trees at a Nursery

Growing trees in containers can be tricky. When you're purchasing, remember the old adage: Buyer beware! Check the following.

Size. Small, younger trees are the more vigorous. When comparing all the trees in the nursery of the same species and container size, choose a specimen somewhere between the smallest and largest. If the size is disproportionate to the container, it may be because the roots are insufficiently developed or potbound.

Caliper and taper. Six-foot-tall container-grown specimens should have a half-to-one-inch trunk caliper (diameter) at six inches above ground level. The central leader and branches should be smaller than the trunk. The tree should be able to stand without its stake, perhaps bending at some level but not from the soil.

Foliage distribution and branch structure. Half the foliage should be on branches growing from the upper third of the trunk, half on branches on the lower two-thirds. The lower trunk should display foliage on short shoots. Large vertical branches should be at least six inches apart.

Roots. If the roots are visible where they attach to the trunk, the tree has been planted too high. If you can't see a root crown at the soil surface, it's been planted too low. Check for injuries or abnormalities there and for thick circling roots near the trunk that would indicate a potbound tree; a few flexible circling roots within the pot can be redirected on planting day. Lift the unstaked specimen by the trunk and note if it moves up before the soil does. If so, you've discovered inadequately developed or badly circling roots.

PERMITS

There's no site that isn't owned or administered by someone. The process of gaining permission goes far beyond convincing that person of your wonderful idea to plant trees. Your job is one of education and enrollment. Your ultimate goal should be for a commitment not only to allow but also to assist you to plant, including permission and help with long-term care. Whether permission is given by a private individual, a group, a public agency, or a corporation, our experience proves time and again that thriving trees are those receiving the care and blessings of the people around them. Trees need guardians. Even if the owners of a property, or an adjacent property, can't help physically or financially, try to involve them in your project in some way. Simply talking someone into letting you plant won't guarantee that the trees will be appreciated and cared for. Save yourself heartache; stop before you get to the arm-twisting stage.

Each property owner will undoubtedly have a different view of trees, and you may need to provide different kinds of assurances and paperwork before you'll be granted planting permission. Policies around the country differ. In many cities, the county tax assessor's office is able to provide the name and address of the owner of the land, but they rarely give out such information over the phone. You'll need to go into the office or write a letter and pay a fee for the service. If you don't have a street address for the site you're interested in, you'll find that most tax assessors' offices will use or give you access to a well-known local street guide to provide information about the parcel of land in question.

Public Agencies

Most cities and agencies with active tree-planting programs have an established permit process. Some city agencies, such as those of Los Angeles and Atlanta, have extensive requirements and a long permit process. You may live in a part of the country that is more flexible, like Sacramento or Austin. However, as urban forestry becomes a popular issue with citizens, more city agencies are tightening their planting regulations in an effort to avoid badly-planned plantings that will cause trouble in the future. Seeking official approval, whether or not it involves paying a permit fee, is well worth your while. City and county staff are a great source of information and usually know which species do well under particular conditions.

Working with Agencies and Officials

▲ Work with *individual* city or county employees.

▲ Realize that agencies and officials exist to help, not hinder. (It's their job to create and maintain sound tree-management practices over time.)

▲ Get a local leader or politician to send a letter of introduction for your group. (This may only require a phone call or perhaps a meeting.)

▲ Have officials explain the permit process and constraints of planting trees.

▲ Keep agencies and officials informed of your efforts and up-to-date through frequent meetings or phone calls. (Try to avoid surprises.)

▲ Let officials get to know and trust you as a group that meets its responsibilities and lives up to its promises.

▲ Know the necessary time requirements so you don't create unnecessary pressure.

▲ Ask for the city or county's help in getting the job done.

▲ Involve officials in your project.

▲ If someone says no, find out what changes are necessary to make your ideas acceptable.

▲ Find out if there is a way that you and your project can help officials meet their goals.

Private Owners

The only way to find the limits of the possible is to go beyond them into the impossible.
ARTHUR C. CLARKE

Land nowadays is a valuable commodity with a variety of potential uses. When you want to plant on private land, you may be surprised by the opposition you face from hesitant property owners. Remember, your job is not to convince but to educate.

Landowners may believe that future income-producing uses of the site will be limited by the presence of trees. They may be concerned about added expenses resulting from cracked sidewalks, damaged utilities, leaf litter, and liability for tree-related injuries and damages. And if they're unwilling to provide maintenance, they may worry that the responsibility will revert to them if your group loses interest in the project. In circumstances like these, you have to think carefully about the consequences of going ahead. Trees are meant to heal relationships as well as the environment. If the opposite happens, something's gone wrong.

Groups that successfully plant trees on private property avoid potential problems by considering the particular concerns of property owners. Before you approach a property owner, improve your chances for success by making sure you can show how and why the site will be improved by your project. Some private, corporate, or institutional property owners may need to retain an option to develop or change a site at some point in the future. In this case, they may require a deal where use of their site for landscape purposes is leased on a month-to-month basis. This may seem tenuous and far from ideal, bearing in mind the long-term needs of the trees, but such arrangements often last for decades without interruption. You may want to either live with the uncertainty or investigate landscape easements, in which the owner signs away development rights and gets a tax deduction from the city or county.

Developing a Proposal

If you're required to write a proposal describing what you want to do and why, remember to make it as interesting and complete as possible—and not too long. Yours may be just one of many proposals the landowner is considering.

The proposal should include your background, your community group's history, and any community projects you've done. If you've received training for tree work, say so; it will add credibility to your background. If you have support from any officials, mention it; it could influence the final decision. Now give a description of your project. You might include a drawing—to

Hackberry
(*Celtis occidentalis*)
zones 2–9

scale if possible. Indicate what you require—money, permission, and so on—and state how the project will benefit the landowner, the site, and possibly the public. Finally, reiterate how the trees will be maintained and how you'll keep the promises you're making. Include endorsement letters from public officials or prominent people to help gain access and credibility. Then keep your fingers crossed!

Planting Permits

As difficult as it sounds and as time-consuming as it can be, the permit process should ensure that appropriate trees are planted in the right place. It also makes possible uniform plantings so a design or species mix can be carried down a street or throughout a neighborhood. (The older communities in many of our towns reflect this, just as they reflect the days before air-conditioning when trees were used to keep homes cool.) Furthermore, during the permit process the agency should research and identify all planned developments, street widenings, and excavations that could have an impact on your plans in the coming years.

Below are some of the typical steps in the permit process based on our experience in Los Angeles where regulations can be complicated. Your city may not follow involved procedures, but these examples should prepare you for what's ahead. In every case, don't write a proposal or proceed with other preparation until you've made an initial phone call to gauge interest. Find the receptive ear first, then put all your enthusiasm into gaining permission.

Parkways or median strips

Call the city or county agency responsible for your street trees and ask for a permit to plant. An inspector may be required to check out your site, in which case you'll need an appointment. If you have to leave a message, call back and be persistent but polite. Understand that the growing public interest in urban trees is overwhelming many cities' capacity to respond appropriately. If someone's gruff with you, bear in mind that they may be having an exasperating day just like you!

At the same time, be sure you have your neighbors' support. Collect the signatures of property owners who want trees adjacent to their property. If someone on the street is not interested or doesn't want trees, leave that name off the petition and ensure no trees are planted in front of that property. Draw up a planting plan showing the frontage of each property along the street and where you want to plant trees. If you'll be cutting through concrete, you or the agency will need to check on underground utilities.

Nothing splendid has ever been achieved except by those who dared believe that something inside them was superior to circumstance.

BRUCE BARTON

Open Space with a Difference

Planting trees in the older section of downtown Atlanta poses unique problems for Trees Atlanta. The entire area is riddled with an underground, and unmapped, maze of coal holes from days gone by. In a display of creative though ill-planned initiative, the more modern town planners simply paved over the chutes. The result? Those digging through the cantilevered sidewalk never know when they're going to hit thin air. Who's responsible for filling in the hole? How can permits be issued when the world beneath the sidewalk is a mystery? Isn't this taking the concern of supplying air to the tree's roots just a little too far? Trees Atlanta puts a special contingency clause in all its funding proposals to account for thin air, brick walls, dead gas lines, and other unknown obstructions that may come up against a shovel at any time.

Date 7/17/89

Permission is hereby granted to Neal Schwedler

Address 12601 Mulholland Dr. B.H. Tel. No. _____ to ~~Plant~~ 12 Tree(s

in front his   Ca. 90240 6506,13,18,19,22,28,29,35,38,44,57 Kraft ___ St. Ave Blv
in side of her property property located at _____
in rear   Number   Name   Quantity

Near _____ St. Ave. Blvd. Lot(s) _____ Block _____ Tract _____
Nearest Cross Street

Kind of Trees to be (planted) Magnolia GrandiFlora   Majestic Beauty
                    ~~trimmed~~   Botanical Name   Common Name

Diam. 1'+ in Height 8'+ ft. Container 15 gal Distance apart 40 ft. Distance from curb 2 :

Note to Property Owner: Trees must be of size indicated above and planted designated distance apart and from cur:
No tree may be planted within 45 feet or less of a corner.

EXISTING CONDITIONS

Width of planting strip 6 ft. Width of sidewalk 4 ft. Width of roadway _____ ft. Total width of street _____:

Kind of existing trees in block Mixed - This is your permit To Plant (12)
Magnolia GrandiFlora's ~~o~~ with Root Control Barriers and metal
tree STAKES.

Distance apart _____ ft. Avg. diam. _____ in. Avg. height _____ ft. Overhead wires no

Condition of trees _____

BOARD OF PUBLIC WORKS
STREET TREE DIVISION

Final Inspection by _____

Application No. 279238 Date 7/17/89   By Dieane Kutel
                                        7-9 AM 230-330 PM   Inspector.

Form 1286—(Rev. 1-83)

DEPARTMENT OF PUBLIC WORKS
City of Los Angeles
BUREAU OF STREET MAINTENANCE
STREET TREE DIVISION
Room 800. City Hall South

Original (Green) Property Owner
Duplicate (Pink) Inspector
Triplicate (Yellow) File

ISSUED IN FIELD

PERMIT TO ~~PLANT~~/TRIM STREET TREES

VENTURA BLVD.   **PERMIT**
                BTN SEPULVEDA BL.
                & LINDLEY AVE

A 151738

Date 1-15 57

Permission is hereby granted to NANCY COLLIS FOR TREE PEOPLE

Address 12601 MULHOLLAND DR   Tel. No. _____ to Trim (247) Tree(s)
in front his CITY PROPERTY   Quantity
in side of her property property located at VENTURA BLVD BTN SEPULVEDA BL & LINDLEY AVE ___ St. Ave. Blvd.
in rear   Number   Name

Near SEPULVEDA BLVD & LINDLEY AVE St. Ave. Blvd. Lot(s) -0- Block -0- Tract -0-
Nearest Cross Street

Kind of Trees to be planted MIX TREES, CRAPE MYRTLES, MAGNOLIAS, HONEY OAKS, & BOTTLE BRUSH TREES
                    trimmed   Botanical Name   Common Name

Diam. 1-5" in Height 6'-20' ft. Container TREE WELLS Distance apart 30-50 ft. Distance from curb 1-3' ft.

Note to Property Owner: Trees must be of size indicated above and planted designated distance apart and from curb.
No tree may be planted within 45 feet or less of a corner.

EXISTING CONDITIONS

Width of planting strip TREE WELL ft. Width of sidewalk 7'-2' ft. Width of roadway 50-100' ft. Total width of street 80-100' ft.

Kind of existing trees in block MIX TREES, THIS IS YOUR AUTHORIZATION TO TRIM (247) VARIOUS MIX TREES MOSTLY, CRAPE MYRTLE
MAGNOLIAS, HONEYOAKS, BOTTLE BRUSH TREES, TO RAISE & LIGHTEN & RETIED & RESTAKE LEANING TREES THAT NEED IT AND
ALSO OK TO CLEAN TREE WELLS OF DEBRIS & UNWANTED GRASS. ALSO DON'T TRIM MORE THAN 30% OR LEAVE STUBS RIPPED LIMBS.

Distance apart 30-50 ft. Avg. diam. 1-5" in. Avg. height 6'-20' ft. Overhead wires NONE

Condition of trees FAIR

BOARD OF PUBLIC WORKS
STREET TREE DIVISION

Final Inspection by _____

Application No. 147593 Date 1-15-57   By OCTAVIO MARTIN
                                        OFFICE HRS 7-9 AM 230-330 PM   Inspector.

Counting What's There

In 1979, David Schrom realized there were no young trees in Palo Alto. "Let's line the streets with food!" he thought. The loquat seedlings he planted generated a demand from the city attorney that he remove them immediately or face a lien on his property to pay the costs of removal. Did he give up urban forestry? No. Riding his bicycle, equipped with a map and a punch ticker, he counted trees along every linear inch of every street in Palo Alto. Twelve neighbors formed a tree committee and conducted a competent amateur inventory, reporting diameter-at-breast height, height estimate, vigor, and location suitability on all 35,000 trees Schrom had counted. They drew up with each resident a three year maintenance contract on trees in front of dwellings and made a recommendation for a shade ordinance: that at twelve noon on the summer solstice, 50 percent of the public pavement would be shaded by public trees, on a block by block basis, in perpetuity. In David's words, he met with "nothing but obstruction." Nevertheless, with 35,000 trees with a forty-year life expectancy, Palo Alto should be planting 750 trees a year. In 1979, they were planting 100. Now they are planting 750. David? He's the head of Peninsula ReLeaf!

Nothing can stop an idea whose time has come.

GOETHE

If an inspector is sent out to your site, he or she will take note of existing trees, parkway size, utilities present, and consider the tree master plan for the city if one exists. It is best to be present at this inspection and show your map and the signatures of property owners. You can discuss possible species at this time. Cities will differ in what they check. In Seattle, for example, the inspector takes note of the historical character of the neighborhood and whether a neighbor's view will be blocked, as well as width of the planting strip, existing trees in the neighborhood, and overhead utilities. Seattle also actively promotes heterogeneous (mixed) planting.

You may be told what species you have permission to plant or given a few choices. In Seattle, three to five choices are offered following the inspection. Ask if the agencies require any particular supplies, such as special stakes or ties. Los Angeles requires all trees on city-regulated property to be planted with root barriers, which are thought to prevent lateral roots from pushing up through the pavement.

If you've obtained written permission from all owners of property adjacent to the planting site and the site has been approved, the inspector will mark the locations for each tree. Then the final tree selection must be made, and your permit will be issued.

City parks

City parks are usually the province of your local city parks and recreation department. They may be accustomed to channeling planting requests through their own tree-dedication program, if they have one, and planting the trees themselves. Give your reasons for wanting this planting to be a community participation event and invite them to be directly involved. Be sure to develop your plan with their guidance and input.

Private land: vacant lot, parking lot, industry

If you don't know who owns the land, ask attached businesses or neighbors or, as stated above, contact your local county tax assessor's office in person or by letter. If you need a legal description of the location, contact city hall. Once you've identified the owner, try to set up a meeting at the site. Be professional. Use recognized procedures, like a proposal (see Developing A Proposal above), and your request will at least be taken seriously.

We'll mention again how important it is to establish credibility. If you or any of your group have special training with trees, it's likely to set you apart as someone who knows a thing or two about the subject at hand. If you've been working with your city-government representative, don't forget to mention that you also have support there. In fact, an introductory phone call or letter from a higher-up never goes astray. Be cooperative. Remember, the final decision will be made by the owner!

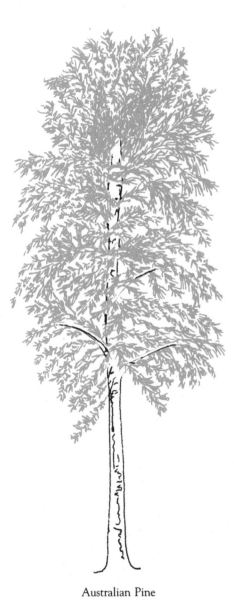

Australian Pine
(*Casuarina cunninghamiana*)
zones 4–7

IF THEY SAY THIS

They break up the sidewalk!
Not if we plant the right kind of tree.

They block the view!
If we plant beautiful trees, you'll still have a beautiful view.

They ruin cars!
The city won't even give us a permit for trees that stain or injure cars.

Criminals can hide behind them!
Gang activity gravitates toward poorly maintained neighborhoods. If we keep our neighborhood clean, paint over graffiti, and do things like planting trees to show the neighborhood is united, we can beat gangs and crime. And crooks have to be pretty skinny to disappear behind a tree.

Cats will get stuck in them.
It will give the fire brigade something to do between fires.

They make the street dark!
Permits regulate tree spacing so there'll be plenty of room for sunlight.

They use a lot of water.
Not drought-resistant species! What's more, providing light shade to lawns or even replacing some lawn space will save water, as lawns are the really thirsty part of a landscape. Trees can help reduce runoff, which will hold more water in the soil. Looking at the big picture, we can ultimately help create a wetter climate and help stop the spread of deserts by planting!

They block my business sign.
They also improve the quality of the street and attract more people. You might want to add a new sign!

They drop leaves and make a mess.
There are lots of trees that don't drop anything.

Birds sit on the branches and do what birds do—all over everything.
You mean sing?

Churches, synagogues, or schools

To avoid wasting time, try going to the top when you first contact an institution. Your suggestion, which may sound strange to a receptionist, could strike just the right chord with the person who ultimately makes decisions. Again, a proposal will probably be expected. Tailor your planting proposal to include the planting plan, the cost and liability of the project, benefits to the constituency, how members or students can be involved, and as much as possible on how the project meets the establishment's needs or goals. Furnish progress reports and final plans. Try to enroll a leader from the institution early on to help develop the plan. If you wait too long, leaders may be reluctant or threatened.

Landfills

Call or write your county sanitation district about the location and site you wish to plant. They may have a master plan that determines what can be planted. They should also have a list of trees that can tolerate the heat and methane generated by landfills. The soil at the landfill should be tested for depth and toxicity. If your local agency has neither the expertise nor personnel on hand to work with you on planting design and specifics, try checking with a sanitation district in a nearby, larger county.

Flood-control channels

Flood-control channels are usually administered by the county. Trees planted here must comply with agency requirements, which vary substantially. Meet agency representatives to determine the issues that would need to be addressed in a proposal if one is needed. Then develop a planting plan and submit a proposal that includes site address and location; flood-control channel name, file code, and station; the landowner's name if the site is an easement; and a drawing of the site and proposed tree species. As with landfills, the soil along a flood-control channel may be contaminated—in this case by herbicides—and need replacing. When plans are final, a permit will be issued.

Railroads

You need to do some detective work to ascertain which railroad currently owns the property you would like to plant and what their long-term plans are. Start by asking your local council representative. The railroad leases out rights-of-way, so you may want to start by trying to get the lease turned over to the city. Develop a proposal that includes the purpose and goals of the project, its area and location, a detailed planting plan that meets all railroad restrictions, your selected tree or shrubbery species, and a timeline

ONE FOOT IN FRONT OF THE OTHER

Don't let impatience kill your good ideas. Give them time to develop. Ideas are like seeds that need the right conditions to sprout. Some conditions happen of their own accord while others will be brought about by your actions. Having the patience to wait for the sprouting is one of your greatest challenges.

Break your big goal into bite-sized chunks to help you take action and to have many points of celebration along the way. These points will sustain you when your larger goal seems elusive. Each step, no matter how small, is a step toward the goal.

In building TreePeople, the successes were often as simple as the planting of one or two trees. Even when suffering defeats on larger goals, little wins can give you hope and energy. During a particularly challenging time, it's helpful to reflect on the fact that, instead of standing still, you're on your path taking it a step at a time.

In 1983, TreePeople learned of a downtown parcel of land that was slated for future development but would be lying idle for a number of years. What about—roll of drums—a temporary urban forest! We developed a plan to show how the planting of donated large trees, the construction of paths and a waterfall, the planting of community gardens to be tended by retirees living in an adjacent high-rise, and the placement of an environmental education kiosk could become a haven for office workers, a teaching tool for inner city youth, a source of food, and a creative demonstration of temporary land use. Our proposal laid out the plan for the removal and relocation of all plant material and other resources. Schools, homeless shelters, and other parks were lined up to happily receive them at the end of the tenure.

As the proposal began attracting widespread publicity and support, the future developers of the site began to fear that they'd never be allowed to build. Despite our pledges of a positive outcome, the proposal was killed after a year. We were heartbroken. Many other projects had suffered while we put all our creative energy and much of our time into this vision.

Six months later, the Community Redevelopment Agency in the neighboring city of Glendale wrote to thank us for our vision. They'd read about it and created a number of small parks right in their central business district. The parks lasted a number of years, and the public was thankful. Our failure became their success.

This visual appeared in a press advertisement developed by McCann-Erickson for Louisiana Pacific, sponsor of the first Marina Freeway Tree Run.

for the project. Establish credibility with the railroad (see Private Land above).

One of the biggest challenges is the fact that the soil is probably sterile and possibly toxic. Most railroads have sprayed the areas under and around their tracks with a variety of defoliants. Plan to conduct a soil test. Very few species will grow or thrive on the treated and sterilized land without replacing the soil.

The Rails to Trails Conservancy is a nationwide network of groups working to convert old railroads into recreation lands. If a local group exists, they may have a plan under way. (See Resources for more information.)

Freeways and highways

Your local highway department may have an adopt-a-highway program. If not, suggest it to them. In California, participants, including civic groups, churches, corporations, and schools agree to plant at least five acres of drought-tolerant, urban-tolerant tree seedlings and establish them for two years. The program is available in many other states, each with its own conditions and requirements.

To ensure safe street and highway plantings, always contact the appropriate agencies for assistance in defining and marking boundaries.

National forests, national parks, and wildlands
In the case of forests and wildlands, you'll be relying on the planting or care prescription of the responsible agencies' resident experts. Forestry and restoration are complex fields requiring a fair amount of training and experience. Agencies like the U.S. Forestry Service often welcome volunteer participation.

Maintenance Permits

Your city tree department may welcome street tree-maintenance assistance if you can prove your commitment, knowledge, and ability; however, as with plantings, there may be a permit procedure.

Large, mature trees need professionals with proper equipment. Where the government is responsible for maintenance of street trees, the homeowner takes on liability when choosing to have the trees pruned by someone other than the city. An inspector will issue a permit for you to prune a small tree—one whose limbs are reachable when you're standing on the ground —if you can offer assurance that you know how to do the job.

You may want to stage an event, working with other individuals knowledgeable about pruning. Consider putting on a training event, bringing in government trainers or private arborists. A few years ago, the Los Angeles City Street Tree Division of Street Maintenance trained TreePeople staff members who, in turn, trained volunteers who went ahead and set up maintenance events. The project did wonders not only for the trees but also for public-private relations. (See Chapter 7 for more on tree care.)

ENHANCED VOLUNTEER COORDINATION

Whether you're working with paid employees, volunteers, agency personnel, or politicians, acknowledgment of everyone's contribution is a crucial part of completing every task, project, and event. If your work becomes an ongoing concern, volunteer acknowledgment and coordination takes on greater importance.

TreePeople is a volunteer-based organization. Although it has a sizeable staff, traditionally every staff member's job has included preparing projects, educating, facilitating, supporting, and acknowledging volunteers in accomplishing the mission of the organization. TreePeople's success is not simply a matter of raising enough money to hire a sufficient amount of people to plant and care for all the trees. Our success has also been in engendering voluntary citizen action.

Ye who would pass by and raise your
   hand against me,
Harken ere you harm me.
I am the heat of your hearth on the
   cold winter nights,
The friendly shade screening you from
   the summer sun;
And my fruits are refreshing draughts
   quenching your
Thirst as you journey on.
I am the beam that holds your house,
The board of your table,
I am the handle of your hoe, the door
   of your homestead,
The wood of your cradle, and the shell
   of your coffin.
I am the gift of God and the friend of
   Man.
Ye who pass by, listen to my prayer . . .
Harm me not!
       NOTICE IN A EUROPEAN PARK

Teaching Forgiveness

Some people come to TreePeople's Citizen Forester Training knowing more about trees than the trainer. Such was the case with Sylva Blackstone, who arrived at the training and immediately jumped in to help Cor Trowbridge, the trainer, explain the technical aspects of tree planting and care. After the course ended, Sylva became active in a neighborhood planting project. The technical aspects were already well handled, so Sylva found herself training, recruiting, and acknowledging volunteers.

Later, Cor joked that she wondered what an expert like Sylva could possibly gain from taking the Citizen Forester Training. Sylva's response? She learned forgiveness—to accept people's shortcomings and support them in accomplishing their goals.

Although most TreePeople staff members work with volunteers in some way, someone has always had the specific job of coordinating volunteers. The job includes recruitment and orientation, facilitation, support, and acknowledgment—acknowledgment being prime on the list of responsibilities. The coordinator makes sure that volunteers are thanked by the project leaders and produces an annual volunteer awards bash.

A number of good models are available to guide you in recruiting and supporting volunteers, and it is not the purpose of this book to be a primer on the subject. A good source of information and support is the network of Voluntary Action Centers. Most major cities have a center, and the national office is in Washington. The local centers maintain a list of people who have contacted them expressing interest in volunteering.

Recruiting

The most powerful form of recruitment for TreePeople is word of mouth. People have a good time, feel needed, feel a sense of community, family, and accomplishment. They share their excitement with others and bring them along for more.

People find TreePeople in a variety of ways. Publicity about our events attracts new volunteers, but for the most part we recruit in a steady low-key fashion. Volunteers and staff regularly address groups, clubs, and churches. An outreach team staffs information booths at fairs. Public service and media-calendar announcements invite new volunteers to a monthly orientation meeting or a bimonthly community gathering.

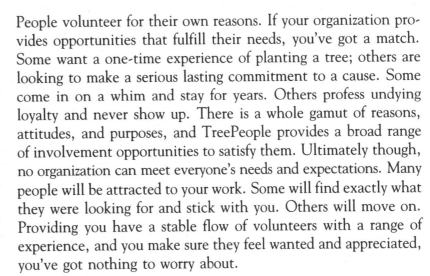

We've been back to water the trees on Ventura Boulevard in Encino. It will be several weeks before we can do it again.

August 6, 1989

Meanwhile, if everyone on the Boulevard gives "their" trees a couple of buckets of water from time to time, the summer may progress without casualties. However, if your trees have died you can make the following Encino Chamber of Commerce contact for a no-charge replacement:

Phil Nordberg
American Business Communications
16154 Runnymede
Van Nuys, Ca 91406

At the gatherings, both volunteers and staff members report on and celebrate recent results and recruit people to assist with upcoming events. Every month we publish a summary of upcoming events in our membership subscription newsletter, *Seedling News*, and produce a more detailed flyer that can be distributed or mailed to those interested in getting involved. Volunteers choose where and when to participate and sign up in advance.

Upon first contact, volunteers are guided to an orientation meeting or spend time with the volunteer coordinator. This meeting is almost like a job interview. When they've found their area of interest, they meet the project leader and sign up. In the days or weeks leading up to an event, a phone team recruits or confirms the participation of those who have expressed interest.

Longevity

People volunteer for their own reasons. If your organization provides opportunities that fulfill their needs, you've got a match. Some want a one-time experience of planting a tree; others are looking to make a serious lasting commitment to a cause. Some come in on a whim and stay for years. Others profess undying loyalty and never show up. There is a whole gamut of reasons, attitudes, and purposes, and TreePeople provides a broad range of involvement opportunities to satisfy them. Ultimately though, no organization can meet everyone's needs and expectations. Many people will be attracted to your work. Some will find exactly what they were looking for and stick with you. Others will move on. Providing you have a stable flow of volunteers with a range of experience, and you make sure they feel wanted and appreciated, you've got nothing to worry about.

Ohio Buckeye
(*Aesculus glabra*)
zones 5–7

Wise Use

Volunteers represent an energy force or resource similar to money. If you have a clearly defined project and clearly defined needs, resources appear, as if magically, to meet those needs. Your challenge is to recognize the resources when they show up, and make effective use of them. For a time in our history, TreePeople staff would spend hours worrying about not having enough volunteers in the organization. We were dealing with the issue in the same way as we would talk about money in the bank. The fact is that during that period we had stopped defining jobs and roles for volunteers and didn't know where to place people when they offered to help. Once we defined the job to be done, the right volunteer usually walked in the door.

Similarly, volunteers don't show up or stick around if they're not needed. Once we had a conscientious staff member who personally covered all the bases at every event. This person often complained of a lack of volunteers that could play a leadership role and was frequently let down by volunteers who didn't show up at events. In follow-up conversations, the volunteers gave the message loud and clear: "You did so well at the events, I figured you didn't need me, and it wouldn't matter if I didn't come."

FUNDING: THE OTHER GREEN STUFF

Life is short and so is money.
BERTOLT BRECHT

Before you even look at how to fund your project, try to work on exactly what you're going to need—in resources as well as money. Remember, the more time, talent, supplies, and equipment that are donated, the less money you'll have to raise. People are your greatest asset. Find out what each person or group can contribute. It may be extra soil, volunteer time, scrap lumber, a contact in city hall, or goods for a bake sale. It may be a large, unexpected check. Remember, your personal relationships are the basis for success.

When you first get a neighborhood group together, have everyone present write down their business and organizational affiliations as well as their addresses and special-interest or talent information. Often we overlook a big personal resource simply because we're too close to it. If you see that happening, don't be afraid to ask. The worst that anyone can do is say no.

We strongly encourage donations from as many sources as possible. TreePeople's annual budget in dollars has always been artificially low when compared to the amount of work the organization accomplishes. The reason? At least as much is donated

WESTWOOD HOMEOWNERS' ASSOCIATION, INC.

P.O. Box 241966
Village Station
Los Angeles, Ca 90024
Tel: (213) 470-8981

President
Joyce Foster

Vice-President
Laura Lake, Ph.D.

Secretary
Lucille Sibley

Treasurer
Jon Lundgren

Directors
Richard Agay
Susan Bryant-Deason
Joyce Foster
Neil Jacoby, Jr.
Neal Kaufman
Laura Lake, Ph.D.
Bruce LaPlante
Jon Lundgren
Don Shoup
Lucille Sibley
R. David Sibley, M.D.
Howard Singer

Mr. James C. Smith, Vice President   October 15, 1989
Real Estate Development
Weyerhauser Mortgage Company
6320 Canoga Avenue, Suite 710
Woodland Hills, CA 91367

Dear Mr. Smith:

To mark the 60th anniversary of the founding of Westwood, the Westwood Homeowners' Association is organizing a project to plant street trees throughout our Association's neighborhood, which is bounded on the North by Wilshire Boulevard, on the South by Santa Monica Boulevard, on the West by Sepulveda Boulevard, and on the East by the Los Angeles Country Club. I am writing to request Weyerhauser's support in this tree planting.

As you know from previous discussions, our Association's neighborhood includes the site of your new office project, "The Atriums." Undoubtedly, the construction of a major office building on Santa Monica Boulevard will have a major impact on our neighborhood. Many residents will naturally feel that the construction project with its attendant noise, dust, traffic congestion, workers' parking on residential streets, and the felling of the two small woods on either side of the Grove apartments will lower the quality of neighborhood life during construction.

New street trees would help to filter dust from the air, muffle noise, and replace trees cut down for construction. Thus, planting new street trees in the neighborhood is a dramatic way to compensate the neighborhood for some of the ordeal that a major construction project unavoidably imposes. Weyerhauser's support for the Westwood Homeowners' Association's street tree planting project would be seen as a generous gesture of goodwill designed to mitigate the negative impact of its construction and to improve relations with the affected residents of the surrounding community.

In return for Weyerhauser's support for our street tree planting, the Westwood Homeowners' Association will publicize your support to our membership through our quarterly newsletter which is delivered to every homeowner in the neighborhood. Every resident would know that Weyerhauser had contributed all the new trees in their neighborhood, and the Westwood Homeowners' Association will undertake to give every credit to Weyerhauser for its contribution. We will be happy to report to all our members at every meeting the progress of the tree planting, and to emphasize that Weyerhauser is supporting the project in order to mitigate the inconveniences inevitably accompanying a major construction project in the neighborhood.

We had begun planning the tree planting project before it occurred to us to seek your support, and we have already done most of the preliminary work. Thus, all we would need is financial help to pay for planting the trees. I am enclosing a copy of the "Trees for Westwood" flyer that was distributed in the neighborhood last month.

...s have already expressed an interest
...ir homes. According to one landscape
... gallon trees is about $40 apiece, and
...135 per tree. Thus, the cost of
...owners who have already expressed

...s that Weyerhauser is offering to pay
...meowners may express an interest in
...l in the flyer that the City might pay
...who want a tree only if it is free are
...ided to the flyer. Also, about half
...trees in front of their homes, so I
...offer to pay for planting a street
...s one without greatly increasing the

...ier forest products companies,
...appropriate way to create goodwill
...nstruction project that many
...nk of a better way for Weyerhauser
...than by offering to plant street

...g to handle all the administrative
...e necessary City permits, securing
...ners. We are also willing to provide
...ct.

...ting project will earn locally for
...espread favorable attention among
...responsible way for developers of
...mental impacts and to placate irate
...s uniquely well placed to benefit
...rototype for corporate/community
...hborhood.

... very favorably impressed by
...i in the past, and I hope that I have
...fforts as you now begin
...this proposal and answer any
...mber in UCLA's Graduate School
...in the evenings at (213) 474-4463. I

Sincerely,

Donald C. Shoup
Tree Planting Coordinator
Member, Board of Directors,
WESTWOOD HOMEOWNERS' ASSOCIATION

cc: Councilman Zev Yaroslavsky
      Commissioner William Luddy

in volunteer time, materials, services, and supplies. From a good deal on a load of gravel to having a video produced gratis, donations can really stretch your dollars, whether your budget is $100 or $1,000,000. It's usually much easier to seek in-kind donations than cash. What's more, every penny saved is one penny less you or your committee will have to raise, so be tight with that cash.

Before we get down to it, here's another piece of advice. Don't make the mistake of thinking publicity will handle fundraising. After some disaster relief work we coordinated in the early eighties, TreePeople's name became a household word in Los Angeles. Even so, we were still putting staff on the Salary Savings Plan (meaning nobody got paid) during the lean summer months, because people just didn't know we needed money. Unlike the for-profit world, getting your name out is not the same as getting the money in.

Analyzing Costs

Tree planting isn't free. In our experience, it costs $100 to $300 to plant a street tree; the larger figure includes concrete cutting and well covers. It typically costs even more when it's done by local government or private contractors.

To help you figure costs we've formulated some rules of thumb. Take into account that different planting sites require varying tree sizes and equipment and that these are average 1990 figures. In budgeting for your planting consider all possible expenses, then turn that into a per-tree amount to use in proposals.

Tree expenses

Seedlings and quarts 12″ or less: $1–$5

1–5-gallon containers 1′–5′: $3–$15

15-gallon container 6′–10′: $35–$75

1″ caliper balled and burlap 6′–8′: $150

2″ caliper balled and burlap 8′–12′: $200

24″ box container 8′–15′: $130–$180 (wholesale)

36″ box container 12′–18′: $400–$500

Related expenses

Stakes (metal): $10

Vinyl tree ties (4 per tree): $0.40 (each)

Soil amendment: $3

Root barriers (15 gallon): $25

¾″ crushed gravel: $3 or $12 per skip

4630 Mary Ellen Ave.
Sherman Oaks, Ca 91423
August 25th, 1988

Ms. Janine Sacks
Neighbors- Daily News
Box 4200
Woodland Hills, Ca 91365

Following is a public service announcement for your publication:

TreePeople needs volunteers to help water street trees along Ventura Boulevard in Encino. Meet Sunday, September 11th, 8:30 am, on the Paso Robles side of Encino Park (16900 Ventura Blvd.) Bring gloves and brown bag lunch. Sylvia Sheppard, Project Coordinator.

Thank you, Ms. Sacks.

Paying for Stamps

How do you find the money that's not for trees or stakes but for stamps and the telephone bill? *Administrative support*, as it's called, is hard to come by. Tucson Clean and Beautiful put together its recommended planting list for the desert environment, then offered endorsements to nurseries that agreed to stock those species and disseminate information about their program. The participating nurseries win because their names appear on a $10 tree certificate that can be bought from Tucson Clean and Beautiful and redeemed at their counter for one of the selected species. The public wins because it receives guidance. The environment wins because the right trees are planted. And Tucson Clean and Beautiful? They get $1 back on every certificate!

Go Shopping

How do we open an office?
Start one in the corner of a supportive business—or in your own living room.

Where do we get office furniture?
From a large company that's retrenching or upgrading.

What about vehicles?
Become a nonprofit. Donating a used car or truck is a great tax deduction!

What can we plant seedlings in?
Milk cartons! Get misprints or those with expired universal product codes (computer stripes) from your local dairy.

How can I afford printing?
Ask big printing firms if they'd be willing to tack your artwork on the end of a big job, to make the use of the excess paper that would otherwise be scrapped. Don't be fussy about paper or colors!

If a big company can't give you a donation, ask if they can let you use their copy machine or their print shop if they have one.

Cutting concrete

Concrete cutting (36″ × 36″ hole): $90.00
(the price will drop for large orders)

Concrete aggregate tree-well covers: $30.00

Other tree-related expenses: transplanting solution, wire cages, and permits. *General expenses*: photocopying, telephone, stamps, gas and transportation, equipment rental, recruitment costs, and publicity. *Amenities*: film for cameras, water, cups, name tags, and refreshments.

Cash for Tree Care

Analyzing costs for tree care and getting it funded are not necessarily easy, but they are straightforward, so we'll deal with them right here.

Tree care for young 'uns is fairly inexpensive; much is done simply by volunteers from a community. As a tree gets older and needs more pruning, expenses grow. These costs are extremely variable but are only incurred every three to seven years, and by the time public trees are this large, many cities assume responsibility. However, if you don't want to leave it to chance, or if

Taking Care of the Mascot

The coral tree is the official tree of Los Angeles. In 1982, a violent storm decimated one of the city's most spectacular displays of coral trees on San Vicente Boulevard. City budget constraints had made pruning possible only every three or four years, so the tree committee of the local property owner's association took on the task of raising an endowment for an annual pruning of these trees whose brittle limbs require meticulous care if they are to survive such storms. The campaign focused on a highly visible cause and a well-defined geographic area. Families and businesses were invited to adopt trees. To get neighbors involved and to bring even more attention to the trees, organizers tied huge red ribbons around each trunk and held a rally beneath the trees where they sold T-shirts, visors, and refreshments. It took a year, but ultimately they raised more than $125,000, and the trees are now receiving the special attention they need.

your trees need special care, consider raising money for their long-term welfare. Here are several options.

▲ Annual collection from homeowners.

▲ Initial, one-time payment of fee.

▲ Trust fund: A 1990 estimate is that $115 invested when a tree is planted is enough to care for it for life. The investment, plus interest, that property owners make up front will keep those trees in the manner to which we'd like them to become accustomed!

▲ Assessment district: Business assessment districts can be set up by business owners to fund improvements such as planting or, in this case, maintaining trees. Each business owner or tenant pays a certain amount into the fund every assessment period. Either the interest or the principal from the fund is used as needed toward the maintenance of the trees.

Borrowing and Bartering Equipment

Equipment is reusable. You'll not need it forever so try not to buy too much of it. You'll limit your creativity if you think in terms of having to raise cash to buy everything (see page 89). Equipment can be borrowed from many sources. The more creative you are, the easier it will be to find what you need.

Does someone owe you a favor? If they have something you need right now, now's the time for them to be magnanimous!

Contact a local tree-planting group if one exists for help with equipment, supplies, obtaining trees, getting permits waived, and other services. Existing groups have been through this before. You may not have to reinvent the wheel.

Other important sources could be the state, county, or city forestry departments. Your street-tree division, street-maintenance department, fire department, parks-and-recreation or public-works department, or general services may also come through for you. Don't view them as strangers; they're there to help and might loan equipment such as shovels, hoses, brooms, trucks, water trucks, skip loaders, bulldozers, augers, jack hammers, and even helicopters! Do you have a state or local conservation corps? In California, the CCC and local corps have a terrific reputation for volunteering support for environmental causes. Utility companies, providing phone, gas, and electricity, are often very interested in getting involved in tree projects. As we've stated, the proper placement of trees affects their ability to function. They may be pleased to have a part in supporting your project by providing manpower, donating printing, or loaning equipment.

Neighborhood Tenacity

What began as door-to-door recruiting for a Saturday neighborhood-cleanup operation turned into the formation of the 5ive Points Community Association. The low-income residents and workers in this mixed manufacturing-industrial district of south-central Los Angeles realized the next step was tree planting. Undaunted by the fund-raising challenge, they suggested each family make a five-dollar per month contribution to pay for trees. This was ultimately supplemented by a Community Development Block Grant and funds from a department store whose warehouse was in the district. They constructed their own water truck, using two fifty-five gallon drums strapped to a trailer and hitched up to a car, then went on to organize outings for their kids, graffiti paint-out projects, murals, and ongoing meetings with business people, schools, and police.

When all else fails, of course, send in the marines! Our armed forces are often there to help. They have enormous amounts of manpower and equipment that can be tapped if you take the time to ask.

Begging and Buying Resources and Money

May I borrow a face tissue? We all know how ludicrous the request is. Who wants it back? It's the same with supplies. Supplies are used once and can't be returned. They're not as easy to come by, but you can still get them. Many businesses will be happy to make in-kind donations to your project.

For the times when you actually have to shell out some cash, we want to make a radical suggestion: pay for it yourselves! It's amazing how many resources exist within a community. You have to dig a bit to find them, but by preparing a list of your needs and circulating it to all neighbors and participants, you can garner a tremendous amount of support. You can either raise cash or cut costs significantly by trying some of the following suggestions.

Get everyone to chip in so you can buy needed supplies. Whether it's $1 or $1,000, we should all look into our purses as well as our hearts to support something we believe in. Even Andy and Katie are dues-paying members of TreePeople. If you can't rely on your closest circle, how can any of them ask others to give? Giving time is great; giving money at some point becomes essential. Raising money from your own circle also reduces the amount you need to raise from the outside.

You'll receive wholesale prices if you buy in bulk. If money up front is a problem, try spreading out payments over several months. What seems like a lot of money may, in fact, be easy enough to raise if everyone in your tree-project group gives a small monthly amount. For example, five dollars per month for seven months buys a tree.

Too many people fail to realize that they actually have within their grasp the means to pay for their project. Discovering your financial power is just one more important facet to all you're discovering right now. What's more, it can become a good test of a group's commitment.

Even so, hold on to as much of that money as you can for the things that are not donated. See if you can interest a supplier or nursery in donating resources. Perhaps you can interest a sponsor. Think about what's in it for them. Nowadays, businesses everywhere, big and small, are looking for ways to show their commitment to the environment. Tree projects are a safe and popular option. Businesses don't donate time, money, or materials to individual property owners to enhance a private residence, but

if the plantings benefit an entire community, businesses can be persuaded to support the cause.

Likewise, local developers who have an upcoming project may also be looking for a way to give back to the community. Are there any other advantages for businesses? Invite them to tell you what they'd like. Offer media exposure, their logo on your flyer, their banner at your planting, an on-site plaque or acknowledgment sign (build in the cost), or a commendation from the mayor, who should be accessible if you're doing neighborhood improvement. Remember to have the acknowledgment fit the contribution. Also, be prepared to say no if you sense something fishy (see page 127).

Others that might consider taking you under their wing and raising some change for you include local business associations like chambers of commerce or Junior Achievement; service clubs such as the Rotary Club or Kiwanis; campus organizations like sororities or fraternities; and religious groups like the Knights of Columbus, Scottish Heritage Club, or Hadassah.

Fundraising events, too, can be a relatively easy path to quick clean money, especially if you have a couple of people with a little experience who will take responsibility for it while you're organizing the rest of the project. How about selling tickets for a car wash? If you want to go bigger than a donated parking lot, try talking to a neighborhood gas station. They could promote the event to their customers and perhaps recruit new customers on the day, especially if they can offer special deals.

Try sponsoring a bake-off or a garage sale. Choose a house that's on a main thoroughfare or post signs at the nearest intersection. Use the occasion to recruit volunteers and to advertise what you're doing. Start a recycling program for cans, newspapers, and bottles. By turning in these items for cash, you've both raised money for your project and helped the environment.

Parties are another painless way to bring in funds. You could throw a block party or organize potluck dinners or spaghetti nights with a ticket price. Raffles are also a time-honored tradition. Try offering small trees or handmade items as prizes.

You could even try an auction. People like a deal. Gather donated products or services like babysitting, home-grown plants, or dinner for two at the current local hot spot. If you really go to town with the auction concept and have a lot of merchandise, you can charge admission too. Ask business contributors for an all-out donation. It's better than having to return the wholesale value to them. It also gives them a full tax refund. Offer them a complimentary admission to your auction. You might even serve or sell refreshments.

Quick Thinking

The Global ReLeaf fund of the American Forestry Association had a $5,000 corporate contribution that had to be used for citizen tree planting in Seattle. For a number of reasons, the chosen recipient —the Washington State Nursery & Landscape Association—had only two hours to put together a program. It pulled $2,500 from its promotional budget, and the City Arborist pitched in $2,500 of his own. The resulting doubled amount— $10,000—was used to fund 500 Washington ReLeaf certificates, redeemable at participating nurseries, that were good for 50 percent off the cost of a Seattle-approved street tree, up to a maximum of twenty dollars. Each citizen was eligible to obtain three certificates and, after a well-covered press conference, they went like hotcakes. Got a promotional idea for the WSNLA? Great! Can they have two hours to think about it?

Think media. Put together a commemorative magazine, newsletter, or book and sell ads to businesses and individuals. What about selling T-shirts, visors, or buttons with your community-group logo? Haven't got one? Get one!

The Fairy Godmothers

Recommiting ourselves to improving the urban environment affords us the chance to recapture our power and self-sufficiency. With such an ingrained history of expectation that government will meet our needs, it can be a challenge to redirect our attention to our own resourcefulness. Given the global-warming debate and the so-called peace dividend, the 1990s are likely to see more government and foundation funding available for urban forestry. There will never be enough, however, to meet the needs of all communities. Never. You heard it here.

Contact local corporations, foundations, and small businesses (the more local the better) to see if they'll entertain a proposal. You could be lucky! The bigger the entity, however, the more time it will take. Allow at least six months for a corporate giving program or foundation to review and make a decision regarding your proposal. Visit your library for foundation directories that can lead you to sources. Bone up on their giving programs. How much do they usually give? Who have they funded in the past? Would a proposal from you make sense? Add every endorsement for you and your group that you can muster. Raising money is just like getting approval to plant. You've got to sell yourself. Don't send anything cold. Phone before you write. You might be able to have your request squeezed into an upcoming meeting—or you might have just missed one.

Your city or state department of forestry may also provide funds for tree projects. Don't overlook the obvious. Beware the trap, though! The apparent availability of grant funds can sometimes lead you to forget about your ability to raise the money from within your community. We all have a tendency to call mom before handling our responsibilities. Grant funds are always limited and usually don't cover your entire project. What's more, communities can lose motivation as a consequence of either receiving or not receiving a grant. If a grant is awarded, if money appears to flow, there's a danger that people power will drop away, and people power is precisely what's needed to accomplish the task. If a grant application is rejected, organizers may lose heart so much that they overlook the possibility of turning back to the community to find the resources and energy for the job.

This advice may sound a little like humbug, and we don't wish to appear hypocritical. TreePeople certainly receives very large corporate contributions every year. But it's not our only source of money, and we still try to maintain the thrift ethic in the organization. The point here is, don't get stuck on how to get the money. Stay creative.

Eyeball to Eyeball

With money in your pocket, you are wise and you are handsome and you sing well too.

YIDDISH PROVERB

Without a doubt, the most successful, and the most difficult, way to raise a large amount of money in one fell swoop is to make what's called a face-to-face solicitation. The thought of such a confrontation is so daunting to most of us that we will go out of our way for years to avoid taking the one single most effective tack to enrolling others in our work. We know! TreePeople avoided it for years! We finally understood that asking for large sums of money is rather like asking for small amounts of donated items or requesting volunteer help on a planting—and we were very good at that. The only difference is that the stakes are higher, and it involves that touchy subject—money. Your best resource is a small paperback entitled *The Art of Fundraising* by Irving R. Warner. (See Resources for further information.) Are you up to it? Fantastic!

Who are your prospects? Work with your committee to identify them and try to get as close to them with your contacts as you can. Does anyone see them on the golf course or sit on another committee with them? How much should they be asked to give? This figure should be realistic. Don't insult them by asking for too small an amount, but don't show your ignorance by being in fantasyland about it either.

Here are some rules for you or for the person who makes the solicitation. When you set up the meeting, let your prospect know you're coming to talk about the project. It's not fair to place an unexpected request on someone from whom you hope to gain support. Don't try to turn yourself into a super slick salesperson. Your openness, commitment, and knowledge will influence your prospect far greater than a canned performance. What is your motive? It's more than just the funding of your project. You want to inspire your prospect and find a way to share your vision so that it becomes real for both of you during the meeting. Breathe deeply. Take some props if you like: maps, drawings, photographs, newsclippings. Do more listening than talking. Answer questions. Acknowledge any idea your prospect may have. If they're good, pursue them. If they're red herrings, try to bring the conversation

Kentucky Coffee Tree
(*Gymnocladus dioica*)
zones 4–8

back to the issue at hand. Turn around objections, which are a natural part of the process. Remember to tackle the objections, not the prospect! Once you've made your specific request, stop talking. Wait for a response, no matter how uncomfortable it makes you feel. Try to leave the meeting with a commitment—and thank your prospect regardless of the outcome. The absolute sign of success is to witness the transition from *you and me* to *us*. This transition, however, may take more than one meeting.

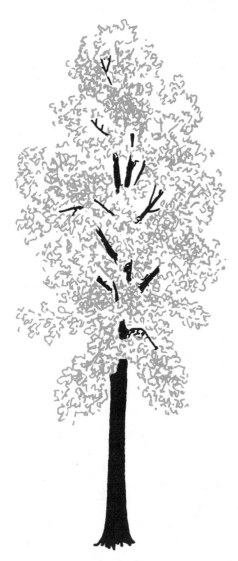

Carolina Poplar
(*Populus canadensis*)
zones 5–9

BE A MOTIVATOR

People do not just give to causes on the basis of objective assessments. Your prospect may have more than one reason to consider contributing to your project. Try to uncover his or her motives and needs and respond to them. In the early part of your conversation, have your prospect speak about those things he or she enjoys or thinks are important or perceives to be wrong. At least one or two of the following points will probably emerge as your prospect's primary reason to give.

▲ to help save the planet
▲ to help create a better environment for children or grandchildren
▲ to help ensure the future health of children or grandchildren
▲ to help conserve energy
▲ to increase property value or attract business
▲ to reduce dust and dirt
▲ to beautify the neighborhood and promote wildlife
▲ to achieve immortality
▲ to gain public recognition
▲ to participate in a historic undertaking
▲ peer pressure
▲ peer competition
▲ to save on taxes
▲ to further networking activity
▲ to promote community spirit
▲ to achieve popularity

4

The Creation Unveiled: Producing Your Event

All the beautiful sentiments in the world weigh less than a single, lovely action.
JAMES RUSSELL LOWELL

Of course, you can plant and care for trees without any hoopla at all. But remember, this book is about nurturing community. A magic develops when people work together and tell the world they're working together. To pull off a successful event requires enormous effort, but it's worth every bead of sweat. There's no high like an event high.

This chapter should have been written by a boy scout, so loud is the message that one must be prepared. We've tried to cover logistics for everything from the pruning and weeding of a couple of street trees to planting projects that may stretch over six months. The first issue tackled under Event Logistics should help you put your project in perspective. Choose from among the information that follows for the scope and scale that best fits your event.

EVENT LOGISTICS

Determining how many trees to plant or maintain over what period of time is one of your most critical decisions. If you bite off more than you or your committee can chew, you can wind up with a failure that could have been avoided. Even if your long-term goal is to plant hundreds or thousands of trees, your first project should be large enough to challenge you but small enough to be manageable, to guarantee an initial success. A good deal of gain, in effect, for very little pain! For building community excitement, enthusiasm, and commitment, go for small wins rather than large failures.

Scope and Scale

No matter the size, set up your project to be accomplished in a single day or in a series of one-day events. It's difficult to maintain leadership or volunteer energy on events that run more than a day each. You should therefore avoid weekend-long events, unless the second is a play day.

Optimal event size depends on various factors: the number of experienced leaders or supervisors available to you; the number of untrained volunteers participating; the difficulty of the site (whether it involves soil digging, concrete removal, or slope, for instance); the size of the trees; and the planting requirements. As a rule of thumb, TreePeople figures it takes a team of two or three well-guided adult volunteers approximately two hours to plant a large street tree. Adding time for the logistical details of set-up and clean-up, you shouldn't expect that team to plant more than two or three trees in a day. This may sound absurd, especially if you're used to personally planting several hundred seedlings a day, but hang in there.

If you have forty large trees to plant over several city blocks, you'll need between forty and sixty people to comfortably accomplish the task in a day. When dealing with large urban trees—with a 15-gallon to 24-inch box, 2-inch caliper balled and burlap, or 12-foot-tall bare root—figure on about one tree per person per day. This rule works well if all work is done the day of the event. If you're working with residents who can't deal well with heavy work, you may want to recruit additional labor sources to help dig the holes either a day in advance or just before the planting.

We observed and assisted at a project where the work was more than the volunteers could handle. Instead of being done in a day or a weekend, it required several more weeks to complete. After the first day, a smaller, fatigued group of volunteers assembled and did the best they could but ultimately put their shovels away to prepare for their work week. In that process, the neighborhood volunteers burned out, and the organizer turned first to the Los Angeles Conservation Corps for donated labor and finally to hired physical laborers to complete the job. Although the trees now look great, the neighborhood has been reluctant to move on to additional projects.

This situation is avoidable with proper planning. If you're a little worried that the project may get out of hand, try recruiting backup teams in advance: youth clubs, conservation corps, high school or college sports teams, fraternities or sororities, corporate volunteer corps, even National Guard personnel.

Preparing the Site for Trees

For some projects, preparing the site means clearing a small area of weeds and grass and poking a hole in the soil. This simple and inexpensive approach is usually employed to plant seeds where the soil layer is deep and well drained; where the slope is not excessively steep; where there are few surrounding space limitations such as buildings, utilities, or other existing vegetation; and where permits are not required once permission is obtained from the property owner.

For projects at developed sites, getting the site prepared might be more involved. You'll need to make sure it's accessible on the day of planting. This might mean getting a gate opened, or having city officials close off the street or lane or post caution signs. At this point, you may need another city inspection (this time from the traffic or police department) to assist you with the logistics of lane closure.

Cutting pavement, concrete, or asphalt, breaking it up, and hauling it away is another major preparation that must be done in good time. You must check for underground utilities at least forty-eight hours before you begin cutting. Nothing can ruin your day like cutting through electrical, gas, or sewer lines! Almost the entire country is now served by a One Call Service that will contact all utilities for you. Check with the American Public Works Association in Chicago for a number in your area, or look in your phone book under *pipeline or cable locating* or the name of your utility. In Southern California, for instance, the company is called Underground Service Alert (1-800-422-4133). *Caution:* Very stiff fines are assessed for cutting concrete without notifying the utilities in advance. In California—under AB 73—those cutting without knowing the law are subject to a $10,000 fine, and those who knowingly break the law are subject to a $50,000 fine.

Once the concrete is out, dig a single test hole if you're planning to plant large container trees; you'll get a better idea of whether tools like picks, digging bars, and augers (drills) will be useful. Soil dries out as soon as it's exposed to air, so if you plan to dig the holes in advance, replace the dirt until planting time.

Preparation is different at undeveloped sites. You may need to establish an adequate layer of soil for planting, such as at landfill sites. The planting area might need to be *graded*, to achieve a smooth horizontal or sloping surface. When planting seedlings to convert a grassy hillside to forest cover, many foresters prefer to *disc* the soil to loosen it and knock down competing vegetation, then remove any rubble and trash. However, this activity can hurt existing trees. It's also possible to prepare such sites without heavy equipment and disruption by hand clearing individual planting sites. This is done by *scalping* a three- to five-foot-diameter circle, removing all vegetation down to mineral soil, which ensures that the seedling won't have to compete for water, sunlight, and nutrients in its first year of establishment.

Soil Testing

You can gauge a good deal about the quality of the soil on your site by looking at existing vegetation. Are the trees and shrubs healthy and thriving, or are they stunted, discolored, or suffering in some way? Inexpensive soil-PH testing kits will help you determine the composition of the soil. It's also possible to send a soil sample away to a testing lab. Some testing services will send you an analysis with a recommendation for amendments needed to improve your site.

It's important to check drainage too. Bad drainage is a common problem in urban environments, and tree roots do not take well to being suffocated by standing water. Here's a simple test. Dig a hole about a foot across and a foot deep; then fill it with

Prepare in Advance

Nothing is quite as disappointing for volunteers as to arrive and have no way to participate because the site isn't ready for planting. At one tree planting in downtown Los Angeles, 100 planters waited for two hours while frantic volunteers cut concrete tree wells inch by inch with handheld saws. By planting time, half the crowd was gone. The Citizen Forester for the planting planned to start cutting concrete at 6 A.M. on the planting day, but the concrete cutter broke down shortly before volunteers arrived. The moral of the story: It pays to have your site prepared well in advance.

water. If the water drains at less than one inch per hour, drainage is poor; one to three inches per hour is good; and more than three inches per hour is excessive. Soil that drains too slowly can be improved by augering (drilling) holes several feet deep every few feet and filling them with coarse gravel. Soil that drains very quickly should be mixed with an organic soil amendment. Consult a professional arborist if you have questions.

Above all else, remember it is best to choose a tree that likes the native soil.

Watering

It is not only what we do, but also what we do not do, for which we are accountable.
MOLIÈRE

Most important of all, newly planted trees must be watered right away. Be confident you can get water to the trees during the planting and afterward. Very deep watering at the beginning establishes all species well—including those that will be drought tolerant. Don't be stingy here. Gallons used now can prevent gallons later on. There are a number of options for water delivery.

Residents or businesses can each water their own tree. Dragging out a hose from each house or business on the day of the planting or tree-care event is the simplest way to water your trees, and it adds to the sense of community. If logistics won't allow this, you can bring a hose with you and use an available spigot.

With some advance notice, and provided there's no fire in the area, your local fire station might be able to bring its engine out on the day of planting to give the trees their first drink. This makes a good visual for media coverage, and the fire companies usually enjoy lending a hand. One note of caution, however: Some fire agencies keep their tankers filled with *light water*—a chemical treatment that enhances fire fighting but is harmful to the plants—making use of their engines impossible for the task. Be sure you check whether this is the case! You can achieve the

same end result by tapping into fire hydrants. You'll need permission, however, and a fee is sometimes involved, as well as special equipment including an eddy valve and a wrench to open the hydrant.

Failing all this, organize a bucket brigade! Trash cans filled with water, coupled with buckets that can be carried by kids or others, is a fine solution. One thirty-gallon trash can will water two street trees or five to six seedlings.

Facilities

Restrooms and drinking water should always be available for volunteers. Locate the nearest restrooms—check at gas stations, fast-food restaurants, shopping malls, neighbors' homes, churches, temples, and other places for permission to use their facilities. If there simply aren't any restrooms around, consider recruiting someone with a mobile home who will loan it for the event. If necessary, you can always rent portable toilets (or possibly borrow them from road-construction or highway agencies). If your planting is in a rural area, bring drinking water in canteens.

Storage

Events are usually on weekends, and nurseries and building-supply companies often deliver only on weekdays. If you're planning a good-sized event, you may need a central, safe, and secure location to store the supplies that arrive in advance. Someone is sure to have a yard you can use, but don't take anything for granted. Arrange for storage well ahead of the event. The best place to store gravel is on the street, but find out if you need any permits or permission before you have it dumped.

Disposal

Whether you're running a planting or a tree-care event, you need a place of disposal. When planting street trees, the planting style and the size of the watering basins will determine whether or not you have soil left over. On a residential street, leftover soil is usually snapped up for gardens, but in a commercial zone, you'll need a method of transport and a place of disposal. With luck, your local street-maintenance or parks department can be talked into lending a hand and a dump truck. If this is not possible, consider putting the soil in the empty tree pots and hauling them to a preapproved site.

Jack Pine
(*Pinus banksiana*)
zones 4–8

You'll have an even bigger disposal challenge if you're cutting concrete. If you contract out the work, make sure that the contractor agrees to haul the debris. If you do it yourself, look for a place where broken concrete is recycled, such as a landscape or building-supply firm that uses it for building decorative landscape walls or a concrete recycling facility. Santa Monica, California has such a facility that turns concrete back into gravel for roads and construction. Again, check with a city agency to see whether the concrete can be hauled free of charge. If all else fails, rent a roll-off debris dumpster. A private waste hauler will deliver the dumpster for you to fill, then haul it off—along with $100 to $200.

If you're planning a tree-care event that involves pruning, removing suckers, or weeding, think about the trimmings. Estimate how much you think you'll be producing. Without experience, this is difficult to measure, but not impossible. Consider the number of trees you're working on and the work you're going to do; then look at the trees. Are there a lot of weeds or suckers? Are the trees small, requiring little trimming, or are they large?

Trimmings, being good organic waste, make perfect mulch. Since you're planting and maintaining trees to help heal the city, your first call should be to see if there's a city service that will use a chipper to convert the trimmings to mulch or compost instead of burying it in a landfill. Mulch the trees you've just aided or see if the city will haul away the leftovers.

Failing that, check to see whether there are any local compost bins you can help fill. Or see if everybody involved in the project can take home and dispose of one tree's worth of waste. You may be able to get permission to use a nearby dumpster. If you've got a lot to dispose of, get permission from several places so you don't completely fill any single dumpster.

Our trusty standby, the trash can, comes in useful again here. You can fill trash cans at the site, then cart them off to be dumped. This works well for small projects but can get cumbersome very quickly on larger ones. Try not to use plastic bags if possible; they won't biodegrade. (See Chapter 7 for further information.)

Be Safe

Safety plays a crucial part in a volunteer event. Be sure to consider safety procedures as part of your planning process, as well as part of your event.

Remember to take along a fully equipped first-aid kit and have on hand the addresses and phone numbers of the nearest paramedics or rescue service, fire station, police department, and hospital emergency room. For large events, assign a qualified volunteer to first aid.

Match the volunteers' physical ability with the site. Keep in mind the terrain and its steepness, proximity to heavily traveled streets, the possibility of bugs and reptiles, or broken glass and other debris in the area. While planting in the mountains or in rural or unfamiliar areas, people can get caught up in the activity and lose sight of the rest of the group. Institute a buddy system so that planters can keep track of each other and don't get lost!

Make sure power equipment and vehicles are operated only by responsible people. Don't allow anyone to ride on tailgates or the sides of a truck bed. And don't move any vehicle without checking for kids, dogs, and the like. Have someone act as a spotter when necessary.

Instruct supervisors and volunteers on the safe way to use and carry tools and don't use any that are broken or faulty. Lay all shovels, rakes, picks, and other tools point down or flat on the ground and keep volunteers well spaced when using tools swung over the shoulder.

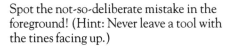

Spot the not-so-deliberate mistake in the foreground! (Hint: Never leave a tool with the tines facing up.)

Run a tree planting effectively to avoid careless accidents. Don't allow anyone—adults or children—to run around, throw things, or play with tools. The only thing participants should be allowed to throw is water—at one another—after a long, hot day!

Communications

For large events spread over several blocks or miles, walkie-talkies will improve your communications and facilitate logistical support. You may want to assign radios to a supply vehicle (for rapid delivery of special tools, gravel, or supplies), the check-in table, a first-aid team, and the event leader. We avoid using radios as much as possible in order to keep our events human, but sometimes they're vital.

If you go this route, use powerful equipment you can rely on. You can rent walkie-talkies from audiovisual supply companies for ten to twenty dollars per unit per day plus insurance, which is worth getting, as they usually cost in excess of one thousand dollars to replace. Better still, recruit a local ham-radio club to assist you. Hams are fantastic support people, and given enough lead time to recruit volunteers for you, they'll be a real asset. Hams are geared up to supply emergency communications during disasters, and they appreciate events such as these as opportunities to drill and sharpen their skills.

Contacts

We've said it before and we'll say it again: let your city councilperson or county supervisor know whenever you're working in the area. They may offer organizing assistance if you let them know ahead of time. Even if you don't need their assistance, it's a good idea to keep them updated so they're aware of your interest in greening your neighborhood.

A few days before the event, call the local police station. Tell the watch commander you and your neighbors will be out planting or maintaining trees. It pays to warn them that people will be working on the street or in a public place. More than once TreePeople volunteers have been stopped by police who thought they might be tree vandals!

Vehicles

Large events require trucks to help move tools, trees, and supplies. Try borrowing from the people in your neighborhood or have them talk with their friends or family members. You can rent large or specialized trucks, such as dumps or water trucks, but this is a costly way to go. It might be possible to arrange for a construction company, public utility, city agency, or even a local National Guard base to provide a vehicle with a driver. Because of liability problems, it's unlikely that any company or agency will loan you a vehicle without a driver, so appreciate that your request may involve them in a financial contribution to pay an employee unless the employee volunteers.

GLEANING

When planning your event, remember the begging, bartering, or borrowing theory from the previous chapter. Get creative. Keep your eyes open for surplus or underutilized resources that could be of service to you. Once you start thinking like a purchaser, your world is limited. When you're a gleaner, everything is a potential resource to your project!

When TreePeople needed trucks to move trees to the mountains, Andy called the Air Force, because he'd seen idle trucks at armories. It took a year for the Force to respond, but ultimately it provided nearly ten years' worth of tree transport convoys. Once we were offered 5,000 cups of yogurt as event refreshment, but there was a catch. The yogurt had to be picked up on a weekday and held in cold storage until Sunday. We asked another dairy if they'd loan us a refrigerated truck, and they came through. When several of our friends tired of having TreePeople's nursery in their backyards, we began looking for another space. We considered vacant car dealerships and gas stations, but ultimately found what looked like underutilized public land around a fire station. After listening to us for three years, during which time our friends lost almost all patience, the City Recreation and Parks Department gave us a permit to take over the forty-five-acre facility. What started as a place to put our seedlings became our Coldwater Canyon Park headquarters on Mulholland Drive—among the most expensive real estate in Los Angeles. It's a pity our buildings are falling apart!

Especially in this country, everywhere we look there are surplus or wasted resources—including people—that can be recycled, or more fully utilized for the improvement work our communities need.

Tools

It is likely that your neighbors have tools: picks, shovels, hoses, and trash cans you can use for small events. For larger events, start by asking volunteers to bring their own tools. If you don't want to rely on potluck, try the following sources. Check close to home: one of your city's agencies might maintain a tool bank for just this purpose. Some fire departments even have a checkout system for hoses and nozzles. If you strike out locally, try your state or county forester or the closest office of the U.S. Forest Service or Park Service, if there is a national forest or park nearby. In all cases, you may need a brief proposal to prove your credibility. Not all agencies will be able to help you, but many have now adopted policies to support volunteer efforts.

If there's a lot of activity brewing in your area, you may be able to convince your city to create a mobile tool bank that can be driven to neighborhood project sites to provide the vital support such grass-roots efforts need. Whatever you do, be sure to set up a tool checkout, as many volunteers in TreePeople's past, who didn't understand that volunteering meant no payment, have figured we'd never miss a shovel or a set of pruning shears. A simple suggestion is to number your tools and your volunteers at the check-in table. You'll still lose things now and then, but it sends a message that you're watching and can't afford to give away equipment.

Food

Volunteers feel appreciated and nurtured when they're provided with food to stave their hunger or drinks to quench their thirst. See if neighbors who aren't up to the physical labor can bake goodies or make lemonade or coffee. It's also likely you can inspire a local business or service club to host that part of your event. Seeing neighborhood improvement going on, local restaurants and fast-food emporiums can usually be persuaded to donate several dozen donuts, hamburgers for lunch, or a number of party pizzas.

Spreading the Word

You can recruit volunteers, create public awareness, and acknowledge those who donated to your project—all through the media. You can also publicize your event with flyers.

For every planting, someone should be responsible for spreading the word. Make simple fact sheets to mail to local newspapers.

All For One and Trees For All

In 1987, a community group with all the energy of the original trio began working on lining the boundary streets of the entire seven-square-mile city of El Segundo in the County of Los Angeles. The Tree Musketeers began by planting median strips, then approached the huge corporations and agencies that occupied the industrial borders of their city and asked them to get behind their plan. In the first two years, the north and south boundaries were planted. Arbor Day 1989 saw a planting on the east side and this year, the agency on the west, which is in the middle of reconstruction, agreed to landscape its entire site within five years. For Arbor Day 1990, the Tree Musketeers organized a *treeathlon*, which includes running, planting, and riding. The key here is that decision making and strategy are the responsibility of the Council of Youth Directors, whose members' ages range from ten to eighteen years!

Check deadlines with each paper. Post flyers on community bulletin boards at supermarkets and other businesses, libraries, and civic buildings in the area. Distribute flyers door to door in the immediate vicinity. Call any local celebrities and politicians to be on hand for the event. Don't forget to have information at the event to give to passersby who may want to get involved in future events.

Be sure your package clearly states the date, time, and place of the event; what exactly is going to happen; who is sponsoring it; and a telephone number to call for more information. Make your flyers attractive, enthusiastic, and readable.

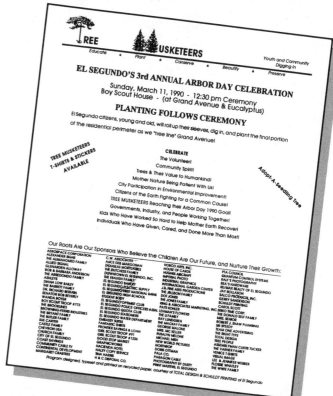

Managing Volunteers

Energetic, die-hard, well-managed volunteers are vital to the success of your event. Once volunteers are on board, let them know they're being counted on. Some people take volunteer commitments lightly and choose at the last minute to drop their obligations. It's important your volunteers understand that they can and will affect the quality of the event if they choose not to honor their commitments. There are ways to do this without scaring people off. You don't want to have to fire anyone. On the other hand, nobody's going to feel good about an event that fizzles through a lack of commitment. The biggest trap is the One-Person-Tree-Machine syndrome. A constant challenge within the

Black Walnut
(*Juglans nigra*)
zones 5–7

TreePeople organization is to train both staff and volunteers to share the workload. TreePeople's vision generally attracts very hardworking and capable people. No matter how efficient one individual is, however, he or she cannot dream, organize, and carry out a project single-handedly. If you appear to have it all together, your committee and event volunteers may perceive they're not needed and just bow out. Ask yourself who's to blame. Is it all their fault or fifty-fifty?

When recruiting volunteers for your event, calculate how many you need, then shoot for 10 to 20 percent more to cover for last-minute dropouts. There's nothing worse than a lack of good volunteers, except perhaps burning out the few you have by making them finish the project, and losing them for the future. While you want to make sure you don't underestimate volunteer numbers, it also isn't great to have too many volunteers and not enough work. They'll wonder why they came in the first place and will be difficult to motivate later on. People do volunteer for the right reasons; they want to work hard for something they care about. But the most widely reported reason for volunteering, across the board, is social. So make sure the volunteers have a good time!

Advance team

To have trees thrive in the urban environment, and to have your reputation thrive in the eyes of the bureaucracy and the public, you must guarantee a high planting or maintenance standard. It's important to have experienced people at your event, who not only know how to plant and care for trees but can also show others and check that it's done correctly. TreePeople has designated several roles that help achieve the best results.

Event developer. This role is necessary for large events. Around TreePeople, this would be the Citizen Forester. It's probably you, unless you've successfully given this job away and assigned yourself to fundraising, recruitment, or another part of the picture. The event developer is in charge of the project from start to finish. The bulk of the work is done ahead of the event. On the day of the event, the role can include running a ceremony, handling media interviews, hosting politicians or dignitaries, and managing photo opportunities, acknowledgments, and evaluation. Depending on the size of the event or group, these activities may be split or shared by a number of individuals.

Event leader. This person will head up the teams on the day of the event. His or her responsibilities include knowing the site intimately and knowing what equipment and supplies are coming. The role includes directing volunteers and answering the logistics questions that will arise during the day.

Again, the success of the event depends on how well it is managed. The leader must stay aware and awake, paying constant attention to how things are working. Volunteers and work need to be divided so that everyone has challenging tasks. If the leader stops leading, as the following story relates, things can easily fall apart.

TreePeople once organized a large and difficult planting with 300 volunteers spread over fifty acres of mountainside. The entire leadership team, who'd been up since 4 A.M. continuously directing volunteers, trees, and supplies to obscure pockets of the forest, independently, spontaneously, and simultaneously noticed that things were going so well that they decided they could stop managing and plant a tree or two. As you can probably understand, it's very hard for tree planters not to plant trees. Within ten minutes the entire planting operation broke down. Hundreds of people were wandering around aimlessly, trying to figure out where and what to plant next! It took forty-five minutes to put the operation back together.

Event supervisors. These are the people you'll train before the day to lead others through the process of planting and maintaining trees. Naturally, if yours is a planting, they'll need to be taught thoroughly and supervised initially to ensure they've got the point, as they'll play a vital role in guiding others at the event. They should be able to supervise up to four volunteers in the process of planting or carrying out maintenance on two or three trees at a time.

Troubleshooters. These people are your problem solvers. Choose volunteers with good judgment, who know how to *power through* rather than complain or give up. They'll have little assigned work on the day of the event other than perhaps being part of a planting or maintenance team, so that if a problem arises they can get things under control without being missed back at the job.

Other jobs. Volunteers can work at a sign-in table for tools and as drivers, or can dispense first aid or refreshments.

EVENT FLOW

Sample Agenda for an Urban Planting

7:00 A.M.   Event developer/coordinator arrives and begins setting up.

8:00 A.M.   Advance team arrives, gets assignments and orientation to the site.

9:00 A.M.   Volunteers arrive and attend a demonstration/ceremony.

1:00 P.M.   Planting complete, cleanup is in full swing.

Lunch celebration begins on the site, or everyone heads for the pizza parlor. Having a lunch break in the middle of the event is a sure way to lose half your crowd, unless you're holding an all-day affair.

National Arbor Day

Usually the last Friday in April, National Arbor Day was first celebrated in Nebraska in 1872. J. Sterling Morton, a journalist, moved to Nebraska when it was treeless and, missing the beauty and benefits of trees, began planting many species around his home. When Morton became editor of Nebraska's first newspaper, he encouraged other settlers to plant trees for soil protection, fuel, building materials, fruit, shade, and beauty. He convinced the Board of Agriculture to set aside a day for planting trees. More than one million trees were planted in the state on the first Arbor Day. By 1894, Arbor Day was celebrated in every state, and in this century the holiday has spread to other countries. J. Sterling Morton was fond of saying, "Other holidays repose on the past; Arbor Day proposes for the future."

To keep things moving, create an agenda with a timeline. Include everything from the time you start to the time you go home with the job completed. An agenda will give the day a general structure and ensure that nothing's left out.

Make a list of what you (or others) are to bring to the site. Check off these items as you load up. Loading up the night before is recommended if you don't like waking up at dawn. If the event is right outside your house, you should have all tools and supplies gathered in one spot the day before.

On the Day

You should plan on having your advance team—developer, leader, supervisors, and troubleshooters—arrive at the site at least one hour before everyone else.

Bring the team together so those who have not yet met can do so, and go over the agenda. Remember, these people are the net that holds everything together. Have a refresher on the planting or pruning style you want to use so all volunteers get the same instructions for that specific site (see Chapter 6), and repeat to supervisors here what you will tell the whole group at the kickoff, so they can pass it along to any late arrivals. Be sure to cover safety instructions and to explain where the bathrooms and refreshments are.

The advance team should then get everything ready for the volunteers (for example, posting no-parking or direction signs, or opening gates to the site). If volunteers arrive early, make sure they're assigned jobs to prevent their standing around getting bored and feeling useless. If you prepare well, everyone can concentrate on getting trees in the ground when things get rolling.

Making It Ceremonial

Ceremonies or press conferences can be an important part of an event. They offer a chance to acknowledge those who made the project possible, including donors, planners, other groups who assisted, volunteers, and anybody else who played a role. A ceremony is also a place to talk about what you're doing in your community and can be used to recruit support for future projects.

Though ceremonies take a lot of work, they're important for large, well-publicized events. If you decide to have a ceremony, ask yourself the following questions: What's its purpose? How long will it last? (Fifteen to twenty minutes should be the maximum.) Who will speak? (It may be you or a member of your group, local officials, celebrities, major donors or sponsors of the project, representatives of the groups that were important to the planning process, or people being acknowledged for their support.) How many people are expected? How many chairs and tables will be needed? Will you need a public-address system?

What to wear and what to bring

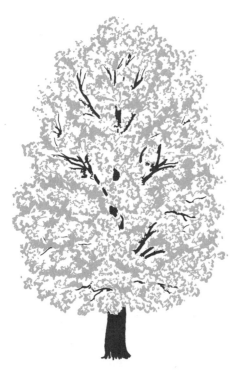

Wear
- △ boots or sturdy-toed shoes (*no* open-toed shoes)
- △ long pants
- △ clothes that can get dirty (because they will)
- △ layers of clothing to adjust with temperature
- △ bandana for all-around usefulness (chosen carefully if work is in gang territory)
- △ gardening or work gloves
- △ hats and/or sunglasses

Bring
- △ something to drink
- △ lunch or a snack
- △ camera and film for before-and-after documentation

Get Down to Work!

If you don't have a ceremony, it's important to have a kickoff gathering to bring volunteers together for an orientation. This meeting is really a ceremony with no pomp and all circumstance! Welcome everyone and thank them for choosing this event over everything they could have done that day. Let them know a little about the planting: who's involved, who paid or sponsored, who did the background work, and what trees are being planted or pruned and why. Give participants an overview of the day and your expectations of them; for example, you can announce that trees, to survive, need to be planted correctly, so you need folks to listen well, to help one another and share tools, and, if possible, to stay for the whole event and help clean up. Explain that a well-controlled event will be a safe, high-quality event. Introduce the event supervisors if you have them and then, depending on the size of the turnout, either give a demonstration or divide the participants into supervised groups so they can go off and have

Flame Maple
(*Acer ginnala*)
zones 2–7

their demo. Ideally, each group shouldn't have more than about fifteen members. With many more, volunteers lose attention and miss vital information. Individuals can then be assigned to their work areas.

It's a good idea to keep someone at the sign-in table to greet late arrivals, VIPs, or news media. It also makes sense to keep a supervisor free to give late planting or pruning instructions. If that's not possible, assign late arrivals to already-working teams so they can get on-the-job training. Even experienced volunteers who go to work without an orientation are more likely than not to be out of sync and to use an incorrect technique.

As the day progresses, the leader, supervisors, and trouble-shooters should continue to monitor the quality of the work and offer correction where needed. If it's going to be a long day, plan on building in rest or refreshment breaks. These can be spontaneous, taken by each team as it completes a tree, or done in unison with the entire group—a good idea for lunch.

Whenever possible, maintain group unity and you'll keep intact a tremendous amount of extra energy in the form of synergy. When a project is long and hard, working alone without the support of the group can be draining. The synergy of the group can carry everyone through the fatigue and keep spirits high. It is this synergy that keeps people coming out for events. Capture it, nurture it, and you and your efforts will be applauded and appreciated throughout the neighborhood, because you'll turn your events into something very special—a celebration of community that people will never forget.

On a similar note, the wrap-up and clean-up is best done with the aid of the entire group. There's nothing more depleting than feeling abandoned to do the dirty work. Cleaning, stacking, counting, sorting the tools, rolling hoses, and even washing vehicles and putting away the tools can be a high when done by the people who've just shared the day together. If it's not done this way, the wrap-up process can take days. The person left holding the ball—most likely you—will resent not having received any help and will probably never want to do the work again. Don't sabotage the process. Let everyone know ahead of time you expect to see a full team till the end. In fact, volunteers who cheat themselves of a good completion often regret it later when they hear about the good time everyone had after the event.

Interim Wrap-Up

Even so, some people will always have a tendency to wander off after they feel the bulk of the work is done. Once again, this dissipates the energy and can send a low signal to those remaining. If this happens, gather the volunteers, thank them, and release those whose heads are already home and taking a bath! Invite people to report on anything special that happened. Have everyone picture the difference their efforts will make. This time is a good time to talk about any follow-up activities you may have planned.

Celebration

Once the day has been declared complete, you may want a completion celebration. This can be as simple as a potluck meal at someone's house or a lunch provided by those who can't work, or as complicated as closing the street for a block party or having a party at a local school or house. A celebration gives everybody a chance to enjoy what they've accomplished. TreePeople hardly ever *plans* one of these, but it's a rare event that doesn't finish with a gaggle of staff and volunteers downing beer and pizza at our headquarters, enjoying the high that comes from a good hard day with the trees, and perhaps catching a little mention on the news once in a while.

Green Ash
(*Fraxinus pennsylvanica*)
zones 3–9

Target: Two Hundred Million Trees

In September 1985, Claire Ekas, the wife of a Queensland farmer, saw a videotape of clips from TreePeople's Million Tree Campaign (see Chapter 5). "I could do that!" declared Claire. She launched *Target: 200 Million Trees by 1988* and set about coordinating one of the world's most spectacular reforestation campaigns.

Claire used the Australian Bicentenary to encourage every possible community group, school, government body, farm family, shire council, and business to contribute to restoring a denuded continent. Many groups were already active but working in isolation. When the campaign closed three years and three months later, the total had reached 201,769,556.

Claire took the follow-up one step farther than TreePeople, acknowledging by letter every person who sent in his or her tree count. She also added humor to the message with slogans like "Put some branches 'round your ranches" and "Possums Need Blossoms."

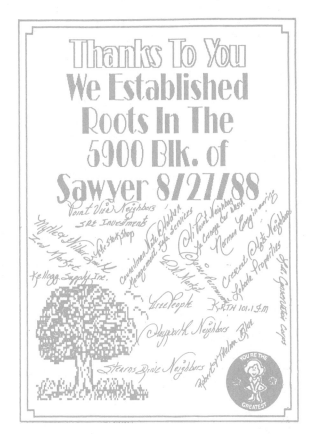

After It's Over

Even though you've perhaps stood in front of the crowd and said thank you, even though you've shaken hands, hugged, patted backs, and shared glasses of champagne or a celebration hot dog, you haven't really thanked everyone until you've written it down. It can be as simple as a postcard or as sophisticated as a plaque, or a typewritten letter with resulting newsclips, photos, or even other letters of acknowledgment from the community that benefited. These people are your volunteers, your donors, media or personalities who showed up, and the folks who greased the skids for you, helped get your permits through, or offered a special deal on supplies. You'll need them for your next project, so make them feel as important as they were. Some communities have even put together photo albums of their event and shared it at a future gathering or in separate meetings. If you plan on doing this again, consider this sort of documentation. It will certainly help you recruit resources next time. Drop a little seedling on the desk of someone really special as a thank-you gift. Such consideration also works beforehand. If you're trying to attract the attention of a potential sponsor, think of appropriate, unusual touches for your communication.

Evaluating Your Event

For help in planning future projects, evaluate your event after it's over. Look at what happened—both good and bad. Acknowledge what worked well and examine that which didn't work so you can find better ways next time. Include your advance team and anybody else interested in the process.

Let everybody give feedback. You might want to use a chalkboard divided into sides listing the good and the not-so-good. Don't try to analyze these thoughts; as in a brainstorm session, get everybody's ideas as a starting point. Then take time to talk about each item mentioned.

Children of the Green Earth's Tips on Working with Children

Children of the Green Earth is a nonprofit educational organization based in Seattle whose work was inspired by the late Richard St. Barbe Baker. The following excerpts are from their book, *Planting Trees with Children—and Making It Work.*

▲ Plan to allow time for sharing the experience with children involved.

▲ Give the children a context for the planting and create a mood for the event. This can be done by telling a story, explaining why the group is planting, for example.

▲ Let the children know the sequence of events and explain that their cooperation is necessary for the tree to grow up healthy.

▲ Dedicate the tree for a special reason or in honor of someone. Have the children give it a name or their good wishes, or recite a poem.

▲ Share a quiet moment after the planting. Help the children envison a full-grown, beautiful tree and imagine the benefits it will provide.

▲ Find out about trees. Gathering the information about the trees you'll be planting helps the children feel more connected during the event—from general planting requirements and care for a particular species, to its folklore and history.

▲ Do something else with trees. A project in art, music, literature, woodworking, or craft helps kids understand the many ways we use forest products. Be sure to tie in the idea of replacing what we use.

▲ Sing a closing song. The Children of the Green Earth song is sung by children all over the world. Motions which accompany the words are:

"From our hearts" (hands on hearts). "With our hands" (hands moving out to center of the circle, palms up as if offering a gift). "For the earth" (kneeling and putting hands on the earth). "All the World Together" (rising and lifting arms overhead and then circling them down to their sides, describing a sphere around themselves).

Kids: The Little Planters with Lots to Offer

Children love tree plantings, and the experience can stay with them for the rest of their lives. Some of our most successful plantings have involved schools and kids. You'll need to keep in mind children's physical constraints, but here are some suggestions for keeping eager hands busy.

Kids will probably have no difficulty carrying light buckets to help with watering. You can also try having them dig holes for trees by taking turns at the shovel. Most children love to sort, so have them count, sort, and pile shovels and other safe, lightweight tools. They can also help you deliver tree ties for staking.

Any child can perform small but important tasks, such as fetching drinks and running messages. Make sure there's a level of involvement for everyone.

An all-children planting is a possibility with smaller trees and plenty of supervision. Make the tasks more interesting with added information and stories.

ANATOMY OF A HUGE EVENT

If for some silly reason you want to take on a huge event, you should know that planning and preparation are the keys to success. Although we're known for producing some monstrous events (see Chapter 5), we don't recommend them as the basis for establishing a program.

Huge events can produce visibility, credibility, impact, and outreach and can galvanize a community to accomplish *the unthinkable*, giving individuals a profound experience of personal power. On the other hand, huge events are costly. They consume large amounts of cash and can burn out staff and volunteers. Along with the goodies, they can produce a dependency on you or your organization, instead of self-sufficiency. Perhaps most insidious, a splashy event doesn't necessarily produce an ongoing commitment to care for the trees that are planted. As powerful as they can be, we suggest you consider huge events with great caution. We offer the following chronicle as an example of what can be accomplished, along with some analysis of costs, successes, and failures.

On January 13, 1990, the anniversary of the birth of Dr. Martin Luther King, Jr., TreePeople produced its largest-ever single-day urban tree planting. The event resulted in the ultimate planting of over 400 trees along the entire seven miles of the boulevard named after Dr. King. Several thousand people showed up to help plant the trees, honor Dr. King, and convert the street into a living monument.

The event was seeded eighteen months previously when Citizen Forester Eudora Russell began talking of a decade-long dream she'd had of turning King Boulevard into a fitting memorial to its namesake. She'd completed her first substantial project and was ready to take on something bigger. Her first letters to the city produced no response, and she finally shared her dream with TreePeople staff. Instead of spending years persuading the city to put millions of dollars into redesigning and landscaping the entire street, she decided to get started on something that could be accomplished much quicker.

Eudora met with the Los Angeles City Street Tree Division and together they chose Canary Island pines as the species.

In March 1989, when TreePeople was offered a small grant via Gallo Wines and AFA's Global Releaf Fund, we used it to launch the King project. Eleven large pines were planted on April 22 in a National Arbor Day ceremony that called attention to the new dream and to the need for a committee of volunteers to

Everybody can be great, because anybody can serve.

DR. MARTIN LUTHER KING, JR.

make it real. After a number of discussions with Andy, the idea emerged for a major celebration on Dr. King's birthday. The aim was to gather the community in the spirit of Dr. King's dream and philosophy, and accomplish the entire planting in one day.

In October, the Southern California Gas Company and the mayor's office expressed an interest in leading the corporate-fund-raising effort. Six months passed during which other pressing issues had taken priority and now, with so little time before the proposed date, January 13, 1990, TreePeople pledged to help Eudora and her committee, despite our strong encouragement that Citizen Foresters organize their plantings with as little outside assistance as possible. Instead of dropping the project on an overloaded staff, we hired a Citizen Forester, Fred Anderson, and assigned him to coordinate all aspects of the production.

Fred began to facilitate the work of the King Boulevard Memorial Project Committee. A logo was designed, and the committee began recruiting broad-based community support. City council staff from the four districts through which the boulevard ran joined the committee, along with a representative from Mayor Bradley's office and staff from a sponsoring local radio station.

To emphasize community ownership, a fund was established at the California Community Foundation to receive and manage incoming tax-deductible donations.

Fred led TreePeople staff in designing a logistics and community-outreach plan. As the plan unfolded it became clear that increasing amounts of staff time would be needed for a successful event. The budget—$130,000—attempted to cover all expenses.

Outreach and Enrollment

We couldn't produce just a planting and walk away because we were committed to community ownership. This project was to be by the people and for the people. Our community outreach included schools, churches, group mailings, and canvassing.

One staff member coordinated an attempt at personal contact (using door hangers only as a last resort) with every home or business within half a block of the entire fourteen linear miles of the boulevard. TreePeople's school-program staff made presentations to over thirty elementary schools near the boulevard while the outreach team worked with three public high schools, two of which had leadership-development programs. We also worked with the Los Angeles Conservation Corps' *Clean-and-Green* Junior High program and were in touch with all the churches to involve their membership. One committee member produced a poster contest to further the message.

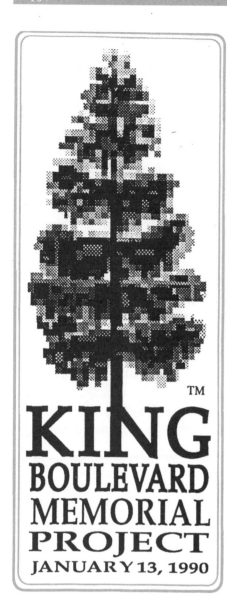

KING
BOULEVARD
MEMORIAL
PROJECT
JANUARY 13, 1990

Interagency Coordination

Early on, we coordinated a meeting with representatives of the Street Tree Division, the Bureau of Street Maintenance, the Traffic Department, police tactical planning, the fire department, the Department of Transportation, and the mayor's office. The event would require official closure of a lane on each side of the street (fourteen miles of signs, cones, barricades, and flags), posting of no-parking signs, and mechanical street sweeping after the event. Even without planting logistics and support, the event represented an enormous burden of manpower and equipment on the agencies. The costs involved necessitated the securing of a city council special-event resolution enabling the agencies to commit and spend unbudgeted resources. The resolution also allowed us to cover the event under our existing one-million-dollar-liability insurance policy.

Logistics

We decided to plant all seven miles simultaneously. Appreciating the difficulty in managing anything on a site that large, we broke the fifty-block-long area into twenty-five two-block units, and set them up as fully independent operations, as if each block were a small planting. Management was to be handled by a block captain (like a mini event leader), hosts and greeters, and a team of planting supervisors. Multiplied fifty times, that amounted to more than 500 people who needed to be recruited and trained in advance. Each unit would be fully equipped with a sign-in table and chairs; supplies including steel tree stakes, gravel, and root-control barriers; tools; trees; a first-aid kit; a walkie-talkie; and a portable toilet.

Delivering the supplies proved a major challenge. Because of the size of the planting, nothing could be delivered in advance. Volunteers needed to be in place for set-up. We planned to rent eight twenty-foot flatbed trucks and to load each with a set of supplies for a group of block-unit stations. The rentals would be augmented by a fleet of trucks provided by TreePeople, volunteers, vendors, and public agencies. We chose to rent the basic fleet for critical supplies to avoid a possible breakdown if a loaned vehicle didn't show.

A police station parking lot roughly midway along the boulevard was designated an interagency communications command post. To avoid bottlenecks, we arranged for walk-in volunteers to sign up at any one of twenty-five registration areas along the boulevard. They would be greeted and signed in, and would re-

ceive a name tag before being grouped with a trained planting supervisor to guide them through the planting of their trees. In this way, we were able to guarantee all trees would be planted by experienced personnel and all volunteers would experience support through the entire process.

Each block captain would be issued a walkie-talkie for emergencies or logistics questions. To enhance the educational aspect of the event, we arranged for the City Bureau of Sanitation to provide recycling bins at every sign-in table. They also provided one of their new recycling trucks to cruise the boulevard and service the bins.

Tools

Although TreePeople maintains a supply of more than 500 shovels, we needed many more for this event. We arranged to borrow an additional 800 shovels from the Bureau of Street Maintenance. We also needed more stake pounders, so we borrowed all we could from the Recreation and Parks Department and the Street Tree Division, and when we still didn't locate enough, the Southern California Gas Company underwrote the cost of the ones we needed to purchase. Tables and chairs to supply each of the block units were loaned by the County of Los Angeles.

Fundraising

Despite our best efforts, TreePeople has rarely finished its fundraising before a project's inception. It gives us ulcers but keeps spirit and energy in our work. Within moderation, we try not to let a lack of money stand in our way. Although many items and services were being donated for this project, a number of service donations fell through. The project was becoming very expensive, but those helping to raise the money didn't see the expense as a major problem.

This project was so big that it equaled a sizeable portion of the entire TreePeople budget, and was far more than we could raise on our own. Besides, with our own annual budget to raise, we were reticent to ask our regular donors to support a project that was supposedly being handled by the community, with TreePeople providing only coordination and training. With so much else to do throughout the year, how could we continue to provide the funding for every community planting project?

Regardless, we set up a system for donor acknowledgment. Corporate sponsors of $1,000 or more were to be honored with a banner on the boulevard. Individuals, schools, and groups were invited to sponsor the planting or care of one tree for $100 and $53 respectively. Each would receive a T-shirt and a certificate.

The fundraising team included personnel from the Southern California Gas Company, the mayor's office, and the King Boulevard Memorial Project Committee. Although we had some political and corporate clout, we had nobody lined up to make a substantial contribution—nowhere near the 50 percent goal one should shoot for before making a public announcement to raise the other half. The gas company made an opening commitment of $10,000 and pledged to donate all the printing costs. Since they were leading another major Martin Luther King Birthday event, they expected to bring in substantial funding to match their generosity along with an endorsement from the other event. What they didn't anticipate was that the planting was viewed by many as funding competition, so no endorsement was made and consequently no high-level corporate support was given.

We were at a critical point, with no cash to cover all the preparation. We set a go/no-go date of a month before the event and just in time, Mayor Bradley made a public commitment to raising the funds. The mayor's leadership was critical. His job was to communicate the need for public involvement to save the project. We held a press conference in which the mayor made a request for assistance.

Unfortunately, it backfired. The following day, a generous, well-placed half-page newspaper article appeared proclaiming that the mayor and the city were going to plant 400 trees on King Boulevard and that the first hundred had already been planted! The public was told that everything was being handled without them—business as usual. We were not able to invite the greater community to help until the day of the event.

We pushed the fundraising as hard as we could and slid into the planting day with a $40,000 deficit, which came out of TreePeople's general fund. We'd even set up a toll-free phone line, compliments of GEO, and with an intensive media effort, invited tree sponsorship. Despite good coverage, including the *Los Angeles Times*, we received only eighteen phone-call donations. Toll-free phone lines, without a telethon to back them up, are not a good way to raise money!

Training

The outreach and enrollment programs recruited a large pool of volunteers to be trained for event leadership. TreePeople staff and experienced Citizen Foresters produced a number of hands-on planting-supervisor trainings in the two months prior to the event. Those trainings alone resulted in the planting of 100 trees. In addition to the trainings, all volunteers were called to participate in a final logistics meeting three nights before the event where they reviewed what they'd learned, met with their block teams, and were given their block-captain, host, or supervisor T-shirts along with a final pep talk. The goal of having 500 people trained in advance was met.

Site Preparation

Many planting sites were in concrete sidewalk that needed to be marked, cut, broken out, and removed. That was the only significant site preparation needed other than lane closure and traffic control on the planting day. Initially, we hoped that city agencies would cut the concrete and auger the tree holes before the planting. As it turned out, they did not have equipment, manpower, or time to do it. We eventually contracted out the concrete cutting, breaking, and debris removal. We decided it would be better for volunteers to dig the holes.

Theory Versus Practice

The best laid plans indeed! One could imagine, considering the variables, that a few things wouldn't go as planned. We weren't disappointed. When you step into citizen forestry, or any substantially uncharted territory, you need to have what former staff member Hunter Lovins called "a high tolerance for ambiguity"; in other words, a lot of patience and an ability to solve problems creatively. Despite apparent breakdowns, the event was an absolute success. A few of the highlights:

Misinterpretations of various commitments and plans caused substantial delays in a number of areas. One example resulted in the concrete-cutting process being slowed to the point of failing to meet the deadline. We discovered this about thirty-six hours before the event and, at the last minute, tried unsuccessfully to hire a fleet of additional contractors. Ultimately, we called our buddies at the gas company, who dispatched emergency crews with jackhammers, which freed the contractors to focus on simple cutting. That left the hole clearing to the volunteers, who placed the broken concrete and debris in the street for removal by the City Bureau of Street Maintenance—a major unplanned city effort and expense.

Instead of delivering twenty-five separate piles of gravel, the building supply firm would drop only one eighty ton pile. Initially, we lined up eighty members of the Los Angeles Conservation

No planting in Los Angeles is approved without a root barrier (the big round thing in the foreground).

Corps to shovel it into 5 gallon buckets, but once again, the Bureau of Street Maintenance came through on the morning of the planting with skip loaders and huge dump trucks. We expected twenty-five piles, but they wound up delicately delivering a mini pile at *each* of the 300 tree sites. Although this saved a lot of volunteer sweat, it caused considerable delay for those waiting at the end of the delivery routes.

We recruited our hams (amateur radio operators) too late, which gave us too few for total event command, so we had to rent fifty walkie-talkies. The flaw with this step, however, was that we had only one frequency! Fortunately, the few hams we recruited managed the communication system, trained all the volunteers, and saved the day.

During the afternoon before the planting, it began to rain. Just as it was getting dark, we discovered that the tree sites we'd mapped out didn't match the markings on the street. All volunteers already had their maps and assignments. Two of us drove and walked the entire route in the rain, counting and reassigning, then used both walkie-talkie and public telephone to communicate the information to the TreePeople office, where staff worked through the night to make new maps.

We'd promised the volunteers that the planting was on—rain or shine. At 4 A.M. when we woke, it was pouring. The initial leadership showed up at the site at six o'clock dressed and drenched. Every block captain was in position by 7:30 and it was still raining. Two key staff members were so sick with the flu that they couldn't get out of bed. By 8:30, the Planting Supervisors were on the scene and the sun began to break through. The public converged at 9:00 and the rain had stopped. The turnout was astonishing, both in terms of numbers and diversity. Blacks, Hispanics, Asians, and Whites from all over Southern California were attracted by the invitation to create a monument.

At 11:00, with stake pounders ringing like bells in the background, we held a press conference and ceremony that was attended by the mayor, city councilpeople, and corporate sponsors. The mayor was visibly moved, having just driven several miles of the boulevard and witnessed the incredible outpouring of human energy and spirit—the citizens of his city out working together. He turned the press conference into a fundraiser by writing a personal check and declaring that no politician would be allowed to speak unless they came to the podium with a check in hand! Every time a check of $100 or more was written, the mayor interrupted to acknowledge it.

The final speaker was the Vice-President for Public Affairs at the Southern California Gas Company. Like the mayor, he was moved both by the magnitude of the event and by the fact that more than two hundred of his employees were on the street volunteering. He threw away his speech and made a surprise announcement: although they'd been the lead giver, they wanted to dig deeper to retire the debt. He revealed that his company had a policy of donating $100 to any nonprofit organization for which an employee volunteered more than eight hours of service. Thus, his two hundred employees' full-day effort resulted in a commitment of an additional $20,000 to the project.

That commitment signified a remarkable process that we often see when executives first get involved in this work. They intellectually support the cause, but when they actually begin to physically participate and have a direct experience, their excitement and enthusiasm go off the scale.

The ceremony concluded with birthday cake—not just at the press conference site but concurrently at all twenty-five registration tables. The major hotels in Los Angeles had organized themselves to bake and deliver enough cake to feed all the planters. Every cake was different; some were works of thematic art, complete with plastic trees and L.A. beach scenes. Imagine: birthday cake for 3,000 people. In Andy's final comments, he gave thanks for a miraculous event, drawing attention to the island of sun in which the planting was taking place. We were surrounded by heavy clouds. It was still raining on the rest of the city.

As each tree was planted, a neighbor was recruited to help water and care for it. All the planters signed their names to clean stickers and fixed them to the steel tree stakes along with the name given to their tree. A final sticker identified the person who'd adopted the tree and committed to its early care.

One last glitch developed. Although we'd prescribed an interagency communications command post and provided the facility (a large motor home), the involved agencies didn't staff it. As a result, logistics difficulties took much longer to resolve. To facilitate solutions, we issued radios to some city staff members, enabling them to work as part of the problem-solving force.

Once the trees were in and the street cleaned up, the leadership team gathered to sort tools and compare stories. And what stories they were: of gang members naming their tree after a friend who'd been killed in a drive-by shooting; of an elderly woman who'd marched with Dr. King dissolving into tears as she recounted the story to planters; of neighbors coming out of houses and of planters being offered cups of tea and coffee. Then the sky opened up with a sun shower, which produced a sight so sweet we all swore no one would believe it if we reported it—a bright rainbow graced the horizon.

To accomplish great things, we must not only act but also dream, not only plan but also believe.

ANATOLE FRANCE

Follow-up

All the people who signed in at the event were sent thank-you notes and a follow-up newsletter. Every couple of months a group of volunteers gathers to do a bit of work and continue to enroll, and thank, neighbors for caring for trees. Even the city has sent a water truck along the boulevard a few times. As we had hoped, the trees are surviving with care and attention from those who live and work nearby.

Additional Analysis

As wonderful and successful as this program was, it's not a model of good citizen forestry. In producing it, we violated one of our basic operating principles: we jumped in and guaranteed the event before the local communities were ready to take it on. In retrospect, another year of outreach would have provided viable community leadership. Even though there was a high percentage of neighborhood involvement, our true goal was to see the local churches, schools, and community groups adopt entire stretches of the boulevard in advance, both for planting and ongoing tree care.

The event left the staff, volunteers, and community members deeply moved, inspired, and gratified. It also left some of us thoroughly exhausted. Most important, the community was left with a new spirit and sense of possibility. Neighbors, politicians, agency personnel, and bureaucrats worked together, forging a new kind of partnership. That partnership produced cooperation, teamwork, empowerment, spirit, and hope—the ideals about which we dream, the things dreamed of by Martin Luther King, Jr.

When we spoke in Portland recently of this event as a failure, one audience member commented that if this was a failure, he'd hate to see our successes! As the book relays, however, our successes are much quieter. They don't all make the news. They happen in backyards and on streets, in classrooms and living rooms, in African villages and on mountain slopes. With luck, you'll soon be one of them.

5

Taking It to the Streets: The Million Tree Story

*H*ire a contractor, and you have a measurable goal. But how do you measure the success of a campaign that inspires ordinary individuals to pick up a shovel? And, moreover, how do you make such a campaign succeed? In Los Angeles, TreePeople has always tried to be the bridge that keeps communication open between the professionals and the public. In the three years leading to the 1984 Olympics, using resources that are not hidden but are often overlooked, Tree-People successfully motivated the public to report the planting of over one million trees. In the media capital of the world, when the *greenhouse effect* still referred to an early crop of tomatoes, TreePeople made tree planting trendy.

This chapter describes lessons learned during the Million Tree Campaign. Our challenge was to inform, enroll, guide, and inspire the public on an ongoing basis—without a public-relations or advertising budget. The less money you have, the more creatively you'll be able to seek out and use free or low-cost resources and techniques. Take these thoughts, adapt them, and apply them in your own community to win the attention of the media, the imagination of your politicians, the dollars of your sponsors, and the hearts of your community.

With the growing awareness that trees are part of the solution to the greenhouse effect, most people will continue to envision acres on acres of forest trees as the sole answer, rather than considering the more specific and effective plantings that can occur in cities. Without a visible, educated constituency in support of urban trees, tree-maintenance budgets, as opposed to quick-fix planting dollars, will take a back seat to what are believed to be more vital issues.

Even though many politicians seem to have been sold on the value of a healthy urban forest, it's probably a much more expensive ticket item than they can anticipate. Hence the reason for marketing urban forestry: to build active support to put public trees on the public agenda.

The steps outlined are written from a private, nonprofit perspective. Most tactics would also be relevant for government agencies, so if you have a good relationship with your city government, you may suggest some of this in your role of advocate for the department in charge of urban trees. A committee of such advocates can provide flexibility to operate outside government constraints when needed and can serve as a place for business and community leaders to contribute their skills and resources. Although the tactics outlined made up a three-year intensive effort, many of them are appropriate for independent use in smaller campaigns.

THE PLAN

Public-education campaigns are similar to planting campaigns. Before you can be organized, you must do your homework. If well planned and guided, such a campaign can provide as much exposure as a multimillion-dollar advertising campaign and can result in far greater public involvement.

First identify the major issues you need to highlight: tackling the greenhouse effect through energy conservation; protecting the environment from the hazards of the depleted ozone layer through shade production; increasing property value; helping the city celebrate its bicentennial; enhancing air quality; feeding the hungry; or galvanizing youth, mitigating the trash crisis, and so on. Make this specific for your city rather than simply copying what worked somewhere else. TreePeople used the approaching Olympics as the reason to galvanize the public, then focused on a number of problems we thought urban forestry could help solve. Others may choose a certain percentage of tree cover, or a certain number of people involved, as a goal.

Know what you want the community to do. Do you just want to engender political support and awareness, or do you want people out planting and caring for trees?

Identify and enroll community leaders who can help you, including those from neighborhood organizations, the business community, churches, and unions, and invite celebrities and the news media to publicize your effort. Consider organizing an informal group of people who want to help accomplish your goal.

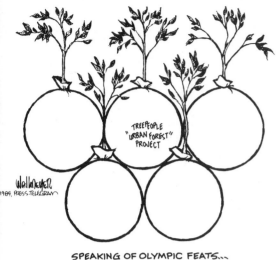

TREEPEOPLE
"URBAN FOREST"
PROJECT

Wallmeyer
1984, PRESS-TELEGRAM

SPEAKING OF OLYMPIC FEATS...

Seek out campaign resources. Look for people and companies who can donate all or most of the materials and services you'll need. However, be careful not to take on any volunteers without first checking the quality of their work! Seek out advertising agencies, public-relations firms, printers, artists, designers or art directors, writers, photographers, a local newspaper, a radio or television station, or concerned newswriters or reporters. TreePeople targeted an international advertising agency, Doyle Dane Bernbach, and persuaded the president to donate some agency time and talent to help produce the Million Tree Campaign.

Also identify possible corporate sponsors. Use your creativity to bring together people with common interests, such as a company that uses a tree as its logo or suppliers known for their philanthropy.

Set the campaign time period. Keep the community posted on your progress, and build in a completion and wrap-up phase. Create several stages so that you can celebrate accomplishments along the way. Each completion gives you the opportunity for a media event.

THE ACTION

Be courageous. People may think you're foolish, but they'll admire and may even support your courage with time, money, talent, resources, or pure sweat.

On July 1, 1981, TreePeople launched a campaign to inspire the planting of one million trees in Southern California before the 1984 Summer Olympics. The campaign was a response to a request from the mayor. The Los Angeles City Planning Department had just released a report that had studied the effect on air pollution of massive tree planting in other cities. It claimed that one million trees, when mature in twenty years, would be capable of filtering up to 200 tons of particulate smog from the air every day. The report concluded that it would take twenty years and 200 millon taxpayer dollars to plant the trees on streets and another 200 million dollars to maintain them. The city turned to TreePeople, the organization it had seen mobilize thousands of individuals to provide volunteer disaster relief during recent floods. The pollution problem was a disaster of sorts too. Its organizational ego inflated from its recent success, TreePeople took on the task.

The figure one million had a good solid ring to it—one that we felt could inspire great volunteer efforts within the community. So, with no prior money allocated, TreePeople's purportedly impossible three-year goal fired the public's imagination.

With an overall game plan but no set rules, TreePeople used the following methods to keep the goal (and the dream) alive in a city of 10 million people and 100 million causes. Note the failures. We learned as much from them as we did from the successes, and thus we'll highlight them as pitfalls that should be approached with caution.

A Pro Bono Advertising Campaign

Doyle Dane Bernbach (DDB) assigned a team to the *TreePeople account*. We used them while they were fresh and inspired. The creative team needed to be briefed on the goals, values, and principles of the urban forest and our campaign, which was obviously vastly different from its usual accounts.

For instance, as the material illustrates, TreePeople was not to be seen as the hero of this campaign. We knew we couldn't do it alone and, in fact, if we had to, we would have failed in our mission to inspire public participation. The advertising agency had a hard time accepting that a client would not want name recognition. We understood the concern, but we were conscious of the natural tendency of people to relegate the handling of problems to others. In this case, TreePeople would handle the trees. Did our strategy work? We don't know. Would more people have participated if our name were up front? As it is, many people who don't know TreePeople's name still remember the campaign to plant a million trees in Los Angeles. "Oh! That was you guys?" they say. In a way, by our own standard, that means we were successful.

This advertisement was a great concept; unfortunately, we didn't have the budget to buy space and run it.

By 1984 there will be one million more trees in Los Angeles. **HELP PLANT THE URBAN FOREST.**

WOULDN'T IT BE
SOMETHING IF THERE
WERE FORESTS LIKE
THIS IN LOS ANGELES?
FORESTS TO BEAUTIFY

Gregory Peck with the newlyweds, 1983.

DDB devised a fully integrated advertising strategy, along with the theme materials and artwork. The tag line was "Turn Over a New Leaf, L.A.—Help Plant the Urban Forest," with one poster line the team couldn't resist—Urban Releaf! (They could not have known the impact the pun would have on the nation's community forestry movement six years later!)

Television
The agency wrote a television script and gave us the job of enrolling the talent. Persistence paid off. After dozens of attempts to enroll celebrities with persuasive letters and repeated phoning, Gregory Peck returned our call and became our spokesperson.

General Telephone (GTE) was asked to provide a video production crew, and a daylong shoot was produced for the cost of sixteen hamburgers. The thirty-second spot got its fair share of air play, because it was a high-quality piece featuring a high-quality household name who was actually committed to the cause; Peck joined our board of directors.

Public-service time on radio is the easiest form of free advertising and the easiest to produce. Most radio stations will accept either a written script or a thirty- or sixty-second tape. They usually require two weeks to get them on the air and will play them for at least a month.

Unless you can continue to furnish the radio stations with new taped scripts, which is a very expensive option, you'll get only about a month's mileage out of each. Far more effective is to mail sets of "live" ten-, thirty-, and sixty-second scripts every month, enclosing a grateful cover letter. These are read by announcers and, when written well and typed clearly, are preferred by the stations to prerecorded tapes. Try to have a professional advertising writer work on these.

Newspapers and magazines will, on rare occasions, run a public-service advertisement. It's much more difficult for them and is very expensive. But with persistence and footwork, one usually can persuade an advertising editor to insert an ad at some time. It's extremely difficult, however, to control when, where, and how big the ad will run. Another option is to enroll a department store that can donate space for your message in its own ads, run a promotion with you that it can advertise, or even pay the costs for running your ad in exchange for an acknowledgment.

Radio

DDB wrote and produced a great radio commercial using Lohmann and Barkley, a local radio comedy team often used for paid commercials. Tapes were delivered to over seventy-five radio stations. Unfortunately, many of the stations refused to run the spots, because they regarded Lohmann and Barkley as competition for their own comic acts.

TreePeople mailed *live announcer* scripts. The message was the same each month, but clever copywriting made it fresh and different every time.

Print

DDB also created artwork for a print ad, but we were unsuccessful in getting space donated. This is much easier if you're in a small town. The *Los Angeles Times* has too many paying customers and so doesn't have much surplus space available. Nevertheless, print ads were run by companies who sponsored other parts of our campaign mentioned below: General Telephone, May Company, Louisiana-Pacific, and Nurseryland. These ads promoted the campaign but also highlighted company efforts.

Most billboard companies provide small spaces to community causes as a public service, but they usually charge to post each board. Some companies even charge monthly.

At great expense near the beginning of the campaign, we produced and printed 5,000 copies of a fantastic book—a forerunner to this one—called *A Planters' Guide to the Urban Forest.* A member of the book's advisory team who was also the horticulture editor of the *Los Angeles Times* got inspired and sold the *Times* on the project. They dedicated an entire issue of their Sunday *Home Magazine* to the thirty-nine best trees for Los Angeles and delivered it to one and a half million homes without costing us a cent! We enhanced its impact with a telephone referral service that directed callers to nurseries specializing in their favorite trees.

Outdoor

Some billboard companies have a great distaste for trees, because they block their boards. Without realizing this, we stumbled into a hornet's nest when we began asking for support. We discovered later that one company had just been prosecuted for a midnight massacre of a dozen trees. Even though our campaign focused on people planting in their own yards, most firms remained cold. Despite the negativity, we found a company that loved the idea and posted 800 boards at no charge. We did have to pay twenty-five dollars for each of the 400 bus signs posted.

DDB produced artwork for the billboards and bus signs, but we were unsuccessful in getting the printing donated. However, we found a printer who let us pay him when we could. Ironically, the final installment was mailed two years later—the month the campaign ended.

You'll always need materials to present the overview of your program to the general public, and it makes sense to have it coordinated with the rest of your campaign.

Support material

DDB designed a brochure that was written by TreePeople and printed by Southern California Edison. "Help Plant an Idea" explained the campaign and how people could participate. We stapled packets of seeds to the front of each brochure, which was labor intensive but eye-catching.

DDB also designed a bumper sticker—"I brake for trees"— that was light-hearted and took advantage of "I brake for animals," one of the bumper stickers popular at the time. Although we paid for the printing of the stickers, we also sold a lot, which underwrote their cost and raised a bit of extra small change.

I brake for trees.

HELP PLANT THE URBAN FOREST.

A PROJECT OF 🌲 TreePeople

Don't assume anything! Entities that look like natural partners to you often have other forces pulling on them, or just a completely different perspective on your campaign. Do as much footwork as you can before you spend too much money or time trying to involve a reluctant sponsor. There's more than one way to skin a cat.

Point of purchase material (POP)

The sign printing and the nursery kits mentioned below were the only print items paid for during the campaign, and they were not necessarily more vital than the free materials to the campaign's success. Our lesson to keep the campaign economical came back to us in spades as we struggled to pay the bill! One tactic—necessary but very time-consuming and often disheartening—was to involve the nursery trade. At a cost of forty dollars apiece, we produced with DDB a packet of materials to be given to 1,000 nurseries in Southern California. The nursery kit contained tree tags, banners that read "Urban Forest Headquarters" and matched the billboards, confirmation forms, and a display mailbox to be periodically emptied by either the nursery personnel or TreePeople volunteers.

Our hope was that each nursery, seeing the value of our campaign for its business, would make a tax-deductible donation to cover the cost. For the most part, we were mistaken.

We were puzzled by the general lack of interest on the part of the nursery industry. Only one major chain, Nuseryland, ran ads announcing their involvement. Because the state association would not endorse a campaign that didn't involve the entire state, we made separate presentations to each regional association in Southern California. One unresponsive group left us feeling particularly disillusioned. Cleaning up after our talk, we found dozens of our brochures left on the seats—but with the little seed packets removed.

Don't go to the trouble of running a campaign unless you make sure everyone hears about it!

Volunteers serviced the nursery mailboxes and hung tree tags.

When we finally realized we were going to be stuck with almost 1,000 kits that would simply get dusty in our storeroom and not do their job, we came down off our nonprofit pedestal and decided to cut our losses and give the kits away. The sales force of Kellogg Supply, a fertilizer company, volunteered to help distribute kits and collect confirmation cards as they made their biweekly visits to customers. Many nurseries displayed the material and thousands of confirmation forms were mailed to us from eager customers who didn't want to use, or couldn't find, the nursery mailbox.

Another major wholesale grower was unsuccessful in mobilizing enough nurseries to participate in a cooperative ad campaign. Despite their lack of interest, several nurseries acknowledged that they benefited financially from our campaign.

News Events

The day after TreePeople committed itself to the Million Tree Campaign, a nursery that was going out of business called, wanting to donate 100,000 seedlings. We called the National Guard and they agreed to deliver the trees in eight forty-foot trucks that stretched a mile along the freeway. What a visual: the army and the environmentalists! We had the mayor unload the first seedling to a kid. A human conveyor belt delivered the trees from the trucks to our own nursery. We got plenty of coverage.

TreePeople has built a reputation for being *media aware*. This description is sometimes leveled as a criticism; however, we take it as a compliment. We've never had a public-relations budget

Make sure your events are interesting! Take the time to design an event with good visual interest. The only way to compete with TV violence is to give the media something more colorful or interesting. Charts, graphs, and celebrities planting trees are all better than a person in a suit behind a lectern.

Use institutions that already exist, such as Arbor Day, Earth Day, or a local equivalent, around which to build an event. Editors are always looking for stories relevant to time, season, or occasion. They also like stories related to other major headlines.

For instance, if there's a major global warming conference scheduled in your town, you might create an event that highlights how your program is helping to cut energy costs locally, thereby reducing carbon dioxide output. Since trees can be part of the solution to many urban problems, many opportunities are available. Another example would be to utilize gang members in a constructive project. That kind of story will always get coverage.

Keep it fresh! Find a new twist every time you stage an event, or the media will become very tired very fast. Serve the media. Coffee and (donated) muffins are good for a start! Then add press releases and a couple of high-contrast black-and-white photos, in case the newspaper reporters don't bring along a photographer. Be thoughtful when setting times for your events. The best time is weekdays at 10 A.M. This will usually give you a fresh crew with time to shoot and edit your story before their schedule gets too hectic.

nor a staff person devoted to that function. In every case, and sometimes in spite of our efforts, the national media attention we've received has been unsolicited—out of the blue. Our best coverage has always been the result of a story we didn't initiate.

Why is this? We believe it has something to do with the points above, plus our genuine respect for most of the media folk we've worked with. They deserve it: they're a priceless resource. Don't overuse them or try to trick them.

TreePeople actually turned down an offered donation of two pickup trucks because after months of negotiation and no commitment, the offer finally came through the evening before one of our big scheduled press conferences. Naturally, the corporation wanted to be there to announce the sponsorship. Our press releases had gone out three days prior with not a peep about this. We valued our reputation for being straight shooters with the media and weren't prepared to annoy them with a surprise change of script on the day of the press conferences.

Tree People enrolled a local TV station, KABC, and a newsman, to produce a five-night miniseries on various aspects of the campaign. KABC took up the cause. They provided regular updates and a *treemometer* to measure progress. In fact, it was their innocent request for our phone number to flash on the screen that finally sent our tree count through the roof. Believe it or not, in the land of the telephone, we'd been asking for planting confirmations in writing—on a postcard or even a scrap of paper. The immediacy and obviousness of a tree hotline and answering machines to take the calls twenty-four hours a day had passed us by.

TreePeople presented KABC with a special award at the end of the campaign and made sure the viewers were acknowledged for the major role they played. Everybody deserves to feel worthy, appreciated, and part of the key to success.

Register Your Trees!
213/273-TREE
24-HOUR HOTLINE
TreePeople

TV news editors are always looking for stories that they can use on holiday weekends, but avoid weekend media events. Most stations have few or no camera crews on weekends, and crimes and disasters are their priority.

Never think of your public-education work as PR. The media don't like giving free advertising, and you're not advertising: you're inspiring and educating the public about something of vital importance to the environment everyone lives in. That's not a commercial item.

Make yourself fully available. It may not look like progress at the time, but when you plant hundreds of seeds, some are sure to grow.

Brief yourself on the group you're addressing. Find out what they've done in the past and what they're capable of doing for your campaign. Don't ram information down their throats at the beginning of your presentation, but be sure to give plenty of options at the end; and if you get a check as well, so much the better. (See page 39.)

BEAN COUNTING

Campaigns like this are enough to give you early ulcers. Your tree count will drive you crazy. When your real job is to encourage high-quality planting and tree care, why do you spend most of the time drumming up enthusiasm and bean counting? The age of the sound bite will turn your highest intentions for communicating care and thoroughness into a one-liner, and that one-liner will be your number goal. Think very carefully before you give yourself this rod for your back.

TreePeople is still apprehensive about a repeat of a campaign for Los Angeles that hangs success on a number. One essential problem with such a campaign is that you will be hailed if you hit the jackpot, and you'll receive sympathy cards if you don't. So you'll go crazy getting to that number. You'll want to cheat. You'll beg people to let you count their trees. They'll ask you if you want to count their rose bushes and vines too. You'll want to fudge your timeline. You'll have long philosophical discussions with your colleagues about whether trees that would have been planted anyway should count and what the geographic boundaries should be. And what you're doing it all for anyway. Everyone will get sick or depressed or leave straight after the campaign—win or lose. You probably think we're kidding.

The Interview and Speaking Circuit

TreePeople recruited and trained staff and volunteers for a speakers bureau. We appeared on TV and radio interview programs at a moment's notice—at 6 A.M. or 12 midnight. Every opportunity to talk was taken. Every rotary club, garden club, or gathering of two or more got a speaker and a slide show.

The Religious Community

TreePeople involved churches and synagogues in some aspects of the campaign. A presentation to the Inter-Religious Council of Southern California inspired leaders of many religions to get involved at some level. A few congregations organized seedling distributions based around an urban-forest sermon, but this didn't result in widespread participation.

Trees are a positive issue and are an important symbol in the ideology of many of the world's religions. Don't expect interest to spread from the top down. Time and again, we were shown that the most powerful direction is from the bottom up! A committed member of a congregation is definitely your best shot.

Many large corporations have in-house printing and video and audio facilities. Having them contribute those resources is usually easier than getting direct funding and is often much more valuable. The important thing is to allow a lot of time. Your project must fit into the corporation's profit-making schedule, which sometimes can take months.

The Corporate Community

Companies can be very helpful. Their executives can provide leadership to both your organization and the community, and their involvement can lend credibility to your cause. Companies can contribute resources, finances, and volunteers. And reaching people where they work is often an overlooked route.

The TV spot we shot with GTE's crew would have cost at least $25,000 (in 1983 dollars) if we'd had to pay for professional services; instead it cost us nothing. Southern California Edison contributed thousands of dollars in printing services over the years. Also, having a volunteer art director employed at a design firm meant help from suppliers, who usually are happy to oblige their client.

Large corporations are also a resource for volunteers. Corporate community responsibility is a big issue these days, and concern for the environment makes it a double whammy in your favor. Big concerns often have volunteer coordinators on staff whose job it is to recruit both executives and rank-and-file workers

Use fun runs for publicity rather than to raise money. You'll avoid disappointment!

Think of easy (for you) and cheap (for them) ways to involve corporations, like our tree-dedication program. For ten dollars each, they can have trees planted in the mountains in honor of customers or employees or just to boost their public image. They're not all going to be $10,000 sponsors, but you can still do great business together.

But be careful. We've been caught many times putting days and months into ideas that never happened. Time is often a necessary investment to realize your dreams. The time wasted can be minimized if you inform a company at the outset that your resources are limited and that, without anything solid, your time is limited too. If they're not happy with that, it's better to end the association right then, as they'll never be able to understand the difference between nonprofit and profit-making concerns, and more heartbreak will follow with both partners feeling cheated. Be careful not to let their involvement divert you from your mission. Simply try to make your agenda their agenda and then let their involvement work for you. Stay open and make the negotiation fun.

for service projects. The most forward-thinking companies are even providing paid release time from daily duties for some volunteers. Also, some companies will contribute funds to organizations where their employees volunteer.

Early in the campaign, General Telephone's vice-president for public affairs joined our board of directors. We began working on a plan that developed into a major two-year commitment from GTE. They invited their people to become Urban Forest Rangers, who would visit local elementary schools with environmental information, stories, seeds, soil mini-greenhouse kits, and followup curriculum packets for the teachers. Almost 700 people volunteered, and GTE underwrote the entire $40,000 cost of the program. The staff and resource time contributed was valued at another $100,000!

GTE's involvement paid off in riches beyond their dreams. Almost 70,000 kids participated, and all their parents found out about it. The positive publicity generated was greater than anything they could have bought, and their vice-president was featured in an article in *Fortune* magazine. Of course, GTE's participation was also a great boost for TreePeople.

Although it didn't come to fruition until after the campaign, TreePeople's friendly, cooperative approach to corporate involvement paid off again when the Southern California Honda Dealers Association committed major dollars and full-page advertisements to a campaign to "Help Make Your Drive More Beautiful" by sponsoring the planting of 1,000 trees a month for three months.

Another example is the Urban Forest Run. Four years in a row, TreePeople closed down a freeway and staged a ten-kilometer run sponsored by May Co., Louisiana-Pacific, The Gap, and Warner Bros., respectively. We had to work hard to get these corporate sponsors but once on board they paid for the T-shirts and other promotional materials distributed. The idea was to demonstrate that freeways could be made human-scale, even if only for half a day. Even with this project, TreePeople managed to make its statement about the power of the individual. The organization had a fairly low profile at the time and, though the run didn't make money, a front-page photo in the *Los Angeles Times* showing thousands of running bodies did wonders for our name recognition.

TreePeople's latest and greatest corporate sponsor is GEO. With the GEO Metro rated the most fuel-efficient car on the road today, we were happy to open discussions that led to our biggest-ever corporate contribution—and to receiving six vehicles to replace old jalopies. The GEO executives and their PR firm

were long-sighted, allowing us to use their contribution to hire more staff at a time when it was really needed in exchange for a long-term contract and the promise of 35,000 trees in the ground. As we've come to know and trust each other, TreePeople has been able to express its vision to a receptive and educated ear. Our GEO partners can now take our agenda and match it to their goals, rather than vice versa, which is the most common frustration in these circumstances. Both parties can feel good about the relationship when the dog is wagging the tail. In our case, that means solid, well-executed programs coming before funding, rather than funding dictating how we spend our time.

Be guided by your intuition. A partnership isn't necessarily right just because it sounds logical. With luck, this time around, the environmental movement is here to stay for a bit. Your work, your integrity, and your image are more important than any corporate partnership, no matter how attractive it can be made to look. Believe it or not, the money from a corporation isn't always worth the cost to your organization. You can fall from grace very quickly and you or your organization can be smeared for life. Beware the corporation that appears to want to give you a blank check. What do they really want from you?

Take some photos of the site before preparation. This step will make a good set of before-and-after pictures to document your work and show it off!

How many subgroups are in your community? Use their internal structure to get your message across. Catch people where they work, where they shop, where they play, and where they live.

Schools, Scouts, and Walking the Streets

TreePeople used its established school program to spread the word. Many schools took on plantings, and a three-year total of 45,000 children planted a tree at home. TreePeople currently reaches over 100,000 kids a year in the classrooms and assembly halls of Los Angeles' schools and on the nature trails of our park headquarters. On safe plantings—those not involving freeways or large street trees—we used scouts and other youth groups who like to get involved in fresh, new group activities.

Free trees often are thrown away, because they have no intrinsic value to the recipient. TreePeople distributed seedlings for one dollar each at fairs and shopping malls and even went door to door offering to plant seedlings in homeowner's gardens —just to spread the word. This action was a wonderful but desperate measure and was very labor intensive. It was dropped after a couple of months.

CONCLUSIONS

We encourage you to set up your program in such a way that you have room to experiment and take risks. It's the creativity that catches attention and inspires others. Don't be discouraged by failure. Look at what worked and also at what didn't. Learn your lessons and move on, trying other variations until you succeed.

Even in the 1990s, there's no certain method for achieving your public-awareness goal. We're all still pioneers in this field. Aside from being creative, one must be persistent. Finding a new way involves the risk of failure as well as the chance of success.

During the Million Tree Campaign, we often felt like rats in a maze, following every possible path. Some succeeded; others were bitter failures. Nevertheless, we'd set our deadline and had no time or money for lengthy and costly research, even though it may have been valuable and economic in the long run. If an idea didn't work within a few months, we'd drop it and move on, with no regrets, fresh for the next idea. We kept thinking one thing was going to do it. That wasn't true. It was an accumulation of many things—most strongly, dogged persistence.

We're still learning from our oversights back then. For instance, how many of the million trees are alive today? We don't know because we didn't build in an assessment factor. Because we emphasized trees planted on private property, we assume a high survival rate. On reflection, we might have done even more to educate people about the need not only to plant but also to commit to long-term care. As this book demonstrates, we're obsessed with stressing maintenance these days.

This lesson is just the beginning. Use it to inspire ever greater and more successful public-education efforts. This chapter was originally a paper delivered at the Third National Urban Forestry Conference in Orlando, Florida, in 1986. It was reproduced and has been sent to community groups around the world. Many have reported the fantasic, original ideas they've been able to put into action from our experience. A lot have reported that the willingness to fail has served them unbelievably well.

By the way, the campaign *was* a success. It certainly didn't turn out according to plan, but we accomplished the stated goal. The people of Southern California—individuals, families, churches, service organizations, cities, the U.S. Forest Service, County Foresters, scouts, and corporations—reached the goal, and those working closely with us celebrated that accomplishment. After three years, four days before the lighting of the Olympic flame, we received word that an apricot tree had been planted in Canoga Park. It was the confirmation of the planting of the millionth tree.

American Elm
(*Ulmus americana*)
zones 3–8

Do the Right Thing: Planting Your Tree

6

Plant a tree. You found several here when you landed on this old earth and you've seen many cut down during your time. You probably cut down a few yourself. The children who are born after you've passed have a right to find a few trees standing. But they will not if every person who passes through this vale of tears cuts down a few and forgets to plant any. Plant a tree. Plant a dozen of them, and then you will have done something for the generations who follow you, even as someone did something for you ages ago.

FORT LAUDERDALE *HERALD*

The simple act of planting a tree referred to in the title *is* pretty simple, as long as you've thought about the type of tree you're planting and the environment you're planting it in. Whether you're planning an enormous event or a weekend project around your home, you'll need to know how to get the trees into the ground.

Wherever you are, wherever you go, planting styles will differ. There is no one right way to plant a tree—there is only the method that works for you and the tree you've chosen. Let your planting research begin here, and follow up with further reading and planting experiences of your own. Ask a local urbanforestry professional or a friendly nurseryman for a planting demonstration, which will confirm or alter what you've read here based on your area's specific needs and requirements. New planting techniques may be discovered next week, so get on the mailing lists of national forestry groups such as the American Forestry Association and the National Arbor Day Foundation (see Resources). Don't be afraid to change your planting methods with new information. You and your planting supervisors will be leaders in the field!

TRAIN YOUR SUPERVISORS

TreePeople has developed a format for planting-supervisor training that works well. It may be more thorough than you would want for a single event, but if you need supervisors for a series of plantings, the effort pays off. We start with a one-hour classroom session, reviewing basic tree biology, fundamentals of planting, and use of supplies, then end with a question-answer period. The

For mine is the old belief. . . .
There is a soul in every leaf.
M. M. BALLOU

instructor hands out a sheet that details and illustrates planting procedures. At the planting site, each new trainee is teamed up with a seasoned veteran for a lesson on how to work with unskilled volunteers and how to plant correctly. Thus, planting supervisors absorb the same information in three ways—by listening, reading, and getting hands-on experience.

ALWAYS DO A DEMO

Tree-planting demonstrations are the best way to get trees planted correctly, so don't be shy about holding them at every event. It's a real shame to spend months or years organizing a planting only to have the trees planted poorly. Many people will tell you they've been planting for years, but an update never hurts.

On the planting day, after you've refreshed your planting supervisors' memories by going over the instructions or by planting a demonstration tree, deputize a handful of experienced supervisors to be quality-control agents, circulating among the planting teams and correcting faulty techniques. If you're planting massive numbers of seedlings over a large site, assign supervisors to pieces of turf and have them examine and approve or correct each planter's first results before giving them more trees. One-on-one supervision is a sure way to catch errors.

Some volunteers will find this attention to quality planting a nuisance; after all, they just wanted to come out and plant trees. Others will be grateful for the knowledge and attention you're giving them. Both groups will appreciate a demonstration that shows a commitment to care that begins before the trees go in the ground. Try to walk the line that makes both groups happy: provide instruction and stress the value of doing a good job, but keep the mood fun and light.

Make sure the person leading the class is someone who communicates enthusiastically and clearly. No amount of expert tree knowledge can make up for a boring or disorganized speaker. If you'll be cooperating with a government agency, this attention to quality and detail is vital; it's often the key issue of concern that agencies have about working with volunteers.

PLANTING TIPS

Dig a hole twice as wide and the same depth as the tree's container.

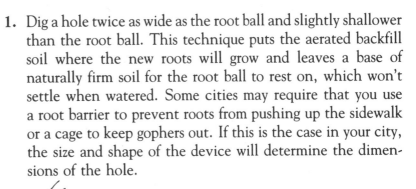

1. Dig a hole twice as wide as the root ball and slightly shallower than the root ball. This technique puts the aerated backfill soil where the new roots will grow and leaves a base of naturally firm soil for the root ball to rest on, which won't settle when watered. Some cities may require that you use a root barrier to prevent roots from pushing up the sidewalk or a cage to keep gophers out. If this is the case in your city, the size and shape of the device will determine the dimensions of the hole.

2. Avoid the *clay-pot syndrome*. Roughen the sides and bottom of your planting hole with a pick or shovel so that root tips can penetrate the native soil. Smooth walls are like cement to root tips.

3. If you are using potted trees, be gentle but firm when removing the container. Making sure to protect the foliage, lay the tree on its side with the container end near the planting hole. Hit the bottom and sides of the container until the root ball is loosened. If the container is metal, use cutters to snip it from top to bottom.

Center the tree in the hole. Test to see that the top of the root ball is level with the surrounding ground. Orient and straighten the tree.

4. Check the root ball for circling roots. If circling roots are left in place, they will continue to enlarge in that pattern after the tree has been planted. Gently separate them, shorten exceptionally long roots, and guide them downward or outward. If roots are severely circled or kinked near the trunk, get another plant. Remember that the tiny root tips that absorb water and minerals for the tree die off quickly when exposed to light and air, so don't waste time.

5. Don't cover the root crown with soil. If soil is added above the crown, which is the place where the roots end and the trunk begins, it will lead to rot at the base of the trunk. Aim to have the top of the root ball about ½ to 1 inch above the surrounding soil surface, making sure not to cover it with soil unless roots are exposed. Check the height of the root crown by laying a straight piece of wood across the top of the hole. Adjust the height by lifting the tree out of the hole (lift it by the root ball, not by the trunk) and adjusting the soil level in the planting hole.

6. Orient the tree while you have the chance. If the tree has a preferred side, turn it toward a prominent viewpoint (such as your kitchen window). If it's lopsided, turn the side with more foliage toward the prevailing wind. This will encourage the other side to catch up. In sunny, arid climates, orient the tree so that the best-shaded side of the trunk faces southwest. Sunburn can kill the cambium, weakening the tree and disfiguring the trunk and bark. When turning the tree, lift it from the base of the root ball, not from the base of the trunk.

7. Sight it upright! Once the tree is in the hole, stand back and make sure it's standing upright. Tilt the root ball until the tree is straight; then backfill firmly under and around the root ball.

8. Give your soil a boost. Though the latest trend in tree planting is not to add amendment to the backfill soil, there are instances when it can be useful. If your native soil is hard to work with (heavy clay) or retains little moisture (very sandy), you can treat it to some organic amendment. The amendment won't be a permanent solution to soil deficiencies, but it will help retain water and air in the soil around the root ball for the first few vital years. If adding soil amendment, always mix it with soil from the planting site; about one part amendment to three parts native soil is a good

Trees outstrip most people in the extent and depth of their work for the public good.

SARA EBENRECK
American Forests

proportion for backfill soil. Some professionals also recommend putting slow-release fertilizer tablets in the hole at this time. See page 162 in the next chapter for more on fertilizing.

9. Tamp the soil as you backfill. Using the heel of your foot, press down firmly to collapse any large air pockets in the soil. This will help stabilize the tree in the hole. Don't wait until the planting is finished; press down every few shovels of soil. Yes, you can tamp too much; excessive pressure (especially in clay soils) will reduce the soil porosity, which is essential for healthy root growth. As usual with trees (and most living things), practice moderation.

Backfill soil around root ball and tamp with your foot.

Build basin tightly around root ball to direct water.

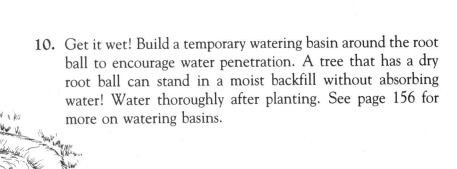

10. Get it wet! Build a temporary watering basin around the root ball to encourage water penetration. A tree that has a dry root ball can stand in a moist backfill without absorbing water! Water thoroughly after planting. See page 156 for more on watering basins.

Fill several times to water deeply. Widen basin to include whole planting area after a month.

Provide two stakes per tree. Use non-abrasive ties in figure-eight pattern.

11. Stake well! Remove the square wooden nursery stake after planting. Stake the tree loosely for protection or support if needed. If the stem can't stand up on its own, stake it so that it stands upright. Plan to remove stakes as soon as the tree can support itself, in six to twelve months. See page 161 for more information on staking.

12. Mulch till you drop! Cover the entire planting area, except a small circle at the base of the trunk, to a depth of 2 to 4 inches with bark, wood chips, old sawdust, pine needles, leaves, or gravel. Mulch keeps the topsoil temperate for root growth, reduces surface evaporation of water, provides nutrients to feed the tree, and slows weed and grass growth around the tree's base. For plantings along a street or sidewalk, concrete or decomposed granite will act as mulch, but you must allow an open area for air and water exchange (see pages 148–149).

TREE STOCK AND SIZES

Your choice of tree size will most likely be obvious according to the site you've chosen. A rule of thumb is that the smaller the tree is when planted, the sooner it becomes established and resumes vigorous growth. The more time a tree spends in a container, the more confined the roots become. The tree will grow slowly and its ability to establish itself in a new environment will be diminished.

Cities vary widely in minimum-size requirements for street trees, ranging from 5-gallon saplings to 24-inch box trees over 2 inches in trunk diameter.

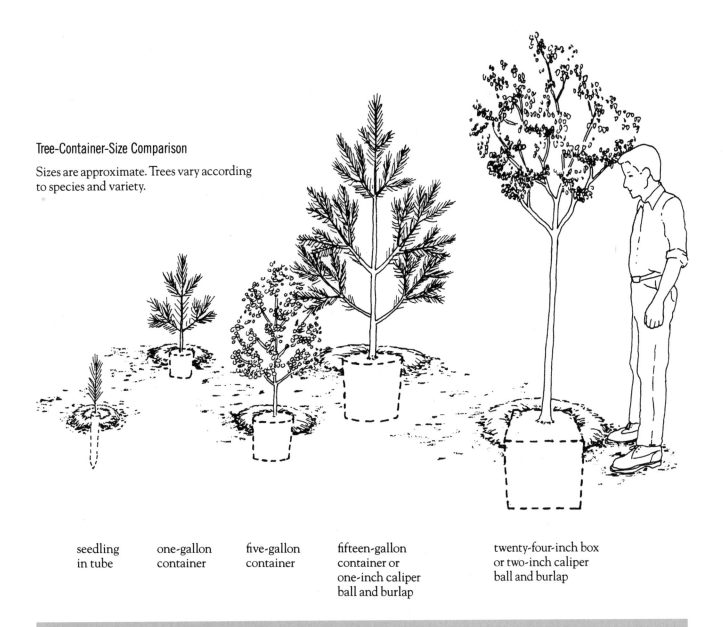

Tree-Container-Size Comparison

Sizes are approximate. Trees vary according to species and variety.

| seedling in tube | one-gallon container | five-gallon container | fifteen-gallon container or one-inch caliper ball and burlap | twenty-four-inch box or two-inch caliper ball and burlap |

	Advantages	Sources	Best time to plant
Seeds *This is a general guideline for working with seeds. As simple as seeds are, working with them is often more complex than working with established trees. You will need to consult local nursery experts to get specific guidance on the best ways to grow trees from seeds in your area.*	△ Large-scale *sowings* are possible in one day. △ Cost is low. △ Only the fittest trees survive initial growth phase. △ They promote deep root systems and are not potbound. △ No transplant shock occurs. △ Planting area is covered with plants quickly. △ Trees are established at site as soon as roots develop. △ No staking is required.	△ Local collecting △ Nurseries △ Seed catalogs △ Fresh fruit and nuts	△ Spring or early summer for frost-tender seedlings △ Year-round if provided with water and care or if grown in a container for transplanting △ Some seeds germinate only after exposure to cold or certain chemicals.
Seedlings (potted and bare-root)	△ They eliminate uncertainty of germination. △ They are easy to transport to planting site. △ Large-scale plantings are practical. △ Most of tree's growth occurs in planting-site environment (less transplant shock than container trees). △ They usually do not require staking. △ Cost is moderate.	△ Neighbor's *volunteer* trees (trees that sprout without being planted) △ Nurseries △ Growers (for large quantities) △ County fire department, forester, or fire warden △ State forester or department of forestry △ Other forestry or conservation groups	△ Late fall or early spring, for the highest possible level of soil moisture. It will *wake up* in spring and begin growing at the optimum time, as long as species is hardy to winter conditions. △ Year-round, weather permitting, if it is watered and cared for. △ Bare-root seedlings must be transplanted when dormant.

Planting Methods

These methods are general. The best techniques will be altered slightly for each species. Consult landscape professionals, enlist the help of local tree groups, confer with city or county tree-planting staff, or refer to written materials listed at the back of this book and at your library.

General planting procedure	Precautions
△ Select or collect the biggest, plumpest seeds of the species from attractive trees. △ Prepare the seeds for germination as per the instructions for your species. Germination requirements can differ greatly. (See Resources for further information.) △ Place seeds in container of soil or directly in ground. Depending on germination rate, the number of seeds per hole will vary. △ Cover with depth of soil twice as thick as diameter of seed. △ Keep soil moist until seed sprouts. (Winter or spring rains may do the job.) △ Protect planted seeds from animals, humans, and frost. This step may entail placing a small mesh tent above or below ground level in soil to protect the seed and its roots, first shoots, and leaves. △ Mulch around seedlings to control weeds.	△ Seeds are not suited to many urban landscapes. △ Landscape effect is not immediate after planting. △ Not all species can be grown successfully from seed. △ Characteristics of the tree may vary from seed to seed. △ Some pregermination treatments are difficult. △ Some seeds and seedlings are lost because of animal and insect damage, harsh conditions, and disease. △ Most food-producing trees must be grafted if grown from seed to produce reliable fruit characteristics.
△ Leave seedlings in container or planting bag in the shade until ready to plant. Work quickly once roots are exposed to air and sunlight. A little exposure can be enough to kill a bare-root seedling before it even gets started. △ Clear an area 3 to 4 feet in diameter, to mineral soil. △ Use your body to shade the planting hole by placing your back to the sun.	△ Seedlings are vulnerable to animal browsing and to foot traffic from animals and humans. △ Seedlings may need monthly watering through the second year to help them become established and increase their growth and survival rate.

Bare-root	Potted
△ In dry climates, you can pretreat the roots with a moisture-attracting agent. △ Dig or pull a hole a few inches deeper than the root system. △ Hold the seedling so that the root crown is at soil level, and make sure that all the roots are pointing down.	△ Measure the depth of soil in the container (the root ball). △ Dig a hole twice as wide and the same depth as the root ball. △ Remove container. △ Place seedling in hole.

Potted and bare-root

△ Fill hole halfway with soil.

△ Tamp soil to eliminate air pockets.

△ Fill remaining hole and tamp soil.

△ Form a watering basin around the seedling.

△ Slowly fill basin with 3 to 5 gallons of water.

△ Mulch inside watering basin.

△ For bare-root seedlings, wait for leaves to appear before watering again (but keep soil moist if in a dry climate).

△ Water thoroughly.

	Advantages	Sources	Best time to plant
Larger bare-root trees	△ Roots grow in native soil; there are no pot-bound roots. △ Tree becomes adjusted to local conditions sooner than container-grown trees. △ They are easy to handle. △ They usually do not require staking. △ Cost is low to medium.	△ Mail-order nurseries △ Retail nurseries △ Wholesale growers	△ Late fall and winter or early spring—during dormancy, before the tree begins to leaf out
Balled and burlapped trees (B&B)	△ Sometimes less expensive than container stock △ Better survival rate than bare-root stock △ Same advantages as container stock	△ Retail and wholesale nurseries	△ Dig and plant most species in spring. △ Fall and winter are fine for warmer climates.
Container trees	△ Large specimens make an instant visual effect. △ Larger size protects trees from animals, vandalism, and mechanical injury. △ They meet many city and county planting specifications. △ Year-round planting is possible if ground isn't frozen.	△ Retail and wholesale nurseries	△ All seasons are fine, even winter if soil isn't frozen.

General planting procedure	Precautions
△ Soak bare roots overnight. △ Cut any broken roots back to healthy tissue. △ Dig a hole large enough to accommodate full root length. △ Make a pile of soil in the middle of the hole so that the root crown will settle at grade level. △ Spread roots over the pile of soil. △ Back fill soil; work in and tamp around roots. △ Water and let the soil settle. △ Readjust tree so that top of root ball is at grade or slightly above ground level. △ Fill rest of hole and tamp soil. △ Soak the tree with water. △ Mulch inside watering basin.	△ Only deciduous fruit and shade trees are sold in large bare-root form. △ Water conservatively after planting until growth begins with warm weather. △ Use trees with healthy, fresh roots. △ Some trees are slow to leaf out.
△ Dig hole twice as wide as root ball. △ Lift tree by root ball and center in planting hole. △ Top of root ball should be 1 to 2 inches above surrounding soil. △ Fill hole halfway with backfill soil (containing 20 to 30 percent organic soil amendment if needed to improve water retention). △ Tamp soil. △ Remove burlap down to backfill level, uncovering half the root ball. △ Water backfill soil and root ball thoroughly. △ Fill remaining hole with soil to grade level, tamping carefully. △ Form watering basin around the hole and water again. △ If needed, stake the tree against prevailing wind. Stake should be anchored in soil beneath planting hole. △ Tie tree to stake loosely. △ Mulch inside watering basin. △ Water root ball thoroughly.	△ Plants are hard to handle due to weight of root ball. △ Circling roots can be a problem (usually near trunk at soil surface). △ Root ball can shatter if not handled carefully. △ Root ball can dry out if its soil is different than native soil.
△ Check for kinked or circling roots near trunk at soil surface. △ Leave tree in container and protect from sun until ready to plant. △ Dig a hole twice the diameter of and slightly shallower than the tree's root ball. △ Roughen the sides and bottom of the planting hole. △ Cut or loosen container and gently remove it. △ Massage outside of root ball to loosen roots; cut tangled roots if necessary. △ Place tree in hole and orient. △ Adjust soil level under tree until top of root ball is about 1 inch above grade. △ Straighten tree. △ Amend backfill soil if desired. △ Fill hole around tree halfway with backfill soil. △ Tamp soil to eliminate air pockets. △ Fill remaining hole with soil up to grade level and tamp (top of root ball should be at grade or slightly higher). △ Untie and remove nursery stake. △ If the tree needs support or protection, place one stake on either side of it outside of root ball (8 to 10 inches from the trunk). △ Secure tree to stake with nonabrasive ties. △ Form a watering basin around root ball. △ Fill basin three times with water. △ Mulch inside watering basin. △ Water root ball thoroughly.	△ Trees must adapt to new site conditions; they may grow slowly for a season. △ For street trees, many cities have precise planting specifications, including a root-control barrier and large specimen size. △ Large container trees are expensive. △ Roots are often kinked and circling from years in various containers.

STAKES AND TIES

Staking trees can do as much harm as good. You'll come across hundreds of different opinions on how to stake your tree. The following gives you some basic rules to follow.

Why Stake?

Trees develop strong trunks by swaying in the wind; however, many nursery grown trees are unable to stand upright without some support. Trees develop a slender, weak stem with little or no taper as a result of common nursery practices such as crowding, rigid staking, and removing side branches along the trunk. These trees will come from the nursery with a wooden stake attached tightly to the trunk with plastic tape. Remove this stake after planting, as soon as you are prepared to tie it to the new stake or stakes.

Where and How to Stake

A tree should be staked if the trunk is not strong enough to support the branches and leaves, or if it needs protection from

intentional or accidental damage. Check the tree each month during the growing season and remove the stake if it's ready to support itself.

The appropriate stake size and material depends on the site. Wooden stakes 2 inches in diameter are fine for most conditions, though some cities require 2-inch metal pipe or ¾-inch rebar for street trees to protect them against vandalism. Install the stakes in pairs on opposite sides of the root ball. On city streets, you can position the stakes either in line with the curb or at right angles to it. Each city has its own rules.

If possible, stake to protect the tree from whatever local elements may harm it, such as strong prevailing winds or heavy foot traffic. For windy areas, arrange the stakes so that a line between them is perpendicular (at right angles) to wind direction. Stake height should be a few inches above the height of the ties, just high enough to keep the tree upright.

Tree-Tie Placement

Attach ties first to the stakes and then around the main trunk. A simple guideline is to attach both ties to the main trunk at the same level—the lowest level that will keep the tree upright. More specifically, ties should be as low on the trunk as possible but high enough that the tree will return to an upright position after it's bent over.

To find the proper height, hold the trunk in one hand, pull the top to one side, and release. Six inches above the height at which the bent-over trunk will return to upright when the top is released is the best tying height. Ties are normally connected between the tree and stake in a figure-eight pattern, with the tie nailed or wired to the stake at the appropriate height. The figure eight protects the trunk from coming in contact with the stake material.

Hillside berm. To prevent water from washing down slope, build wall on lower side of slope to hold water up around root ball.

Tree-Tie Materials

Tree ties are made of a number of nonabrasive, nonbinding materials, such as plastic tape, vinyl, webbing, or pieces of tire (often with wire attached to the ends). Whatever you use, its point of contact with the tree should be a broad surface to minimize rubbing or girdling (cutting into the expanding trunk).

Watering Basins

Watering basins are especially important for newly planted trees in climates where rainfall is inadequate. As you dig the planting hole, set aside clods of soil to use later in making a 3-to-4-inch-high berm, or wall, for the basin. For seedlings, bare-root, and small container trees, a wide (3-foot-diameter) basin is appropriate to contain water in the backfill area. Watering basins are also built for catching runoff on steep slopes. To make a hillside berm, form a U-shaped, or *boomerang*, berm on the downhill side of the tree.

Container trees have special watering needs, because the soil in the container is compacted and can reject water. Watering basins for newly planted container trees should be temporarily constructed tightly around the edge of the root-ball area to force water into it and keep the roots moist. After a month or two the watering basin should be widened to supply water to the whole planting area. Another idea is to build a regular 3-foot-diameter basin and add a temporary inner berm around the edge of the root ball. After planting, water the inner basin weekly and the outer basin monthly. After one to two months, remove the inner berm.

Root-Control Barriers

Root-control barriers are required for plantings on city streets in several California cities, and much controversy exists over their effectiveness. They are designed to protect hardscapes (paved areas) by directing root systems down and away from the soil surface. Root barriers come in many forms, from round cylinders that encircle roots and direct them downward to herbicide strips that guard the sidewalk curbs. Root-control treatments are fairly new, so no conclusive results are available as to how mature trees will respond in the coming years.

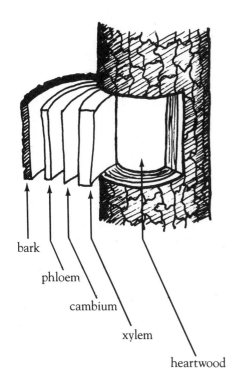

bark

phloem

cambium

xylem

heartwood

WHAT'S GOING ON INSIDE THAT TRUNK?

The trunk and branches of a tree contain its plumbing system and give it structure above ground. The bark protects the tree from injury and disease.

If you could picture a tree without its bark, you would see a sheet of cells as a cloak wrapped around the wood. This layer of cells is called the *cambium*, which produces a new layer of woody tissue each year. The cambium cells divide to make the trunk, branches, and roots grow thicker.

Next to the cambium, toward the interior of the tree, are water-conducting vessels called *xylem* (zī-lem). One year's growth of xylem is known as an *annual ring*, and it is the youngest layer of wood. Young xylem cells transport water with dissolved mineral nutrients from the roots to the leaves. As the cells age and are replaced by newer vessels, they become inactive and get clogged with wastes and resins, and their walls become rigid. The core of inactive xylem cells in the middle of the tree is called *heartwood*.

Between the rough outer bark and the cambium is a thin layer of food-conducting vessels called *phloem* (flō-em). Phloem tissue transports sugar manufactured in the leaves (and other organic compounds) to areas where materials are needed to produce new growth or to storage areas for future use.

Have a Good Time

Plant a tree. Do it!
TOM CRUISE
EARTH DAY 1990

Keeping all of this valuable instruction in mind, the best way to learn about tree planting is to get out there and do it. There are plenty of books to read, but there's no substitute for the real thing. We hope all this *how-to* information has got you itching to dig a hole; it may not be the perfect planting hole the first time, but you'll get a feel for it after a couple of tries. Trees are forgiving: they'll probably survive in spite of your attempts to do everything perfectly! A final word about planting: *tree care begins before your spade hits the turf.* The care you take in choosing a healthy tree and planting with its needs in mind will be reflected in the tree's health as it grows. The next chapter describes the tree-care journey you'll embark upon when your planting is behind you.

7

It's Not Easy Being Green: Caring for Urban Trees

It takes five years to plant a tree.

ALDEN KELLEY
TREE SOCIETY OF ORANGE COUNTY

A tree's needs are few and simple: healthy soil, air, water, and light. We all know trees have grown without human help for thousands of years. So what's the fuss? Why can't the trees we plant in the city fend for themselves? Why does it take five years of care to be sure that an urban tree will survive its infancy?

Unfortunately for the urban forest, towns and cities have not been designed by the laws of nature, but by the law of human supply and demand. Trees are included as amenities and are established in an artificial habitat that usually falls short of supplying basic needs. In this setting, trees are further stressed by pollutants and by human-inflicted injuries. It is necessary to give urban trees special care, not only for their survival and well-being but also to protect people and property from the hazards trees can become when abandoned to a hostile environment.

Urban Soils Are Not Like the Forest Floor

The urban underground habitat is particularly ill-suited for healthy tree growth. The soil is typically a mixture of subsoil, bedrock, and construction wastes, compacted to a density that eliminates 80 to 90 percent of the soil porosity through which air and water must move. Drainage is frequently so poor that routine irrigation leads to a waterlogged environment in which the roots are unable to grow. The nutrient level may be too low for normal tree growth or too high in sodium or trace chemicals, making them toxic to trees.

Trees are planted close to concrete or asphalt surfaces and are routinely installed near established trees. Compacted soil conditions, and light and frequent watering schedules designed for lawns, encourage tree-root growth close to the surface, forcing the roots to grow near driveways and sidewalks. When the manmade structure becomes damaged as a result, the roots are cut back or the tree is removed.

The living and dead look well together in woods. Trees receive a most beautiful burial. Nature takes fallen trees gently to her bosom—at rest from storms. They seem to have been called home out of the sky to sleep now.

JOHN MUIR

MORE THAN JUST A PILE OF DIRT

What Is Soil?
Soil is a mixture of mineral particles, air, water, and organic materials. The mineral particles are made of rocks battered by water, wind, heat, and cold into minute pieces. The organic materials are decaying remains of plants and animals. The solid components of soil provide thirteen of the sixteen elements that plants need to grow.

Soil Texture
Soil particles have varying shapes and sizes, and the proportion of particle types give the soil its texture. For instance, *clay* particles are microscopically small, flat wafers that cling together easily. Clay soils are typically called heavy and look dark and moist. Clay particles have large surfaces that are able to hold water and nutrients, but unless the particles are clumped together, there is often little room for air between them.

In contrast to clay is *sand*. Sand grains are relatively large and round or irregular in shape, naturally forming large pores between the grains. Sandy soils are thought of as light and are easy to dig in, but water—and the nutrients dissolved in it—will drain away quickly. Between clay and sand is *silt*, and the combination of all particle types, along with organic matter, is called *loam*. Loam has a nearly ideal combination of soil texture and pore sizes. It usually holds a good balance of moisture and nutrients and is loose and aerated.

Water moves through the soil in air pockets between particles. When the soil is saturated, water fills the openings between particles. As the soil drains, these air pockets fill with life-giving oxygen for the roots and microorganisms. The normal combination of soil features is approximately 50 percent soil particles, 5 percent or more organic matter, and 45 percent pore space.

Fighting for Life above the Ground

The urban habitat can be just as harsh above ground as it is below. Overhead utility lines, buildings, and trafficways often occupy the space into which a tree's branches normally grow. The consequent clearance pruning is often performed with little regard for the tree's structure or health.

Soil Fertility

Plants require sixteen chemical elements for healthy growth. Three of these elements—carbon, hydrogen, and oxygen—are provided by the air and water. The other essential elements are provided by the soil, and if any are deficient, this will adversely affect the growth of your tree. Deficiency symptoms usually show up in leaf discoloration or in abnormal growth patterns; a number of problems may cause nutrient deficiencies even though all elements are present in the soil. An arborist or urban forester may be able to recognize the problem and point you toward a solution.

The acidity or alkalinity of soil, which is expressed in pH units, affects chemical reactions and can influence the availability of nutrients to the tree. Acid soil has a low pH, while alkaline is higher, with a pH of 7 being neutral. Most trees grow better in soils that are slightly acidic, while some kinds do well in alkaline soil. Find out if the pH of soils in your area may cause problems for the species you want to grow. You may want to test your soil before you plant, then choose a tree that will like growing there! Simple and inexpensive pH meters and test kits are available at retail nurseries or garden centers. Better yet, ask a local expert for advice. Also see Resources for more on soils.

Magnified Soil Particles and Root Hair

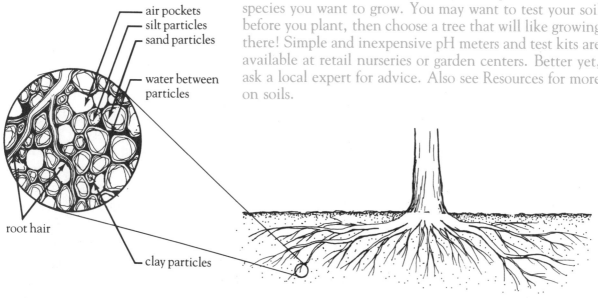

air pockets
silt particles
sand particles

water between particles

root hair

clay particles

A System That Works

One Citizen Forester and two TreePeople volunteers have staged their tree-care event so regularly they have it down to a science. It takes their ten-person crew only three hours to care for fifty trees over two miles of a major Los Angeles thoroughfare.

When volunteers arrive, they gather for a refresher demo, then divide into teams by task. The pruning team, which has the most sophisticated job, leaves first to get ahead of the group. The watering team follows close behind, laying out full buckets at each tree (not emptying them yet!). Two well-cleaning teams set about clearing trash and sucker growth from around the tree base. Two clean-up crews follow, picking up leftover debris and watering the trees. Two small trucks circulate around the site, distributing water and taking trash to the dumpster. When the task is complete, everyone gathers for a brown-bag lunch and debriefing.

Maintenance crews wound the bark of trees with devices for trimming grass around tree bases, interrupting the flow of food from the leaves to the roots and thereby starving roots. Mowers and other motor-driven vehicles collide with trees, and people carve their initials in bark or break off limbs carelessly, tearing away bark and exposing the wood to decay organisms.

The light a city tree receives may be all or nothing. Trees next to buildings can be shaded most of the day or subjected to full sun plus reflected light from light-colored walls and windows.

City trees are frequently doomed to short lifetimes by improper management in the production nurseries. One of the most common flaws in container-grown stock is circling roots. Trees that cannot develop a normal root system may blow down, or their roots may strangle one another.

Be an Intensive Care Unit

As a certain little frog is accustomed to reminding us, it's not easy being green, especially in the city. That's why you can make a huge difference by paying attention to urban tree care. You'll find that the amount of work required to keep a tree growing and glowing isn't very time-consuming. Many trees require only a little upfront attention to be saved from an early death or the gradual loss of health and vigor.

Tree-care operations shouldn't be perceived as drudgery, either. The nurturing of trees and plants is a soul-renewing activity, full of rewards. You'll feel a great sense of accomplishment when you look up at a towering tree and know you are personally responsible for its health and presence.

SCHEDULING TREE CARE

It's easy to lose track of maintenance tasks, because the work is spread over weeks, months, and years. Before taking the time and effort to plant the right tree in the right place the right way, do everyone a favor and keep track of the care those trees are going to receive. A tree-care schedule can ensure that all necessary tasks are done on time, especially if your trees are on private property where no regulations guide maintenance. A tree-care schedule should spell out what and when watering, mulching, weeding, monitoring, and pruning tasks need to be done.

It's also a good idea to assign each task to a specific person or group and make the responsibility clear. Some organizations keep group calendars with all tasks clearly marked. The amount of attention you pay to tree care should equal that which you pay to planting. Show your commitment to the trees!

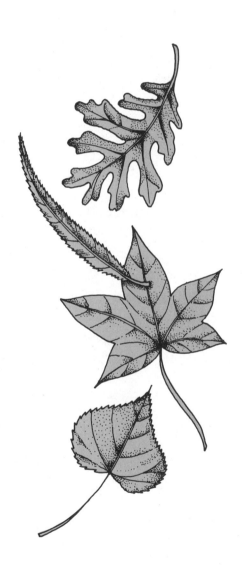

WHAT'S GOING ON INSIDE THAT LEAF?

Leaves have a lot of responsibility: they produce food for all parts of the tree.

Leaves produce food by a chemical process called *photosynthesis*. It is the only natural process that makes food from substances that are not foods, and it is one of the few sources of oxygen to the atmosphere.

The materials required for photosynthesis are carbon dioxide, water, light, and *chlorophyll*. Cell layers inside the leaf contain millions of tiny green chlorophyll cells, which give the leaf its color. Carbon dioxide from the air enters the leaf through small openings called *stomates*, while water is carried up by xylem vessels from the roots. When sunlight passes through the leaf, chlorophyll captures sunlight energy and uses it to combine the other elements to produce sugars, which the tree uses for growth and storage. The other byproduct of photosynthesis, oxygen, is released through the stomates.

Leaves control the amount of water present in the tree through a process called *transpiration*. When water is scarce, some trees' stomates close completely or partially, minimizing water loss.

Leaves of some trees change color in the fall. Shorter days and lower temperatures cause a decrease in green pigment, so the yellow and red pigments in the leaf become visible. Air pollution may also affect leaf color. Ozone and sulphur dioxide, chief components of smog, enter through the stomates and attack the chlorophyll cells, yellowing leaves and needles.

The normal life span of a leaf ranges from less than a year to five or more years, depending on the species. Some trees lose all their leaves at the end of the growing season, then put out a crop of new leaves in the spring. Trees that shed all their leaves annually are *deciduous*. *Evergreen* trees have leaves that live for more than a year, so they remain green year-round. Most evergreen species undergo a seasonal surge of new growth in the spring, and they usually shed old leaves in greater numbers at that time. Evergreens can be either of the needle-leaf or the broad-leaf species.

WHO DOES WHAT?

Assuming responsibility for the care of all the trees you plant can be difficult if you're a zealous planter. If you can't be the one looking after the tree, it shouldn't be planted before you have a commitment from an agency, organization, or individual to provide maintenance for at least the first few years. If you plant it and no one adopts it, you must assume the responsibility for tree care. It is also more difficult to enroll someone in caring for a tree that has been planted by someone else.

Many tasks must be left to well-equipped, trained, and authorized professionals. In most instances, if an operation requires taking one or both of your feet off the ground, don't attempt it. Likewise, root pruning and sidewalk and curb repairs should not be done by a nonprofessional.

You can encourage healthy growth and head off maintenance problems by caring for trees in the following ways during the first three to six years after planting.

△ watering accurately

△ pruning dead or diseased limbs and sucker growth

△ training to provide strong branch structure and adequate clearance for the site

△ ensuring that stakes and ties are properly installed, adjusted, and then removed when they begin interfering with the tree

△ mulching

△ clearing trash and weeds from around trunk base

△ reporting conditions that require professional attention (for example, diseases, pests, or damage)

△ reporting conditions caused by professional malpractice (such as topping, equipment-induced injuries, or inappropriate irrigation)

△ requesting immediate replacement of dead trees

Though you are planting with every intention of being a diligent tree-care giver, there's only so much you can do without professional training. As the tree grows, it will be increasingly difficult for members of your community group to carry out the required work without help from a professional. Tree-care operations are vital to newly planted trees for the first three to five years after planting. Once the trees reach a size at which they must be pruned for clearance to city requirements or when any major work must be done, liability and safety issues require that city crews or contractors take over the job.

Care for trees planted on property other than the parkway strip is another story, as in the case of parks, vacant lots, front- or backyards, flood-control channels, and play or mall areas. On these sites, maintenance is the responsibility of the planting organization, unless the agency in charge of the site agrees to take over as trees grow. All trees planted on private property are the responsibility of the property owner.

WATERING

A study by Dr. K. D. Coder states that "eighty to ninety percent of the variation in tree growth is because of water supply problems." Try asking any professional how often you should water a tree. Most likely he or she will give you an answer like "get to know your tree" or "it depends. . . ." We know how it feels to be on both sides of the watering question, so we're taking a deep breath and offering a suggested watering schedule to start you off. For a tree planted in spring, water the root ball twice a week for the first month, then widen the watering basin to include the whole planting area and water weekly for the next two months.

A TREE LOVER

"The more I learned about pruning, the more I practiced on my own trees, the more I could see—almost hear— some of the trees in my neighborhood crying out for help. I found myself imagining how I'd prune a particular tree: where to make the cuts and how the tree would look. Finally I decided to just do it. I grabbed my pruning saw and shears and a pair of loppers, walked around the block, introduced myself to an elderly neighbor, and asked if I could work on her tree. Once I assured her I was doing it for love rather than money, she gave me the go-ahead. The work took less than an hour and felt so good that I did it again with another neighbor's apple tree. Aside from doing something charitable, I've discovered that the time invested is continuing to pay me back. Nearly every day I deliberately walk by the trees to admire them and see how they're doing. The pruning was a creative act that liberated the tree's grace and beauty. Now when I walk by, I feel not just tremendous satisfaction but something else—I feel a degree of safety and warmth, like I'm in the company of friends."

Decrease to every two weeks, sticking to that schedule until fall, and water monthly throughout winter if you live in a mild climate. Water every four to eight weeks through the second and third years after planting. A tree chosen appropriately for any particular climate, once established (after about three years), shouldn't need watering more than three or four times between July and October unless there are drought conditions. Your watering schedule and the volume of water applied each time should vary with soil texture. For instance, clay soils store twice as much water as sandy soils. If your soil is sandy, irrigate sooner with less water; if heavy clay, space waterings farther apart but add more water each time.

Of course, rain must be taken into account (in general, it takes one inch of rain to soak down six inches in clay loam and the same to soak down ten inches in sandy loam, depending on how moist the soil was before the rain). Frequent overwatering can be as serious a hazard as underwatering.

HOW CAN I TELL IF MY SOIL IS WET OR DRY?

You can tell approximately how much water your soil will hold by examining the soil around the tree. The following guidelines can help in deciding whether or when to change your watering schedule. Watch leaves for signs of wilting to be sure the time between irrigations is not too long.

Check texture. Is it mostly sand or clay? Does it have a lot of fine particles, smaller than sand grains (silt)? If, as is normal, it is a mixture of these, which one is more abundant?

Smell the soil. Does it have the odor of fresh, rich garden soil or woods soil? Or does it have a rank, soured smell, something similar to a faint odor of sewer gas? Use the table at right to interpret your examination results.

Regardless of soil texture, the following conditions indicate excessively wet soil.

▲ There is a rank smell.
▲ Water can be squeezed out of the ball of soil.
▲ There is water in the bottom of the hole.

One way to be sure about soil moisture is to use a soil probe before watering and examine a core sample from a foot under the soil surface, both from the root ball and from the backfill soil. You should only have to do this a few times to get to know your soil's water-holding capacity. Though many kinds of scientific measurement are available, watering trees is not an exact science. *Your intuition will be your best watering guide!* When you become a tree guardian, you'll have a heightened awareness of how much it's rained recently and how long it's been since you watered.

It's important to water deeply and slowly, using a hose or drip irrigation system. This encourages the growth of deep roots, which anchor well, make the tree more drought tolerant, and are less likely to encounter and damage curbs and sidewalks. If the water is only sprinkled on the ground, it seeps no deeper than the surface and the tree develops surface roots. If water is poured onto the ground faster than the soil can absorb, it will run off, doing the tree no good.

Soil Characteristic	Diagnosis
Half or more sand Won't form into a ball, or else crumbles easily.	Too dry
Forms into a ball, crumbles readily under pressure. Has a smell like fresh soil, or freshly wet sand or cement.	Okay
Reacts as above, but when ball is squeezed it leaves a film of moisture on your skin. May have a sour soil odor.	Too wet
Half or more clay Won't form a ball, or else crumbles very easily; dusty.	Too dry
Can be readily formed into a ball, and crumbles under pressure. Smells like fresh, damp soil from a field, garden, or woods.	Okay
Sticks to shovel or trowel when dug. When formed into a ball, acts like modeling clay: doesn't crumble readily, but breaks into large chunks or extends like a ribbon. Leaves a film of water on your skin when squeezed.	Too wet

Pay attention to newly planted container and ball-and-burlap plants that are in leaf. During the early part of their growing season, they will need water more frequently than at the nursery. Container root balls hold less water in the ground than they do in the container. Also, the root systems of balled-and-burlapped plants are greatly reduced when the plants leave the nursery. In arid climates, watering is the most vital care you will provide for trees. Don't forget it!

Maintaining Watering Basins

Six months after planting, schedule a maintenance event to visit the trees and widen or eliminate the watering basins you built so carefully around the root ball. Check the root crown to see if it's buried, and remove that excess soil.

PRUNING

Pruning can ensure a structurally strong tree and help keep it healthy by removing dead, diseased, or damaged wood and branches that will grow to interfere with one another. Proper pruning can also increase the quality or size of fruits, nuts, or flowers; direct and control growth; and ensure public safety.

Every Cut Is a Wound

Every pruning cut in live wood injures the tree and opens the cut area to the possibility of infection. Every removal of foliage reduces the tree's capacity to sustain itself. Be certain, therefore, that each pruning cut will benefit the tree enough to offset the resulting injury and leaf loss and the chance of infection. Also, make each cut in a way that causes the least injury and ensures healthy recovery.

Trees can be pruned year round. Some people think that trees should be pruned when they're dormant; others advise pruning during the growing season, when the tree has energy to heal quickly. Check with an expert for information about your species' pruning needs.

Proper pruning technique takes advantages of the tree's natural protective mechanisms. A protective chemical zone resides within the *branch collar*, a donut-shaped bulge at the base of the branch where the trunk and branch tissues meet. When the collar is left intact after pruning off a branch, the trunk tissue is not damaged, so the trunk is less likely to become decayed.

The wrongs done to trees, wrongs of every sort, are done in the darkness of ignorance and unbelief, for when the light comes, the heart of the people is always right.

JOHN MUIR

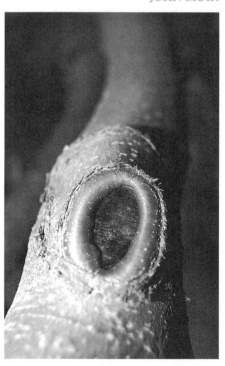

PRUNING DIAGRAM

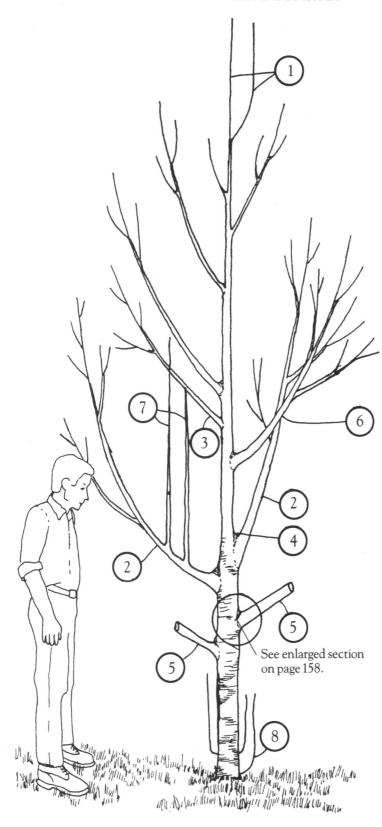

See enlarged section on page 158.

What to Look for

1. Forked top. If left on the tree, this will cause the development of two leaders, thus wasting growth energy. Later, as the two tops get larger, the fork may split and damage the tree.

2. Remove for street-tree clearance.

3. Parallel branch.

4. Branch growing at a sharp angle. When this branch becomes larger, it may rub on the trunk, split out, or even cause rot to develop by giving water a chance to collect.

5. Temporary branch.

6. Crossing branches. These interfere with each other's growth and create bad form.

7. Water sprouts.

8. Basal sprouting from the root crown. This saps energy from the tree, looks messy, and can collect trash.

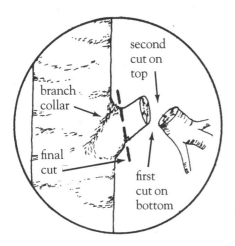

Whether or not you can locate it on the branch of the species you're pruning, visualize this collar and cut outside it.

Cutting a living branch

Make the top of your cut just outside the branch-bark ridge, if apparent, in the crotch between the trunk and branch. Angle the cut outward from the top part, roughly opposite the branch-bark ridge, to the point where the branch collar ends.

The angle formed should be equal to the angle between the branch-bark ridge and the trunk. For a branch smaller than 4 inches, if you can't find either the branch collar or the branch-bark ridge, start the cut ⅛- to ¼-inch from the source stem and angle the cut outward 10 to 20 degrees. For larger branches, increase the dimensions of the cut.

Cutting a dead branch

A dead branch still attached to a tree usually will have a collar of tissue formed around its base. This tissue is trunk tissue. Prune the dead branch outside the collar, making sure not to cut into it.

Pruning Priorities

Go easy with those pruning shears! The more foliage trees have, the more they can grow. In fact, when you're pruning, never remove more than one-third of the leaves and branches; doing so will severely weaken the tree. Keep side branches unless you suspect they'll be damaged by traffic; these branches help to produce a thicker trunk.

Dead and broken limbs are your main concern, and there shouldn't be many of them. On planting day, check the tree for dead or broken limbs and for large stubs left by the nursery. Go ahead and prune them off, leaving the branch collars intact. You can always be sure that these branches should be removed.

Don't leave stubs. When you figure out where the branch collar is, cut as close to it as possible. Cutting beyond this, or leaving a *stub*, interrupts the circulation of sap in the branch and upsets the healing process.

Don't flush cut. A flush cut is a pruning cut that is even with the branch or trunk surface, thus removing the branch collar and cutting into tissues in the trunk. It creates a wound much larger than the collar area and opens up the trunk tissue to decay organisms.

One event put together by a TreePeople volunteer was less of a burden than a planting and produced instant results at least as gratifying as putting trees in the ground. A main thoroughfare in Los Angeles was lined with beautiful young trees in wells that were being choked by trash, weeds, and sucker growth. The beauty of the trees was virtually hidden by five-foot suckers. A day's work brought the trees back to the street. It was like creating a whole new planting of large trees—in one day.

Promote a ban on topping! Topping, a practice employed by untrained tree workers and by utility companies to protect power lines, shears off the top part of the tree regardless of branching structure, causing dense new growth that is weakly attached and increasing the likelihood of damage from wind. Topping reduces both tree value and life expectancy. If an existing tree is likely to interfere with overhead obstructions, the proper technique is to thin or shorten branches periodically to direct growth away from wires. Miles better is to plant a tree that is small when mature.

Don't paint wounds. There is no evidence that conventional wound dressings stop rot. In fact, some dressings create conditions favorable for rot. Allow the tree's protective mechanisms to work as nature designed them.

Make three cuts when removing large branches. If the branch you're removing is too large to be held and controlled with one hand while you cut with the other, three separate cuts should be made. First, to avoid having the bark tear away as the branch falls, make a partial cut one-third to halfway through the branch, about a foot away from the main stem and on the underside of the limb. Next make a complete cut a little farther out on the branch to remove the bulk of it; then make the final cut just outside the branch-bark ridge and branch collar.

Removing water sprouts and sucker growth can be a lifetime commitment. Species that are naturally large, multistemmed shrubs and have been trained to a single trunk will often produce suckers around the base of the trunk. The most effective way to eliminate them is to pull them off when they are very small, ideally by removing the buds at the bases. If they get large enough to require shears or loppers, you know those suckers will rise again! Be sure you're willing to undertake this maintenance task before you purchase such a tree. One positive note: removing sucker growth can be a very satisfying work project with existing trees!

Care for your pruning tools. Dull shears or saws make jagged cuts, which are more difficult for a tree to heal. If you are pruning a tree known to be infected with a systemic disease (such as fireblight), disinfect pruning tools with household disinfectant between each cut.

Remember, pruning either shortens or removes branches, and it is permanent. Your main job is to remove dead or broken branches and sucker growth at the base of the trunk.

Training Young Trees

Another type of pruning is called *training*. The objective in training is to help the young tree develop a strong branch structure. Properly trained trees will require little corrective pruning as they mature. The following guidelines will help you identify trees that need training. It's best at this point to call in a certified professional or experienced pruner to help you select the main branches so that you don't mistakenly maim your favorite tree.

The growth habit of a tree and its function in the landscape determine how much it needs to be trained. Trees with a strong central *leader*, or main trunk, and a conical shape like conifers, liquidambar, and pin oak will probably need little or no pruning. On the other hand, round-headed trees or trees with irregular growth habits don't naturally develop a strong branch structure but can be trained as follows.

1. Keep the leader dominant. If several shoots are competing to be the tallest, select one and prune back the others. A forked top is an example of competing leaders.

2. Select the lowest main branch at a safe and appropriate height, depending on the use of the tree. (Most cities have specifications for the clearance requirements of street trees.) The position of a limb on a trunk remains essentially the same throughout the life of the tree. In fact, as a branch increases in diameter, the distance between it and the ground decreases.

3. On large-growing trees, select main branches that are at least six inches vertically apart. When parallel and spaced closely together, main branches will be long and thin and have little structural strength. Main branches should be less than three-quarters the diameter of the trunk just above the branch.

4. Remove or cut back branches attached to the trunk at a sharp angle. A wide angle between branch and trunk allows strong connective wood to form in the crotch and all around the branch attachment. A narrow angle of attachment may have bark imbedded in the crotch, leaving no room for connective wood to form and making the attachment weak. As foliage grows and makes the limb heavy, it's likely to split off and damage the tree.

5. Branches that cross one another should be removed.

6. Keep small shoots as temporary branches along the trunk for a few years. Leave small branches along the trunk below the lowest main branch and between main branches, and keep

There's always the time-honored method of breaking off the stake and leaving the remainder in the ground, but it's not half as satisfying or as clean a job the whole thing. You can for a shovel blade into some stakes at ground level and raise them, but what about the ones that are entwined in tree roots and can't be budged?

Local Los Angeles tree saver, Alex Man has developed a tree-stake removal tool. The tool resembles a large plumber's pipe wrench. You tighten the wrench jaws around the stake, then pull the end of the tool handle back and forth (not up and down) several times to break the roots loose. An eight-foot-long wood lever (two-by-four), mounted on an adjustable fulcrum stand, slips under the tool jaws next to the tree stake. By pulling down on the end of the lever, you can pull almost any stake out of the ground. For more information on how to construct your own stake remover, write to Alex at P.O. Box 1711, Santa Monica, CA, 90406.

If you're stuck without Alex's tool, you can use a piece of chain to tie the lever to the stake and any fulcrum (rock, cement block) you can find. This method is definitely a step back into the stone age, but it does the trick!

them shorter than 12 inches long. These small branches should be kept on for one to five years after planting to increase lower-trunk size and taper and to protect the trunk from sun and vandals.

REMOVING STAKES AND TIES

Removing stakes and ties is an often-neglected job—even by people who plant trees for a living. Just look around your city streets if you don't believe us! There are lots of trees choking to death out there. Stakes and ties should be viewed as temporary, in constant need of removal or replacement as the tree grows. This is a valuable service that you can provide.

Stakes

When you come across a tree that has the original square nursery stake still attached, remove it. If the tree can't support itself, tie the tree to support stakes loosely, in such a way that it is upright but can sway in the wind.

For trees you've planted, go back and remove the support stakes six to eighteen months after planting. If any stake is rotten or broken, or if it interferes with the tree's growth, remove it and replace it if needed.

Tree Guards

If the tree still needs protection from outside hazards but can stand on its own, try installing protective barriers or tree guards. For seedlings and small trees, a number of tree guards are on the market; you also can make them from wire and small stakes. You can use three or four short stakes (2½ feet above ground) around the trunk of a large tree to protect it from maintenance equipment. For more serious protection from vandals or vehicles, the stakes should be four to five feet tall, made of two-by-fours or equally strong material, such as metal pipe or rebar, and connected by cross-pieces at the top.

Ties

Fix ties that have broken or slipped down. Check for ties cutting into the tree. If the tree has grown around a wire, don't try to remove it, but loosen it as much as possible and cut off any free ends. Replace ties made of materials that can cut into the bark, such as wire or rope. Remove any ties you see beginning to bind, or ties on trees that can stand on their own.

WEEDS, MULCH, AND FERTILIZER

It's best to maintain an area at least two feet in diameter free of turf and weeds around the base of tree trunks. Turf and weeds compete for water and nutrients, and some produce chemicals toxic to other plants. A small turf-free zone around a tree also reduces the need for mowers to come close. After four or five years, tree roots are extensive enough that other plants close to their trunks are not as much of a problem, although mower operators should still exercise caution. One energy-saving way to control weeds is to apply a thick layer of mulch.

Trees should be mulched at the time of planting. A two-to-four-inch layer of mulch in a two-to-six-foot-diameter circle around the base of the tree (or within the watering basin) will control most weeds, protect the soil from compaction and erosion, conserve moisture, moderate soil temperatures, and improve the soil as it degrades.

Leave a small circle bare around the tree's trunk to deter fungus, diseases, and rodents. Mulch should stay in place for as long as possible.

Mulch is commonly made of organic substances, such as composted or shredded bark, wood chips, dry leaves, dried lawn clippings, or similar materials. Inorganic mulches such as decomposed gravel, pea gravel, marble chips, and concrete well covers do not need to be replaced and are usually better suited for trees along city streets than for those in home landscapes.

Much debate surrounds the use of fertilizers. Some professionals recommend no soil amendments or fertilizer be added to trees, since the tree must ultimately adapt to local conditions. Others recommend the application of fertilizer to furnish essential nutrients, especially if the tree is under stress or producing food. Nitrogen is almost always deficient in the soil, and some tree experts feel that a modest amount of nitrogen should be applied to trees regularly. If you suspect fertilizer is needed, take foliage exhibiting mineral-deficiency symptoms to your local nurseryman and determine the plant's exact needs. See Resources for further information.

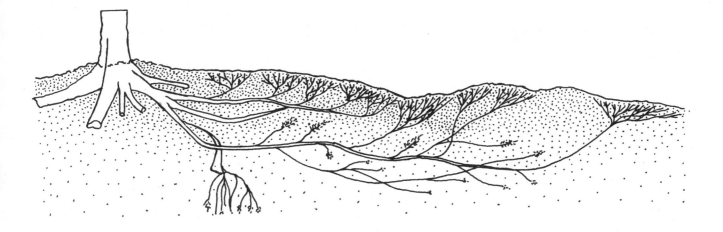

WHAT'S GOING ON UNDERNEATH THAT TREE?

Roots have two important jobs to do. They anchor the tree to the ground so that it can stand erect, and they absorb water and nutrients for all the processes that take place in the tree, from photosynthesis to root growth. Roots will grow best wherever they can find water, oxygen, nutrients, and warm temperatures—typically within the top three feet of soil. Contrary to the popular myth, the root system does not mirror the tree above ground. A better analogy is to imagine the complete tree as a wineglass set on a dinner plate, with the roots extending far beyond the crown.

There are two main types of roots: absorbing roots and structural roots. Absorbing roots are masses of fine feeder roots that take in water and nutrients. They cover an area several times the leaf spread of the tree, but they seldom grow thicker than ⅛ inch and may live only a short time. Absorbing roots grow in horizontal fans near the soil surface. These fans are eventually attacked and consumed by soil organisms.

Structural roots provide the framework for the root system. There are several major roots on a tree, radiating outward and downward from the base of the tree. They are *woody*, grow thicker every year like branches, and have bark. Structural roots primarily grow horizontally and seldom grow deeper than 3 to 7 feet.

MONITORING FOR PROBLEMS

For the first year after planting, inspect your trees every month when watering. For the following two to four years, try to inspect your trees every six months. It takes at least one full growing season for trees to adjust to a new site after transplanting (not including the season of planting), so problems may not show up immediately. They may begin when the roots grow beyond the root ball and into the surrounding soil.

If you find a problem or potential problem, get help immediately! Sources of assistance include local nurserypeople, landscape professionals, university-extension or agricultural commissioners' offices, and private groups. When providing an expert with information about your tree, start by naming the tree species and then describe the problem. What are the symptoms? Is any part of the tree dead or dying? Are there mushrooms at its base? Is the trunk scraped or girdled? If possible, take a photograph of the tree parts that exhibit symptoms of illness or damage. Take a sample of the infected foliage with you, showing the arrangement of leaves on the stem and both healthy and diseased tissue. A thorough tree inspection may uncover evidence of:

△ pest or disease infestations

△ inhibited or stunted growth

△ binding or restriction due to stakes and ties

△ broken, dead, or diseased branches

△ inadequate clearance from traffic under and around the tree

△ wilted, curled, or distorted leaves or dried-out buds

△ leaf color abnormalities (spots, yellowing, or brown margins); early leaf drop

△ cracks in bark from sunburn

△ sucker growth at the base or on the sides of the tree's trunk

△ holes or substances oozing from the trunk

△ a sickly appearance; lack of normal leaf luster or sheen

△ a site that appears unmaintained or abandoned and invites vandalism

△ litter or weeds around the tree base

△ dead or dying trees nearby, which may infect surrounding vegetation

△ severe erosion, sunken holes in the root-ball area, or an inadequate watering basin that threatens the young tree's water supply

△ flooding or poor drainage

△ holes, gouges, or strange growths that might indicate disease or vandalism

△ surface roots beginning to grow

△ algae or mosses around tree base, indicating excess watering

△ burrowing rodents, such as gophers and ground squirrels

△ a heavy layer of soot or particulate matter from air pollution (can be hosed off)

If you're not certain how to treat the tree for whatever problem your inspection reveals, contact a tree professional. Take a moment to prepare yourself for the person's questions by collecting the following information.

△ *How and when the tree was planted.* Sometimes a problem may be as simple as the fact that the tree container was never removed!

△ *Water and drought history.* The effects of drought or letting the tree's roots become extremely dry may not show up until months or years later.

△ *Previous uses of the site.* If the area was used for parking, cars may have compacted the soil. If the site was used for garbage disposal or storage of old oil or machinery, the soil may be contaminated with chemicals.

△ *Activities at surrounding sites.* If a neighbor has recently fumigated or applied herbicide to his or her soil, it may be the cause of your tree's poor health. If a surrounding parcel or building has been treated for a pest infestation, it might have caused pests to migrate to your trees. If neighbors have overwatered, runoff from their yard may cause problems for your trees.

△ *Care of surrounding vegetation.* What nearby plants are receiving fertilizer? Does nearby vegetation drop leaves that make the soil acid?

△ *History of growth.* How old is the tree? Has the weather recently been abnormal? Was past growth especially vigorous or slow? Was the tree ever blown over or severely cut back?

CHOOSING A TREE-CARE PROFESSIONAL

Unfortunately, some people enter the tree-care business with no experience, training, or certification. While it's a toss-up as to whether they leave your tree looking pretty or decimated, either way they could unknowingly cause severe, irreparable damage. Topping or unintentional disease spread can lead to future liability and an ugly tree with all sorts of potential health problems.

Fortunately, a way exists to tell a tree-care professional—one who'll know how to prune or properly diagnose and treat your tree—from those who are just in the business of cutting, topping, shaping, and cleanup. The International Society of Arboriculture (ISA) is a professional association that provides a number of services, including a testing and certification program. Those in the business of tree care must demonstrate a certain level of competence, knowledge, and experience to be certified.

Ask to see ISA certification but don't stop there. Make sure to get and check a couple of references. It's not even too extreme to actually look at the work that's been done by someone you're planning to hire to ensure that your aesthetic styles match. Good tree care is expensive. Make it worth every penny.

A PRAYER FOR TREE CARE

Now that you know what it takes for trees to be planted and grown in urban environments, you'll begin to notice the trees around you. You'll notice not only the beautiful shapes, colors, flowers, and fruits of the trees in your city but also the bad pruning, stakes that need removal, unkempt tree wells, and trees dying from wounds, drought, and pollution. Become a special kind of gardener—a tree guardian. Start caring for trees the way you care for your friends, your body, and your car: give them the care and love needed to keep them alive for you. Begin by finding one tree in the city that *speaks* to you, then wash its leaves, give it a drink, and see if it needs any special care. Then take on another and another. Check up on them every once in a while to see how they're doing. To quote a recent six-year-old participant at TreePeople, if you take care of trees, they'll take care of you.

Afterword

WHERE DO WE GO FROM HERE?

No shade tree? Blame not the sun but yourself.
ANCIENT CHINESE PROVERB

If you've read this far, we do have some expectations. We expect that you've started looking differently at your yard, your street, and your neighborhood. If you've no trees at all, we hope you'll feel as if you've been blind. If a green neighborhood has kept you comfortable, perhaps you're feeling nervous about the lack of young trees growing up or the maintenance of what's there. Maybe you've even put pen to workbook.

However, this book should take you beyond what's possible when neighbors start working with neighbors. The dream includes an ongoing relationship with your city's staff in which they are excited and able to routinely help you with your projects: cutting concrete, supplying tools, hauling debris, and matching costs of trees and planting. It includes an end to confrontation and turf battles and a beginning of knowledgeable citizen support of appropriate urban-forestry budgets. Getting citizens jazzed about planting is half the equation. The other half involves respect for our professionals and a safe way for them to share their knowledge.

GET ACTIVE

Create a citizen tree board or join an existing one. Help build a professional urban-forest management system for your area by working with interested council representatives. Meet whoever is in charge of city trees in your area. What support does that person need to get the job done? Do you, or can you, share objectives? Try to work together.

Challenge your young people to take their city back, to dream of how it could be, and to begin taking action to make it happen. We do not subscribe to the philosophy that assumes we must work with kids because everyone else is a lost cause; this book makes that clear. However, young people have a natural capacity to dream big dreams. They don't mind looking crazy. Encourage them, whenever you can, to investigate the state of their urban forest, ask questions of elected officials, make big plans, raise trees and bond with them, plant on their campuses and in their communities, and participate in ongoing care. This activity can happen only if environmental stewardship is made a part of the school curriculum. We believe these skills will be vital for the new environmental ethic that is emerging around the world.

THE BUCK STOPS HERE

The current outpouring of support for planting is encouraging and most welcome. Trees are becoming popular critters. They're politically correct and noncontroversial. They're up there with motherhood and apple pie. But that's all symbolism. Your job is to choose good trees and good homes for them, to plant them well and take care of them. We hope this book sets you on the path more profoundly than any stirring speech or promise. Regardless of any national program that may come our way, the role you play in your community is the most important. Nobody on the outside knows what's needed in your neighborhood except you and your neighbors. Other folks may plant trees there, but you're the ones who'll be around to keep them alive. From our perspective, a national program should be a celebration of what each of us is doing independently, in a spirit of cooperation, to put our country and our environment back together.

Community urban forestry is a brand new field and Tree-People is only one of several groups playing a leadership role. Because the movement is growing so rapidly, it's stretching us beyond our ability to respond with the competence and personal attention we demand of ourselves. We wrote this book so you could take the ball and run with it, surpassing us with your energy and creativity, and to give you permission not only to succeed, but to fail and plug on, as we have and will doubtless continue to do.

We've learned from conducting Citizen-Forester trainings that this material is greatly enhanced when people are able to share their experiences and together work through their ideas, problems, frustrations, and successes. This book is likely to raise even more questions for you. We encourage you to become uncommonly inquisitive and to appreciate that the future of the urban forest is in your hands as much as it in the hands of anyone else. Take heart, have courage, enjoy the ride!

WHAT IS TREEPEOPLE?

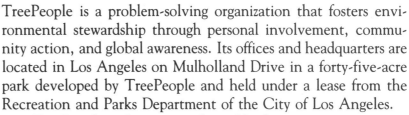

TreePeople is a problem-solving organization that fosters environmental stewardship through personal involvement, community action, and global awareness. Its offices and headquarters are located in Los Angeles on Mulholland Drive in a forty-five-acre park developed by TreePeople and held under a lease from the Recreation and Parks Department of the City of Los Angeles.

TreePeople seeks to move the public from opinion to action. Rather than expecting change through legislation, the organization encourages its constituency to use its power to personally improve the environment.

Legally and financially TreePeople is similar to many other nonprofit (501(c)3 tax-exempt) organizations. It is incorporated, governed by a board of directors, and has a paid professional staff. It receives its most basic and dependable financial support from a rapidly expanding base of 25,000 dues-paying members, and its budget is supplemented by the contributions of corporations and foundations and by occasional contracts with government agencies.

The following is meant not to impress, but to provide a window on the long and steady evolution of the organization, to give you hope and courage. Note particularly the rise of community action at the National Urban Forestry Conferences, the steady growth of grass-roots membership support, and the way TreePeople has responded to unforeseen circumstances.

1973

We plant trees not for ourselves, but for future generations.
CAECILIUS STATIUS, 220–168 B.C.

The first *Los Angeles Times* article, "Andy vs. the Bureaucratic Deadwood," appears in April with a public request for four thousand dollars to fund what is to be the first TreePeople activity (although no actual organization exists at this time), a summer tree-planting program of 8,000 trees in the San Bernardino National Forest. By summer, $10,000 is raised. The California Conservation Project (CCP) is created as a nonprofit corporation to handle the money needed to do the tree planting. Sears, Potlatch, and American Motors are the first major contributors.

1974

Year Two begins with a goal of 10,000 trees potted during the week of Arbor Day. Agencies involved include the California Division of Forestry, California Air National Guard, U.S. Forest Service, Los Angeles Urban Forest Council, L.A. Bicentennial Committee, Southern California Edison (SCE), Camp JCA, ACTION (Peace Corps/VISTA), and numerous civic groups and schools. The public unofficially renames the California Conservation Project "the tree people." *TreePeople News*, the first newsletter, is published in December announcing the new Tree Dedication program.

1975

The organization receives its first grant—$5,000 from ACTION.

1976

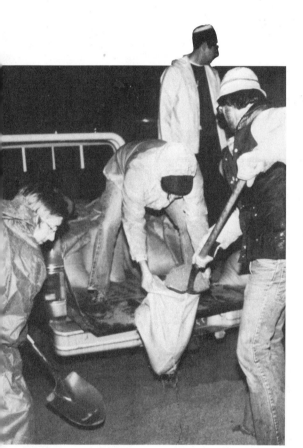

The Los Angeles City Recreation & Parks Department grants TreePeople a conditional-use permit of its Mountain Fire Station 108 for developing a small-scale nursery to grow seedlings. The Atlantic Richfield Company (ARCO) donates a '50s vintage fuel truck, which becomes TreePeople's water truck.

1977

ARCO and TreePeople create the Growing Concern community tree-planting program. In November, TreePeople officially takes over the Mountain Fire Station grounds as its headquarters; the site is immediately designated as Coldwater Canyon Park. By the end of this fourth year, TreePeople has planted 50,000 trees.

1978

Severe rains and local flooding give TreePeople its first experience in mobilizing volunteers for disaster-relief work, resulting in the headquarters being designated L.A.'s Emergency Resource Center. Programs now include tours of the park and facilities, the Little Treehouse summer workshop, community seminars, tree plantings, overnight mountain eco-tours, and classroom presentations. The California Department of Education's Environmental Education Program awards TreePeople its first education grant, and 15,000 schoolchildren are reached in the first year. By year end, TreePeople's tally is at 80,000 trees—5,000 of them in urban areas. The park's nursery houses 10,000 seedlings. At the American Forestry Association's (AFA) First National Urban Forestry Conference in Washington, D.C., community activists, including TreePeople, meet in the halls to network. And it's official—the California Conservation Project, Inc. is now TreePeople, Inc.

1979

The membership program begins. In March, TreePeople closes the Marina Freeway for a Tree Run, sponsored by Louisiana Pacific and KZLA. The closure, a first for an L.A. freeway, attracts 5,000 runners and makes California transportation history by requiring special legislation in Culver City, Los Angeles County, and the California State Legislature.

1980

TreePeople's Forestry Team is launched with the planting of sixty large trees, set up for a Xerox Corporation employees' group wanting a worthwhile civic-improvement project. In February, 3,000 volunteers (responding to 1,200 calls for help) are mobilized to assist local homeowners in volunteer-organized emergency-relief effort during excessive rains and flooding. For the first time, TreePeople activity becomes a media event. Andy Lipkis appears on *The Tonight Show*, and Johnny Carson makes a personal contribution to replace tools lost during the relief work. On the tenth anniversary of Earth Day, 2,000 people attend a celebration at the TreePeople headquarters. The Global 2000 ("Doomsday") Report is released by the President's Council on Environmental Quality and proclaims planetary devastation by the end of the century unless paths of unprecedented global cooperation and action are found.

1981

The City of Los Angeles Planning Department drafts an Air Quality Management Plan that calls for the planting of a million trees to help comply with the air-quality standards of the 1970 Clean Air Act. The city estimates the trees will require twenty years to plant, at a cost of 200 million dollars. It turns to TreePeople. In response to this forecast, its recent disaster-relief success, and the Doomsday Report, TreePeople launches the Million Tree Campaign. (See Chapter 5.)

1982

At AFA's Second National Urban Forestry Conference in Cleveland, Ohio, Andy Lipkis gives a twelve-minute presentation on community involvement.

1983

TreePeople publishes its *Planters' Guide to the Urban Forest*, a book designed to take community groups and individuals through the maze of urban tree planting. The *Los Angeles Times Home Magazine* devotes an entire edition to the Million Tree Campaign, including a pictorial guide to suitable trees for planting around the home. TreePeople is featured in *Fortune* and *Omni* magazines. After essentially being a family affair, the TreePeople Board of Directors begins regular meetings and elects public members.

1984

The organization attempts to save some of the hundreds of thousands of surplus bare-root fruit trees that are burnt at the end of the selling season. Almost 26,000 are donated from wholesale growers in California's Central Valley to be trucked to Los Angeles under refrigeration, pruned, bagged, and distributed to low-income families and Indian reservations through food banks, churches, and schools. Several volunteers spend two weeks camped at a downtown refrigerated warehouse coordinating the project. (The trees bear fruit within a year.) The millionth tree is planted in the San Fernando Valley, four days before the Olympic torch is lit. To celebrate, staff and volunteers go to the mountains and plant 7,000 seedlings in one day. Andy and Katie vacation abroad, where their presentations help launch programs in London and Ireland. TreePeople takes on its largest urban planting to date, a 1.5-mile stretch of the Long Beach Freeway.

1985

Ronald Reagan gives the Voluntary Action Award to GTE for its assistance during the Million Tree Campaign. TreePeople's contributing membership stands at 1,500. A direct-mail campaign is launched to solicit new members.

1986

In the days following a devastating fire, TreePeople coordinates

the hasty evacuation of waterlogged books from the Los Angeles Central Library. (According to the Library of Congress, this effort sets a record for removing more books in less time than any previous evacuation effort.) Three days later, two TreePeople volunteers fly to Africa with 6,000 surplus bare-root fruit trees, set aside the previous February during the annual local distribution. (This action follows a year of research to match available trees with suitable recipients, climates, locations, cultures, and soil types in five countries. Over the next three years, 1,200 additional trees are distributed with the cooperation of humanitarian assistance groups, indigenous organizations, and government agencies.) After the experience of the Million Tree Campaign, the Citizen Forester Training is established, to place more emphasis on quality of planting and maintenance than on quantity of trees planted. Andy and Katie's plenary-session presentation of the Million Tree Campaign receives a standing ovation at AFA's Third National Urban Forestry Conference in Orlando, Florida.

1987

Susan Becker, director of the Africa Fruit Tree project, visits all fourteen villages to find survival rates between 80 and 90 percent. Andy and Katie speak in Australia on behalf of Target: 200 Million Trees, a national effort inspired by the Million Tree Campaign. (A year later, the target is reached one month before the deadline.) TreePeople's work in schools is renamed the En-

vironmental Leadership program. This year it reaches 30,000 children. Staff levels move from ten to eight and end the year at fourteen.

1988

TreePeople members now number 10,000. To help L.A. prepare for its goal of creating citywide mandatory recycling within three years, TreePeople offers its Environmental Leadership program and develops a recycling component for its curriculum. During the school year that follows, 60,000 children—double the number stated in the contract—go through the program.

1989

TreePeople's internal management enters a new era of professionalism with the addition of a managing director to serve and guide a staff that jumps from fifteen in January to thirty-one in December. The organization is recognized by the United Nations and covered by Charles Kuralt's "Sunday Morning," the global telecast "Our Common Future," and an article in *Time* magazine. TreePeople holds a workshop in Tanzania on Home Economics and Horticulture for twenty-six trainees; two are from the African villages that received fruit trees. They return to their communities as teachers, prepared to establish and run self-sufficient fruit-tree projects. At AFA's Fourth National Urban Forestry Conference in St. Louis, Missouri, citizen groups are more present than ever, and half a day is set aside for their presentations.

1990

TreePeople's largest-ever urban planting—7 miles long and more than 300 trees in one day—honors the birth and vision of Dr. Martin Luther King, Jr. With the increase in public concern for the environment, TreePeople's phone now rings on average every forty-one seconds during the workday. Membership jumps from 15,000 to 18,000 in the first three months. Over 100 graduates of Citizen Forester Training now actively organize plantings. The Environmental Leadership program reaches 107,000 schoolchildren this year. The White House invites input from TreePeople in the development of the National Tree Trust. In April—Earth Day month—TreePeople appears in *Smithsonian*, *Mother Jones*, and *Life* magazines, *East West Journal*, *Audubon*, the *Wall Street Journal*, and the *New York Times*. In the first five months of the year, TreePeople assists at or runs thirty plantings, resulting in more than 18,000 trees in the ground.

1991

Los Angeles hosts AFA's Fifth National Urban Forestry Conference in October. TreePeople invites every one of you to attend and swap success stories!

USDA Plant Hardiness Zone Map

RANGE OF AVERAGE ANNUAL MINIMUM
TEMPERATURES FOR EACH ZONE

ZONE 1	BELOW -50°F	
ZONE 2	-50° TO -40°	
ZONE 3	-40° TO -30°	
ZONE 4	-30° TO -20°	
ZONE 5	-20° TO -10°	
ZONE 6	-10° TO 0°	
ZONE 7	0° TO 10°	
ZONE 8	10° TO 20°	
ZONE 9	20° TO 30°	
ZONE 10	30° TO 40°	
ZONE 11	ABOVE 40°	

Resources

The following is an eclectic and in some cases utterly subjective collection of publications that we've gone back to more than once. We hope they will astound you with facts, inspire your children, satisfy your curiosity, tell you stories, occasionally depress you, but ultimately uplift you on your journey.

Books

Baker, Richard St. Barbe, *My Life My Trees* (Findhorn, Scotland: Findhorn Publications, 1970).

Berger, John J., *Restoring the Earth* (New York: Alfred A. Knopf, 1985).

Brown, Lester, *State of the World 1990* (New York: Norton, 1990).

Caplan, Ruth, and the staff of Environmental Action, *Our Earth, Ourselves* (New York: Bantam Books, 1990).

Cherry, Lynne, *The Great Kapok Tree* (Orlando, FL: Harcourt Brace Jovanovich, 1990).

Dr. Seuss, *The Lorax* (New York: Random House, 1971).

Earth Works Group, The, *50 Simple Things You Can Do to Save the Earth* (Berkeley, CA: The Earth Works Press, 1989).

Elkington, John, Julia Hailes, and Joel Mackower, *The Green Consumer Guide* (New York: Penguin Books, 1990).

Giono, Jean, *The Man Who Planted Trees* (Chelsea, VT: Chelsea Green Publishing Company, 1985).

The Global 2000 Report to the President (New York: Penguin, 1982).

Harris, R. W., *Arboriculture* (Englewood Cliffs, NJ: Prentice Hall, 1983).

Huxley, Anthony, *Green Inheritance* (Garden City, NY: Anchor Press, Doubleday & Co., 1985).

Johnson, Craig W. et al., *Urban and Community Forestry: A Guide for the Interior Western United States* (Ogden, UT: U.S.D.A. Forest Service, Intermountain Region, 1990). Copies are available through Extension Publications, Utah State University, Logan, Utah, 84322-5015, (801) 750-1363, at $13.50 per copy.

Joseph, Lawrence E., *GAIA: The Growth of an Idea* (New York: St. Martin's Press, 1990).

Kourik, Robert, *Designing and Maintaining Your Edible Landscape Naturally* (Santa Rosa, CA: Metaphoric Press, 1984).

Moll, Gary, and Sara Ebenreck, *Shading Our Cities* (Washington, DC: Island Press, 1989).

Myers, Norman, *GAIA: An Atlas of Planet Management* (Garden City, NY: Anchor Press, 1984).

Newman, Arnold, *The Tropical Rainforest: A World Survey of Our Most Valuable Endangered Habitats—With a Blueprint for Its Survival* (New York: Facts on File, 1990).

Perlin, John, *A Forest Journey* (New York: Norton, 1989).

Ranger Rick's NatureScope: Trees Are Terrific (Washington, DC: National Wildlife Federation, 1989).

Seeds of Woody Plants in the United States, Agriculture Handbook No. 450 (Washington, DC: Government Printing Office, 1974).

Shigo, A. L., *A New Tree Biology Dictionary: Terms, Topics, and Treatments for Trees and Their Problems and Proper Care* (Durham, NH: Shigo and Trees Associates, 1986).

Warner, Irving R., *The Art of Fund Raising*, rev. ed. (New York: Bantam Books, 1984). Available for $7.50 directly from the author at 11650 Riverside Dr., #6, North Hollywood, CA 91605. (Even if you don't need to raise millions, Warner's psychology will help you muster what you need, and help you do it in the right way.)

Species-Selection Books

Little, Elbert L., *The Audubon Society Field Guide to North American Trees* (New York: Knopf, 1980. These guides are available by region. Consult the appropriate guide for your region.

EASTERN STATES

Brockman, C. Frank, *Trees of North America: A Field Guide to Major Native and Introduced Species North of Mexico* (Golden Press, 1968).

Dirr, Michael A., *Manual of Woody Landscape Plants: Their Identification, Ornamental Characteristics, Culture, Propagation and Uses* (Champaign, IL: Stipes Publishing, 1990).

Grimm, William Carey, *The Illustrated Book of Trees with Keys for Summer and Winter Identification*, rev. ed. (Harrisburg, PA: Stackpole Books, 1983).

WESTERN STATES

Perry, Bob, *Trees and Shrubs For Dry California Landscapes* (San Dimas, CA: Land Design Publishing, 1987).

Sunset Western Garden Book (Menlo Park, CA: Lane Publishing, 1988).

Technical Bibliography

Buchhorn, R., D. Jones, and D. Robertson, eds. *Urban Forestry Handbook: A Guide to the Management of Urban Bushlands* (Victoria, Australia: Department of Conservation, Forests and Lands, Melbourne region, 1989).

Chan, F. J., R. W. Harris, and A. T. Leiser, "Direct Seeding Woody Plants in the Landscape," Leaflet 2577 (University of California—Davis, Division of Agricultural Sciences, January 1977).

Coder, K. D., "Tree Watering," "Drought and Trees," "Diagnosing Tree Problems" (Extension Forest Resources, University of Georgia, April 1989).

Coder, K. D., "Trees and Soils" (Extension Forest Resources, University of Georgia, March 1989).

Harris, R. W., Department of Environmental Horticulture, University of California—Davis. *Arboriculture: Care of Trees, Shrubs, and Vines in the Landscape* (Englewood Cliffs, NJ: Prentice Hall, 1983).

Harris, R. W., Jack L. Paul, and Andrew T. Leiser. "Fertilizing Woody Plants," Leaflet 2958 (University of California—Davis, Division of Agricultural Sciences, August 1977).

Harris, R. W., W. D. Hamilton, W. B. Davis, and A. T. Leiser. "Pruning Landscape Trees," Leaflet 2574, University of California—Davis, Division of Agricultural Sciences. Reprinted January 1978).

Harris, R. W. et al., "Staking Landscape Trees," Leaflet 2576 (University of California—Davis, Division of Agricultural Sciences, March 1982).

Moll, G., "The Best Way to Plant Trees," *American Forests*, March/April 1990.

Moll, G., and J. Urban, "Planting for Long-Term Tree Survival," *Shading Our Cities*, ed. by Gary Moll and Sara Ebenreck (Washington, DC: Island Press, 1989).

Ornamental Trees, Time-Life Gardening Series (Alexandria, VA: Time-Life Books, 1988).

Shigo, A. L., *A New Tree Biology Dictionary: Terms, Topics, and Treatments for Trees and Their Problems and Proper Care* (Durham, NH: Shigo and Trees Associates, 1986).

Shigo, A. L., K. Vollbrecht, and N. Hvass. *Tree Biology and Tree Care: A Photo Guide* (Durham, NH: Shigo and Trees Associates, 1987).

Sunset Western Garden Book (Menlo Park, CA: Lane Publishing, 1988).

Taylor, N., *Taylor's Guide to Trees*. Based on *Taylor's Encyclopedia of Gardening*, 4th ed., rev. by Gordon P. DeWolfe, Jr. (New York: Houghton Mifflin, 1988).

"Tree Care" pamphlet (Illinois Department of Conservation, Division of Forest Resources).

Tree City USA Bulletin, "Living with Urban Soils" (Nebraska City, NE: National Arbor Day Foundation).

Urban Forestry Handbook: A Guide to the Management of Urban Bushlands (International Society of Arboriculture, Western Chapter, "Pruning Standards." No publication date.)

World Forestry Center and Robin Morgan, consult. *A Technical Guide to Community and Urban Forestry in Washington, Oregon and California* (Portland, OR: World Forestry Center, 1989).

Periodicals

Ranger Rick. Published by the National Wildlife Federation, this monthly magazine is for ages six to twelve.

Urban Forests: The Magazine of Community Trees. Available free from the National Urban Forest Council via the American Forestry Association.

Utne Reader. Eric Utne publishes "a field guide to the emerging culture" bi-monthly, using extracts from a multitude of publications to present a fresh and thought-provoking overview of selected subjects in each issue.

Whole Earth Review. Provides "the conscious reader" with the most contemporary tools and ideas for environmental, social, cultural, and political activism. It refrains from taking an editorial stand in an effort to present a variety of positions.

World Watch Magazine. This bimonthly magazine of the Worldwatch Institute provides a global framework for organizations working on energy, environmental, food, population, and peace issues.

National Organizations

There are countless valuable local organizations, known best to you, to speed your way in this venture. The following national organizations may be of particular help.

American Association of Nurserymen (1250 Eye Street, N.W., Suite 500, Washington, DC 20005, 202-789-2900) sets the standards for nursery stock and can send you a list of its certified members. Member or not, any nursery should be asked if it adheres to these standards.

American Forest Council (1250 Connecticut Avenue, N.W., Washington, DC 20036, 202-463-2468) represents the forest-products industry and is sponsor of Project Learning Tree, a teacher-training program and curriculum packet for school-age children.

American Forestry Association (P.O. Box 2000, Washington, DC 20013, 202-667-3300) is a powerhouse of information for citizen foresters. It is the current underwriter of the National Urban Forest Council and its publication is called *Urban Forests: The Magazine of Community Trees*. Publisher of many excellent works, including *Shading Our Cities*, *American Forests Magazine*, and the *Urban Forestry Home Workbook* series, AFA also sponsors the National Urban Forestry Conference and Global ReLeaf, a national and now international network of citizen groups working to put life back into urban forests. We recommend you become a member to take advantage of this great resource.

California Rare Fruit Growers (Fullerton Arboretum, California State University at Fullerton, Fullerton, CA 92634, 714-773-3250) has members around the world. It publishes a quarterly newsletter and a yearbook, and local groups meet to discuss the growing of unusual fruits.

Cooperative Extension Service organizations are usually sponsored by the county and offer programs through local colleges and schools.

The Foundation Center (79 Fifth Avenue, New York, NY 10003, 212-620-4230) is a clearinghouse for over 170 libraries around the country that are geared to assist grantseekers. Your nearest will be a precious resource if you decide to form a nonprofit corporation.

International Society of Arboriculture (P.O. Box 908, Urbana, IL 61801, 217-328-2032) produces a set of tree-pruning standards that should be used as minimum requirements for both private and municipal tree-care contracts. It provides ongoing education to

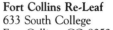

its members via regional meetings, annual conferences, and the *Journal of Arboriculture*. It sponsors vital research to advance the knowledge of planting, pruning, feeding, and even improved species development. It produces a list of certified members and several guides and directories including a new book on city ordinances—the *Municipal Tree Manual*—which is available directly from ISA for twenty-five dollars.

National Arbor Day Foundation (100 Arbor Avenue, Nebraska City, NE 68410, 402-474-5655) is the sponsor of Tree City USA, a program to encourage and acknowledge the work of public and private sector alike in the beautifying of American cities. Single copies of *Tree City USA* bulletins, including those on tree selection and soil analysis, both of which we highly recommend, are available free of charge from the foundation.

National Volunteer Center (1111 N. Nineteenth Street, #500, Arlington, VA 22209, 800-637-7799) is a clearinghouse that provides technical assistance and training, operates a library service, and distributes publications. They can refer you to your local center, which could be a valuable resource for project volunteers.

National Wildlife Federation (1400 Sixteenth Street, N.W., Washington, DC 20036-2266, 202-797-6800) is the world's largest organization of private citizens promoting the wise use of natural resources. It publishes books, magazines for members (including *Ranger Rick*), and other educational materials like the "Backyard Wildlife Habitat" packet, which is free of charge and filled with ideas for creating a safe and happy home for other creatures.

Rails to Trails Conservancy (1400 Sixteenth Street, N.W., Suite 300, Washington, DC 20036, 202-797-5400) works with local recreation and conservation organizations to convert abandoned railroad corridors to public trails.

TreeNet (P.O. Box 52105, Durham, NC 27717-2105, 919-493-1087) is a national urban-forestry electronic-information network that includes legislative bulletins, model ordinances, employment listings, and urban-professional and congressional databases.

Worldwatch Institute (1776 Massachusetts Avenue, N.W., Washington, DC 20036, 202-452-1999) is a research organization concerned with identifying and analyzing emerging global problems and trends and bringing them to the attention of leaders, opinion makers, and the general public. The institute publishes *State of the World*, an annual report of its findings, along with the bimonthly *World Watch Magazine*.

Tree Groups

The following is a partial (and very limited) list of established private tree groups. Before you start anything, if you live where they are, call them! Also try calling or writing to the American Forestry Association (listed above) for details. AFA maintains a contact list of groups that are active under the Global ReLeaf banner. You can also contact your local government or state forester for information on active groups, or simply contact the group below that's nearest to you. It's likely they can refer you to someone closer to home.

California ReLeaf
c/o Trust for Public Land
116 New Montgomery Street
San Francisco, CA 94105
(415) 495-5660
As well as having information on all California groups, this statewide coalition has developed a resource handbook as a companion to this book and a replicable model for other states. Contact them for a copy.

Dallas Parks Foundation
400 S. Record
Dallas, TX 75202
(214) 977-6653

Environmental Action Coalition
625 Broadway
New York, NY 10012
(212) 677-1601

Fort Collins Re-Leaf
633 South College
Fort Collins, CO 80524
(303) 224-2634

Friends of Trees
P.O. Box 40851
Portland, OR 97240
(503) 282-2155

Irvington Forestry Foundation
P.O. Box 2772
Indianapolis, IN 46206
(317) 736-9500

Neighborwoods
220 S. State Street
Chicago, IL 60604
(312) 427-4256

Philadelphia Green
Pennsylvania Horticultural Society
325 Walnut Street
Philadelphia, PA 19106
(215) 625-8280

Tree New Mexico
Alvarado Square T-NM
Albuquerque, NM 87158
(505) 848-4554

Trees Atlanta
96 Poplar Street N.W.
Atlanta, GA 30303
(404) 522-4097

Trees Forever
5190 42d Street N.E.
Cedar Rapids, IA 52402
(319) 373-0650

Trees For Houston
P.O. Box 13096
Houston, TX 77219
(713) 523-8733

TreeUtah
P.O. Box 11506
Salt Lake City, UT 84147-0506
(801) 972-9322

Tucson Clean and Beautiful
P.O. Box 27210
Tucson, AZ 85726
(602) 791-3109

When thoughts, dreams, concerns, fears, and hopes about an idea all pounce on you at once, they can hamper the clarity that's essential for any successful project.

Are you unsure of the first step to take? Have you been derailed by setbacks real or imagined? Do you want an almost foolproof way to cover details for your upcoming project? Have you ever lost sleep over the fear you've forgotten something vital? If so, these workbooks, based on TreePeople's own project development checklists, will be an invaluable tool.

Even if you're superconfident, use them to capture your ideas, to assist you to the next level, to measure your progress, to congratulate yourself as you complete each step, and to compare your original vision with your finished product. They'll not only help you find shortcuts for future projects, but will be priceless guides for those who become inspired by your success.

Sharpen your pencil!

Planting Project
Workbook

TAKE A PEEK

Take a walk around your neighborhood to get to know your urban forest. What catches your eye? Record both good and bad.

Who takes care of your urban forest?

THE VISION PROCESS

How would you like things to be? Do you have a picture of your future urban forest? (Jotting things down now can help you if the going gets tough. Remember, this is your vision.)

Developing the vision

What size project do you imagine organizing? When would you like to see it completed? How much time are you willing to put in?

GOAL SETTING

Check what's important to you.

△ bringing neighbors together
△ neighborhood pride
△ creating area identity
△ improving business
△ providing long-term neighborhood change
△ raising property values
△ providing attractive outdoor areas
△ bringing nature to the city
△ providing seasonal variety
△ providing colorful flowers
△ beautifying your neighborhood
△ providing play apparatus
△ producing more oxygen
△ decreasing pollution
△ natural air-conditioning

△ insulation in winter
△ conserving energy
△ producing shade
△ producing food
△ producing wood
△ repairing or reducing fire damage
△ creating noise barrier
△ creating visual screen
△ decreasing dust
△ creating a wind break
△ improving soil quality
△ decreasing soil erosion
△ creating wildlife habitat
△ as a dedication or memorial
△ other _____

MAKING THE VISION REAL

Who are you going to share this with? (Yes! Names and phone numbers and times to talk with them.)

Positive or negative feedback: (Does it alter your plan?)

HOLD ON A MINUTE!

Your local government representative _____

Telephone number _____

Special contact person _____
(This person could be a county or state representative if appropriate for your site.)

What existing efforts can you link up with, or invite to join your project?

Possible locations

What sites can you find that match your goals and vision?

△ neighbors' backyards
△ parkway strip
△ business-area sidewalk
△ along front lawns near the sidewalk
△ median strip
△ undeveloped parkland
△ city or county park
△ industrial site
△ school
△ parking lot

△ vacant lot
△ freeway
△ flood-control channel
△ landfill
△ railroad right-of-way
△ church, temple, or other private building
△ power-line right-of-way
△ land spandrel
△ other _____
_____

Some feasible targets   Some wild dreams

List here the one or two colleagues that now share your vision and are your partners in this project.

Name	Address	Phone	Expertise

CANVASING THE NEIGHBORHOOD

What are you asking people to do?

△ give general feedback on ideas   △ fill in a contact sheet for later
△ come to a meeting   △ give permission to plant
△ give money   △ help organize

Who's going to help canvass?

How will you do it? Check one or more:

△ phoning   △ door-to-door
△ flyer   △ neighborhood group newsletter
△ letter   △ other _____

What response did you get?

PLANNING THE MEETING

Create your agenda here.

Who will lead the meeting? _____ Phone _____

Who will speak about trees? _____ Phone _____

Location _____

Directions _____

Date _____

Time _____

How many people do you expect? (Think about seating, supplies, refreshments.) _____

Do you have:

△ a displayed agenda
△ a blackboard or writing tablet
△ a sign-in sheet
△ name tags

△ a neighborhood map
△ audio-visual equipment and
   material (slides or video)

AFTER THE MEETING

Did any resources show up at the meeting that will be valuable to your project?

People committed to: By when:

Fundraising _____

_____

_____

Volunteer recruitment/neighborhood enrollment _____

_____

_____

Permit or permission process _____

_____

_____

Investigating site and species selection _____

_____

_____

Hosting and chairing next meeting _____

_____

_____

Other _____

Next meeting date, location, and time _____

TAKING IT TO THE STREETS

If you feel ready to do a major public-education campaign in your city, use the following to give you a jump start.

What is your main selling point? Do you want to have a public goal?

What do you want the public to do?

Identify a working group for this education project.

Name   Phone

_____

_____

_____

_____

_____

_____

_____

_____

What connections can you find to a public relations firm, an advertising agency, or a major newspaper or electronic media outfit? Have you seen PR or advertising material you admire? Find out who produced it, or use it as part of your brief—for content, style and so on.

List key local media personalities or reporters. They will be your lifeline if they support you.

Name	Affiliation	Title	Phone

List public service directors for your TV and radio stations.

Name	Affiliation	Title	Lead time needed

What TV- and radio-interview programs are your targets? To what groups would you like to be invited to address as a speaker?

SITE SELECTION

Now things should be a little more real, and everyone's involved. What site have you settled on?

Address _____ Map Coordinates _____

Site specifications

Overhead space for mature tree _____ Parkway or median width _____

Distance from nearest sidewalk or walkway _____

What will block the tree's spread? _____

△ Will trees be in a lawn? (Frequent light watering poses a potential problem with surface roots.)
△ Should trees be drought tolerant, smog tolerant, or salt tolerant? (Circle choices.)
△ Would leaf or fruit litter pose a problem?

Special site conditions _____

_____

_____

Site inventory

Surrounding vegetation	*Topography*	*Sunlight*	*Slope*
△ irrigated lawn	△ flat land	△ morning	△ steep
△ other trees	△ hilltop	△ afternoon	△ level
△ shrubs	△ hillside	△ all day	△ moderate
△ non-watered ground cover	△ broad valley bottom	△ partial shade	
△ chaparral	△ canyon bottom	△ shade	
△ other _____	△ close to a creek or wash	△ reflected off wall or street	
	△ other _____	△ street lights	
		△ other _____	

Soil Type: Inspect a shovel full of soil. Is it heavy, wet clay that clumps together, or is it very sandy? If you've tested the soil pH level, report here. This information will be helpful when you choose your trees.

SPECIES SELECTION

What type of tree do you want?

Type of tree	Shape	Density
△ evergreen	△ spherical	△ compact (dense)
△ deciduous	△ oval	△ sparse (open)
△ conifer (needle-leaf)	△ spreading	
△ native	△ slender	
	△ pyramidal	

What characteristics do you want it to have?

△ flowers (what color and season?) _____
△ fall color
△ wildlife attraction
△ fruit or nut production
△ desired growth rate _____

What do you now have to choose from?

Species	Good points	Potential problems

Have you seen one? _____

Who has what you want? Who has the best stock? Who is most convenient or can deliver? Who has the best prices?

Nursery	Phone	Contact

PERMITS

Sketching out the permit or permission process here will help with your project timeline. Your expectations will probably differ from reality. Note the actual time it takes to get permission and the process you need to go through. This step will help you and others in future projects.

Who has jurisdiction over the site (public agency or private landowner)?

Contact name _____

Address _____

Phone and best time to call: _____

List owner's objections (if any) and your response.

DEVELOPING A PROPOSAL

Who will write the proposal? _____   Phone _____

Technical advisor (if any) _____   Phone _____

When will you follow up to see if it's been received? _____

When is a decision expected? _____

Permission _____

Describe step to be taken	Contact	Expected completion

ANALYZING COSTS

Equipment (including rental costs)

ITEM	NUMBER	SOURCE/CONTACT	PHONE	COST	TOTAL
Trucks					
Tools					
Other					

√ Check items you hope to have donated.

Professional services

Concrete cutting

Number of holes _____   Size of holes _____

Cost per hole $_____   Total cost $_____

Agency doing cutting _____   Phone _____

Soil testing

Agency doing testing _____   Phone _____

Cost for testing $_____

Other _____

ANALYZING COSTS (continued)

Publicity costs

Items printed _____ Cost $_____

Items mailed _____ Cost $_____

Phone calls _____ Cost $_____

Other item _____ Cost $_____

Other item _____ Cost $_____

Other item _____ Cost $_____

Supplies

ITEM	NUMBER	SOURCE/CONTACT	PHONE	COST	TOTAL
Trees					
Stakes					
Tree ties					
Root barriers					
Gravel					
Well covers					
Soil amendment					
Other					

√ Check items you hope to have donated.

ANALYZING COSTS (continued)

AMENITIES	NUMBER	SOURCE/CONTACT	PHONE	COST	TOTAL
Film (b&w print and color slide)					
Water					
Cups					
Name tags					
Refreshments					

√ Check items you hope to have donated.

Cash for tree care

How are your trees going to be maintained in the future?

△ annual collections from homeowners
△ initial fee
△ assessment district
△ trust fund
△ no cost involved—agency will maintain
△ other _____

BORROWING AND BARTERING EQUIPMENT

What local resources do you have? List tree groups, government agencies, utility companies, armed services, and conservation corps.

BEGGING AND BUYING RESOURCES AND MONEY

Other donations

ITEM	DONOR	ESTIMATED VALUE
Equipment		
Supplies		
Trees		
Permits waived		
Printing		
Services		
Other		

Budget

EXPENSES (ITEMIZED)	INCOME (LIST SOURCE AND AMOUNT)

Total expenses $_____

Total income $_____

Brainstorm a list of potential project sponsors.

Sponsor	Phone	Who Can Approach

What fundraising techniques are you going to employ?

THE FAIRY GODMOTHERS

List funding institutions that will consider a proposal.

Name   Phone   Contact   Date due

EYEBALL TO EYEBALL

Who can help you make the following face-to-face solicitations? _____

Prospect	Address	Phone	Target amount

SCOPE AND SCALE

You should aim to have your project finished and cleaned up in one day. To help determine if this is possible, use the following list.

How many trees do you intend to plant? _____

What size are the trees? _____

What size is your site (length, width, blocks)? _____

Are you in more than one location? _____

How many trees will you assign to each supervisor? _____

How many volunteers will be needed for each tree? _____

How much time will each tree take, given your prescribed planting style? _____

Therefore, to accomplish your event in one day:

How many supervisors do you need? _____

How many able-bodied volunteers do you need? _____

Be sure that you've thought of the long-term maintenance for the trees you're planting now.

How will they be maintained for the next three years?

△ all neighbors or businesses adopt the tree in front of their property
△ community group maintenance team
△ hired firm or neighborhood arborist
△ other group in the neighborhood
△ school kids (hired or volunteer)
△ agency takes over care
△ other _____

How will they be maintained ten or twenty years from now?

△ government agency
△ hired firm or neighborhood arborist

PREPARING THE SITE FOR TREES

What site preparation is needed? Check and report.

△ gaining access _____

△ cutting pavement _____

△ digging test hole _____

△ checking for underground utilities, phone _____

△ clearing vegetation _____

△ testing soil _____

△ locating water source _____

△ locating restrooms _____

△ locating temporary storage for tools and trees _____

△ determining disposal method for soil and debris _____

△ locating site to dump gravel _____

ASSEMBLING EQUIPMENT AND SUPPLIES

EQUIPMENT	NUMBER	SOURCE/CONTACT	PHONE	✓ ORDERED	✓ RECEIVED
Trucks					
Shovels					
Picks					
Stake drivers					
Trash cans					
Buckets					
Hose (length and size)					
Walkie-talkies					
Brooms					
Cones					
Barricades					
Chairs					
Tables					
Signs/Tape					
First aid kit					
Other					

SUPPLIES	NUMBER	SOURCE/CONTACT	PHONE	√ ORDERED	√ RECEIVED
Trees					
Stakes					
Tree ties					
Root barriers					
Gravel					
Well covers					
Soil amendment					
Other					

AMENITIES					
Film					
Sign-in sheets					
Name tags					
Pens					
Water/cups					
Food					

TWO WEEKS BEFORE YOUR EVENT

△ meet inspectors on site
△ cut concrete
△ get permit (in hand)
△ take *before* pictures
△ find drivers
△ reserve borrowed tools
△ recruit truck loaders
△ recruit set-up crew

△ recruit clean-up crew
△ designate a spokesperson for the press
△ send a reminder to volunteer groups
△ tell volunteers what to wear and bring
△ make a map *to* the site
△ make a map *of* the site
△ other _____

_____

SPREADING THE WORD

Who is responsible for mass volunteer recruitment?

Name _____   Phone _____

Recruitment _____

△ flyers
△ local signs
△ telephone
△ local organizations
△ door-to-door campaign
△ mail notices
△ word of mouth

△ presentations
△ newspaper calendar
△ news story
△ public-service announcements
△ press release
△ other _____

List groups with volunteer potential.

Name	Contact	Phone	Number expected

SPREADING THE WORD (continued)

List here the points that need to be covered in communications.

List VIPs you want to invite to your event. Include celebrities, sponsors, politicians, police watch commander, and so on.

Name	Address	Phone

MANAGING VOLUNTEERS

List your planting supervisors here.

Name	Phone	Trained?

List other members of your advance team.

JOB POSITION	NAME	PHONE
Event leader		
Troubleshooters		
Sign/Sign-out		
Tools		
Drivers		
First aid		
Refreshments		
Photos		
Clean-up		

Who are your planters? Use this list after your event to help with acknowledgments.

Name	Address	Phone	Showed?

ON THE DAY

Timeline

TIME	
	Group meeting to load tools, etc., into trucks to get to the site
	Set out tools, trees, etc.
	Set out signs with directions to the site
	Supervisor orientation before volunteers arrive
	Volunteers arrive
	Planting demonstration and volunteer orientation
	Planting begins
	Break for lunch
	Resume planting if necessary
	Clean-up
	Closing—announce first maintenance date
	Return tools
	Other

Other activities

TIME	
	Ceremony
	Celebration
	Other

Day of the event, on site

△ first-aid and water available

△ buckets/trash cans set out

△ post parking/no parking signs

△ all tools laid out

△ post signs directing planters to site

△ meeting/demo with supervisors

△ make sure site is accessible (gates open, etc.)

△ name tags to supervisors

△ sign-up sheet out

△ pick up refreshments

△ have permit on site

△ other _____

_____

Before leaving for site, run a check on all needed tools and materials.

Supplies

△ canteens, cups
△ emergency information
△ fertilizer
△ film (b&w print/slide)
△ gravel
△ name tags
△ pens, pencils
△ plastic drainage pipe
△ root barriers
△ sign-up sheet

△ stakes, tree ties
△ tree well covers
△ trees
△ water, drinks
△ well covers
△ other _____

_____

_____

Equipment

△ auger
△ barricades and signs
△ brooms
△ buckets
△ camera
△ can cutters
△ concrete saw
△ fire hose
△ fire tools
△ first aid kit(s)
△ garden hose
△ generator
△ gloves
△ public-address system
△ picks, post hole digger
△ pliers, hammer

△ pruners, loppers
△ rakes
△ shovels
△ stake driver
△ staple gun
△ traffic cones
△ trash bags
△ trash cans
△ truck(s)
△ walkie-talkies
△ wire cutters
△ other _____

_____

_____

PLANTING DEMONSTRATION

Be sure all these points are covered with your supervisors when you meet to discuss the planting style for the day.

△ how deep and wide the hole should be
△ how to remove tree from container
△ how to adjust tree so root crown is at correct level, and so tree is upright and oriented correctly
△ how much soil amendment and fertilizer to use (if any)
△ how to backfill and tamp
△ how to stake and tie
△ how to mulch
△ how to water and where the water will come from

MAKING IT CEREMONIAL

What's the purpose? _____

How long will it last? _____

Who will speak? (Refer to your VIP list.) _____

Who will be in charge of logistics, equipment, and supplies? _____

Who is your press spokesperson? _____

Who is the official event photographer? _____

CELEBRATION

How do you want to celebrate?

Who will be in charge?

SCHEDULING TREE CARE

Look at what care your trees will need in the future. This schedule does not need to be final, but it should give you a framework.

WORK TO BE DONE	FREQUENCY	DETAILS
Watering		
Mulching		
Trash pick-up, weeding		
Pruning		
Tie removal or adjustment		
Stake removal or adjustment		

ACKNOWLEDGMENTS

Who else, other than those listed on previous pages, do you need to acknowledge? Consider donors, agencies, and media, and check your sign-in sheet.

Name	Address	Helped with

EVALUATING YOUR EVENT

What worked?

What didn't work?

Improvements for next time

Tree Care Project
Workbook

TAKE A PEEK

Take a walk around your neighborhood to get to know your urban forest. Do you see trees that are in need of some tender loving care? Check for girdling ties, low broken branches, and sucker growth.

Who takes care of your urban forest? Do they do the job to your satisfaction?

THE VISION PROCESS

How would you like things to be? Do you have a picture of your future urban forest? (Jotting things down now can help you if the going gets tough. Remember, this is your vision.)

Developing the vision

What size project do you imagine organizing? When would you like to see it completed? How much time are you willing to put in?

GOAL SETTING

Check what you want to accomplish.

△ taking responsibility for the trees you or others have planted
△ bringing neighbors together
△ making business areas more attractive
△ providing long-term neighborhood improvement
△ teaching people the importance of tree care
△ creating attractive outdoor areas
△ helping trees grow faster and healthier
△ discouraging vandalism
△ rapid transformation of blighted area
△ other _____

MAKING THE VISION REAL

Who are you going to share this with? (Yes! Names and phone numbers and times to talk with them.)

Positive or negative feedback: (Does it alter your plan?)

HOLD ON A MINUTE!

Your local government representative _____

Telephone number _____

Special contact person _____
(This person could be a county or state representative if appropriate for your site.)

What existing efforts can you link up with, or invite to join your project?

Possible locations _____

What sites can you find that match your goals and vision?

△ neighbors' backyards   △ vacant lot
△ parkway strip   △ freeway
△ business-area sidewalk   △ flood-control channel
△ along front lawns near the sidewalk   △ landfill
△ median strip   △ railroad right-of-way
△ undeveloped parkland   △ church, temple, or other private building
△ city or county park   △ power-line right-of-way
△ industrial site   △ land spandrel
△ school   △ other _____
△ parking lot
                                         _____

Some feasible targets   Some wild dreams

List here the one or two colleagues that now share your vision and are your partners in this project.

Name   Address   Phone   Expertise

_____

_____

_____

CANVASING THE NEIGHBORHOOD

What are you asking people to do?

△ adopt a tree
△ come out for one work day
△ commit to regular work days
△ give money

△ fill in a contact sheet for later
△ help organize
△ come to a meeting (see pages 184–85)

Who's going to help canvass?

How will you do it? Check one or more:

△ phoning
△ flyer
△ letter

△ door-to-door
△ neighborhood group newsletter
△ other _____

What response did you get?

TAKING IT TO THE STREETS

If you feel the need for a major public-education campaign in your city, use the following to give you a jump start.

What gripe, challenge, or problem do you want to address? What message do you want to give to the public?

△ We need better tree care.
△ Tree butchery must stop.
△ Our trees need individual care.
△ We need tree-protection ordinances.
△ We need an urban-forest management system.
△ We need an urban forester.
△ City budgets for tree maintenance must be increased.
△ Other _____

What do you want the public to do?

Identify a working group for this education project.

Name   Phone

_____

_____

_____

_____

_____

_____

_____

_____

Have you seen PR or advertising material you admire? Find out who produced it, or use it as part of your brief—for content, style and so on.

List key local media personalities or reporters. They will be your lifeline if they support you.

Name   Affiliation   Title   Phone

_____

_____

_____

_____

_____

_____

What TV- and radio-interview programs are your targets? To what groups would you like to be invited to address as a speaker?

SITE SELECTION

What site have you settled on?

Address _____ Map Coordinates _____

What type of work do you want to do? _____

Not all trees require the same care. If you're happiest removing weeds and fixing tree basins, an area with trees in dire need of trimming would not be the best idea. You won't feel the same sense of satisfaction looking at the finished product.

Type of work you want to do

△ watering
△ mulching
△ weeding
△ pruning or training
△ removing dead trees
△ fertilizing
△ washing pollutants off leaves

△ cleaning tree wells
△ fixing watering basins
△ removing sucker growth
△ removing/replacing tree stakes and ties
△ other _____

_____

PERMITS

Do you need a permit or permission?

Who has jurisdiction over the site? (public agency, private landowner)

Contact name _____

Address _____

Phone and best time to call _____

List owner's objections (if any) and your response.

ANALYZING COSTS

ITEM	NUMBER	SOURCE/CONTACT	PHONE	COST	TOTAL
Trucks					
Gasoline					
Tools					
Permits					
Printing					
Supplies					
Tree ties					
Stakes					
Mulch					
Fertilizer					
Spray-wash equipment					
Other					

AMENITIES					
Film					
Water					
Cups					
Name tags					
Refreshments					
Other					

√ Check items you hope to have donated.

ANALYZING COSTS (continued)

Cash for tree care

How are your trees going to be maintained in the future?

△ annual collections from homeowners
△ contract with private maintenance firm
△ assessment district
△ trust fund
△ no cost involved—agency will maintain
△ other _____

BORROWING AND BARTERING EQUIPMENT

What local resources do you have? List tree groups, government agencies, utility companies, armed services, and conservation corps.

BEGGING AND BUYING RESOURCES AND MONEY

Other donations

ITEM	DONOR	ESTIMATED VALUE
Equipment		
Supplies		
Trees		
Permits waived		
Printing		
Services		
Other		

Budget

EXPENSES (ITEMIZED)	INCOME (LIST SOURCE AND AMOUNT)

Total expenses $_____   Total income $_____

BEGGING AND BUYING RESOURCES AND MONEY (continued)

Brainstorm a list of potential project sponsors.

Sponsor	Phone	Who Can Approach

What fundraising techniques are you going to employ?

SCOPE AND SCALE

You should aim to have your project finished and cleaned up in one day. To help determine if this is possible, use the following list.

How many trees will you work on? _____

What size are the trees? _____

Does this species have any special care needs? _____

What size is your site (length, width, blocks)? _____

Are you in more than one location? _____

How many trees will you assign each supervisor? _____

How many volunteers will be needed for each tree? _____

How much time will each tree take, given the operations you're performing? _____

Therefore, to accomplish your event in one day:

How many supervisors do you need? _____

How many able-bodied volunteers do you need? _____

PREPARING THE SITE

What site preparation is needed? Check and report:

△ gaining access _____

△ locating water source _____

△ locating restrooms _____

△ locating temporary storage for tools _____

△ determining disposal method for trimmings and debris _____

ASSEMBLING EQUIPMENT AND SUPPLIES

EQUIPMENT	NUMBER	SOURCE/CONTACT	PHONE	✓ ORDERED	✓ RECEIVED
Barricades					
Brooms					
Buckets					
Chairs/tables					
Cones					
First aid kit					
Hose (length and size)					
Loppers					
Mattocks					
Picks					
Pruning shears					
Saws					
Regular shovels					
Square-tip shovels					
Signs/tape					
Stake drivers					
Trash cans					
Trucks					
Walkie-talkies					
Other					

SUPPLIES	NUMBER	SOURCE/CONTACT	PHONE	√ ORDERED	√ RECEIVED
Stakes					
Tree ties					
Mulch					
Soil amendment					
Other					

AMENITIES					
Film (b&w and color slide)					
Sign-in sheets					
Name tags					
Pens					
Water/cups					
Other					

TWO WEEKS BEFORE YOUR EVENT

△ meet inspectors on site
△ get permit (in hand)
△ take *before* pictures
△ find drivers
△ reserve borrowed tools
△ recruit truck loaders
△ recruit set-up crew
△ recruit clean-up crew

△ designate a spokesperson for the press
△ send a reminder to volunteer groups
△ tell volunteers what to wear and bring
△ make a map *to* the site
△ make a map *of* the site
△ other _____

_____

SPREADING THE WORD

Who is responsible for mass volunteer recruitment?

Name _____   Phone _____

Recruitment

△ flyers
△ local signs
△ telephone
△ local organizations
△ door-to-door campaign
△ mail notices
△ word of mouth

△ presentations
△ newspaper calendar
△ news story
△ public-service announcements
△ press release
△ other _____

List groups with volunteer potential.

Name	Contact	Phone	Number expected

SPREADING THE WORD (continued)

List here the points that need to be covered in communications.

List VIPs you want to invite to your event. Include celebrities, sponsors, politicians, police watch commander, and so on.

Name	Address	Phone

MANAGING VOLUNTEERS

List your tree-care supervisors here.

Name	Phone	Trained?

List other members of your advance team.

JOB POSITION	NAME	PHONE
Event leader		
Troubleshooters		
Sign-in/Sign-out		
Tools		
Drivers		
First aid		
Refreshments		
Photos		
Other		

Who are your volunteers? Use this list after your event to help with acknowledgments.

Name	Address	Phone	Showed?

ON THE DAY

Timeline

TIME

	Group meeting to load tools, etc., into trucks to get to the site
	Set out tools, signs with directions to the site, etc.
	Supervisor orientation before volunteers arrive
	Volunteers arrive
	Tree-care demonstration and volunteer orientation
	Project begins
	Break for lunch
	Resume tree-care activity if necessary
	Clean-up
	Hand out flyers with date, time, and place for next event
	Closing
	Return tools
	Other

Other activities

TIME

	Ceremony
	Celebration
	Other

Day of the event, on site

△ all tools and vehicles in place
△ buckets/trash cans set out
△ first-aid and water available
△ have permit on site
△ make sure site is accessible
△ meeting/demo with supervisors

△ name tags to supervisors
△ pick up refreshments
△ post parking/no parking signs
△ post signs directing volunteers to site
△ sign-up sheet out
△ other _____

ON THE DAY (continued)

Before leaving for site, run a check for all needed tools and materials.

Supplies

△ canteens, cups
△ decomposed granite
△ emergency information
△ film (b&w/color/slide)
△ name tags
△ pens, pencils, markers, tape
△ permit

△ sign-up sheet
△ stakes, tree ties
△ water, drinks
△ other _____

_____

Equipment

△ barricades and signs
△ brooms
△ buckets
△ camera
△ fire hose
△ first aid kit(s)
△ garden hose
△ generator
△ gloves
△ picks, post hole digger
△ pliers, hammer
△ pruners, loppers
△ rakes

△ shovels
△ square tip shovels
△ stake driver
△ staple gun
△ traffic cones
△ trash bags
△ trash cans
△ truck(s)
△ walkie-talkies
△ wire cutters
△ other _____

_____

TREE CARE DEMONSTRATION

Be sure all these points are covered with your supervisors when you meet to discuss tree-care techniques for the day.

△ how to water
△ strict pruning guidelines
△ how to adjust or remove stakes and ties
△ how to mulch
△ how to clear weeds and trash from the tree well
△ what to do with dead trees

MAKING IT CEREMONIAL

What's the purpose? _____

How long will it last? _____

Who will speak? (Refer to your VIP list.) _____

Who will be in charge of logistics, equipment and supplies? _____

Who is your press spokesperson? _____

Who is the official event photographer? _____

CELEBRATION

How do you want to celebrate?

Who will be in charge?

SCHEDULING TREE CARE

How often will you care for these trees? Think of yourself and your team as adoptive parents, providing care now and in the future. This schedule does not need to be final but it should give you a framework.

WORK TO BE DONE	FREQUENCY	DETAILS
Watering		
Mulching		
Weeding		
Pruning		
Tie removal or adjustment		
Stake removal or adjustment		

If trees are already mature, who will do major pruning when needed?

△ government agency
△ hired firm
△ neighborhood arborist

ACKNOWLEDGMENTS

Who else, other than those listed on previous pages, do you need to acknowledge? Consider donors, agencies, and media, and check your sign-in sheet.

Name	Address	Helped with

EVALUATING YOUR EVENT

What worked?

What didn't work?

Improvements for next time

The People of TreePeople

TREEPEOPLE
12601 Mulholland Drive
Beverly Hills, California 90210

△ Please send a free copy of "Ten Tips for Environmental Responsibility" and let me know how I can become a member of TreePeople and receive *Seedling News*.

NAME _____

ADDRESS _____

CITY _____ STATE _____ ZIP _____

To get your free copy of "Ten Tips" immediately, call 1-800-333-3969, ext. 326TP.

TREEPEOPLE
12601 Mulholland Drive
Beverly Hills, California 90210

△ Please send me at no obligation more information about Citizen Foresters, including how I can order resource materials and learn about training programs in my community.

△ You may pass my name on to a tree-planting organization in my community or let others in my area know about my interest in citizen forestry.

NAME _____

ADDRESS _____

CITY _____ STATE _____ ZIP _____

Send me my free packet of tree seeds with complete germination and planting instructions for a tree species suited to my part of North America.

Compliments of GEO

Refer to the zone map on page 176 and circle here the tree species best suited to your area. Circle only one please.

△ Flame Maple   zones 2–7   minimum temperature -50°
△ Green Ash   zones 3–9   minimum temperature -40°
△ Sycamore   zone 10   minimum temperature 30°

NAME _____

ADDRESS _____

CITY _____ STATE _____ ZIP _____

HOME PHONE _____ WORK PHONE _____

Mail this order to: Free Tree Seeds, c/o Jeremy P. Tarcher, Inc., 5858 Wilshire Boulevard, Suite 200, Los Angeles, California 90036.